alba house DIVISION OF THE SOCIETY OF ST. PAUL STATEN ISLAND, N. Y. 10314

Raymond B. Fullam, S.J.

EXPLOR ING VATICAN 2

Christian Living Today & Tomorrow

Imprimi Potest:
    Robert A. Mitchell, S.J.
    Provincial Superior of the New York Province

Nihil Obstat:
    Richard A. Clark
    Censor Deputatus

Imprimatur:
    Walter A. Foery, D.D., Ph.D.
    Bishop of Syracuse
    January 25, 1969

The nihil obstat and imprimatur are official declarations that a book or pamphlet is free of doctrinal or moral error. No implication is contained therein that those who have granted the nihil obstat and imprimatur agree with the contents, opinions or statements expressed.

Library of Congress Catalog Card Number: 79-90777.

Designed, printed and bound in the U.S.A. by the Pauline Fathers and Brothers, 2187 Victory Blvd., Staten Island, N.Y. 10314 as part of their communications apostolate.

EXPLORING VATICAN II

OUTLINE OF CONTENTS

PART FOUR – WITNESS, THE INVOLVEMENT OF CHRISTIANS IN UPLIFTING COMMUNITIES OF THE WORLD

EXPLORING VATICAN II

CHRISTIAN LIVING TODAY AND TOMORROW

TOPICAL TABLE OF CONTENTS

INTRODUCTION

The Purposes of this Book

The main purpose of this book is to assist people in gaining a deeper understanding of the renewed spirit aroused within the Church-community by the Second Vatican Council. They will thereby be better able to apply this renewal to their contemporary Christian living. Letting the Council messages speak directly and clearly will go far to dispel misunderstanding regarding the direction in which the Church is moving. Great benefit will be derived from personal exploration into the Council's messages and from private reflection on the trends in the Church today.

As the Council's lengthy decrees are unavoidably rather ponderous with repetition and formal development, the effort here has been to present key passages from the conciliar documents which disclose, in simplified and more readily digestible form, the spirit of Vatican II and the intimations of its messages. The passages have been selected for their inherent pastoral and practical value, as well as for their suitability for study, discussion, and meditation, whether by clergymen, religious, or laymen.

Exploring Vatican II is structured to stand by itself as a guide to Christian living in contemporary times. The sub-title reveals both the approach and the spiritual nature of the work. The author's brief comments deliberately take a middle-course approach, avoiding extremes while indicating trends in the Church-community. Also, his approach is reflective rather than offering direct commentary in order to encourage the reader to experience his own insights into the Council's messages. He further felt that it was more appropriate to have all scriptural quotations derive from the conciliar passages rather than to include any himself in a work of this kind. It is hoped that the reader will be uplifted by this work and be proud to be a part of the Church's forward-looking spirit.

Beyond the foregoing there is an additional purpose to the book. For those who wish to derive a religious experience from it, similar to making a spiritual retreat, the work is modeled on the Spiritual Exercises of St. Ignatius. It is from his deep insight that the present book draws its organization and the dynamics of its progression. As explained in the Supplement on The Jesuit Way for Assisting Contemporary Christians, there is a parallel between the four parts of the book and the four progressive stages of the Ignatian Exercises designed to bring the interested reader into phase with the action of the Holy Spirit in his life. What the Holy Spirit attempts to accomplish in an individual's spiritual advancement, His benign activity likewise fosters in the total Christian Church as the community comprised of all the People of God. Hence, the four stages of the Ignatian insight for the spiritual development of the individual are applied, in *Exploring Vatican II,* to "Everyman" as the collective Christian community.

Trends in the Church Today

There is clear purpose behind the direction in which the Catholic Church is moving. It is not by chance that some former customs, practices, and structures have come to a stage of transition. Certainly, the central teachings of the faith have not and never will change, due to their divine origin. However, just as the gospel message is meant to be relevant to all generations, the Church also must ever be dynamic and constant in applying our Lord's teachings to the current needs of people through newer means and methods.

It will be profitable to glance at some of the historical movements which led up to Vatican Council II. During recent decades various developments within the Church-community have clamored for answers to some pressing problems. For instance, prior to Pope John XXIII's convening a world-wide council, Pope Pius XII had for years been publishing encyclicals on up-dating the Church, on rejuvenating the liturgy, on saving the faith of doubting youth, on revising the training for the priesthood and religious life, on presenting the requirements for inner-city and rural social order, and on several other topics such as economics, justice and world peace.

This same Pope encouraged scholars to explore newer insights into holy Scripture in the light of modern discoveries regarding former civilizations and man's intrepretation of ancient languages. During his

pontificate, theologians were also discussing the matter of open dialogue with fellow-Christians and non-Christians alike. The study of
theology which heavily stressed defense of the faith in earlier ages
began placing more emphasis on the Christian existentialists' applications of dogmatic, moral and pastoral theology. Finally, the adminis-
trative processes for conducting ecclesiastical affairs had long been
under careful study with a view to their revisions where found to be
archaic. Likewise, the up-dating of canon law was deemed appropriate
to meet the needs of God's people in contemporary times.

In order to understand adequately where the Catholic Church is
going, it is essential to consider the world-wide implications behind and
the reasons for the various movements and changes that are taking
place. It is for the benefit of the immense global needs of the Christian
community that the Council inaugurated revisions which affect the
faithful in every country, diocese, and parish. Since the efforts of the
Church were not as productive as desired in several parts of the world,
certain re-evaluations were deemed necessary. It is for the benefit of
making the practice of the faith more truly meaningful and effective
throughout the entire world and for future generations that local
churches are now necessarily touched by the recently authorized renewals. Though she may not retain the same outward appearance everywhere, the Church will always be essentially the same with consistency
of belief, worship, and purpose beneath a variety of structures, adaptations, and customs. Under the guidance of the Holy Spirit , the authentic renewals should result in bringing Christ's gospel message to more
people of varying nations, cultures, and conditions in a fast-moving
world.

Some predictable revisions will have long-lasting effects within
the Church-community. The administration of ecclesial matters by the
hierarchy will, likely, be altered along more democratic lines. Federations of priests and organizations of the laity will be called upon to
provide closer coordination within the Church in matters of concern for
the faith. Changes affecting the externals of the Mass and the sacraments will continue as needed. Some religious practices and customs
will be further re-evaluated and newer ones devised as more suitable for
modern generations. Since alterations of training have already been
incorporated within diocesan seminaries and religious congregations,
the way of life and methods of apostolic works of future bishops,
priests, nuns and brothers will look noticeably different to meet the
needs of the changing times. Certainly, also, the laity will be given
increasing responsibility and will have more voice in matters of com-

mon interest. Varying types of national, diocesan, and parish structures will spring up and there will be a general revamping of traditional societies on the parochial level. However, though sameness of custom may somewhat disappear, oneness of faith will certainly remain.

Vatican II did not intend to outline every detail required for renewal and adaptation. Yet the Council documents, signed by the Holy Father and 2,300 bishops, clearly present the guidelines whereby all Christians, as well as the various synods of bishops, commissions of theologians, and federations of the clergy, the laity, and the religious can all work together toward renewing the effectiveness of the Church in modern times.

The Arrangement of this Book

Exploring Vatican II can be a richly rewarding adventure. The person seeking to learn "the mind of the Church" will be enlightened by the conciliar passages which are directly quoted. The central messages of the great Council are organized within this book in four progressive parts, each building on the previous one and leading into the next. *Renewal* (Part One), individually and collectively, is the constant function of Christians in order that Christ's gospel message may be put into practice in every new age. *Commitment* (Part Two) to our Lord and His cause follows as a normal consequence when His followers have become renewed in Christ. *Unity* (Part Three) in faith and in the liturgy is the inevitable effect of being committed to Christ's cause. *Witness* (Part Four) to Christ in the world is the natural flowering of the individual as well as of the renewed, committed and united Christian Church-community.

The twelve chapters which develop this four-part progression, offer a reflective approach for pondering the passages from Vatican II. This spiritual attitude should assist the reader to achieve the general renewal envisioned by the Council, with the help of the guiding Holy Spirit of Christ.

The central messages of all sixteen documents are here presented, with more emphasis deliberately placed upon the four constitutions because of their importance and universal application for Christian living in modern times. The quotations from the Council documents are consecutively numbered for quick reference. The translation of the documents is the America/Guild/Association Press edition copyrighted in 1966 by America Press and published by Guild-Association-Herder and Herder. To facilitate analysis and foster discussion, the Index and Study Guide provides cross-references to closely related material. The Supplement shows how this work is readily adaptable for making spiritual meditations and religious retreats.

The Need and Value of Vatican II

Vatican Council II offers a valid vision of deep spiritual insight into Christian living today while lending prophetic direction to the People of God for tomorrow. In his address at the opening of the second session of the Council, Pope Paul VI epitomized the hopes and spirit of the Vatican II era. "The Church is a mystery," he insisted, "It is a reality imbued with the hidden presence of God. It lies, therefore, within the very nature of the Church to be always open to new and greater exploration."

In these days, with scientific and technological advances so prevalent, with tensions and temptations so grave, adult Christians must read beyond the signs of the times`else our present youth or coming generations may simply turn their backs on the Church as irrelevant to their needs. We must truly pray for wisdom and trust in the guidance of the Holy Spirit behind the Second Vatican Council that planted the seeds which must be cultivated now so that the harvest may soon be plentiful. The current trends within Catholicism will affect the lives of people for many generations to come.

The exploration of the conciliar documents should prove most interesting, stimulating, and sanctifying. Now that the excitement has somewhat settled after the first few years of expected post-conciliar turmoil, we may explore the Council's messages with objective perspective and more readily discover their hidden riches. For indeed, the conciliar documents are a resplendent treasury containing a review of sacred Scripture, a handbook of Catholic teaching, a compendium of current theological trends, a summary of pastoral guidelines, and a study of contemporary human conditions. Our modern Christian living will be enhanced by our exploring Vatican II.

Raymond B. Fullam, S.J.

DOCUMENTS

At the end of each passage directly quoting Vatican II is given the paragraph of the Council document as officially numbered. For example, (World, No. 42) means that the conciliar quotation is taken from that passage-number as found in the "Pastoral Constitution on the Church in the Modern World." The following list sets forth the key-word used throughout this book to designate each document of Vatican Council II.

World   Pastoral Constitution on the Church in the Modern World, (Gaudium et Spes).

Revelation Dogmatic Constitution on Divine Revelation, (Dei Verbum).

Church   Dogmatic Constitution on the Church, (Lumen Gentium).

Liturgy   Constitution on the Sacred Liturgy, (Sacrosanctum Consilium).

Laity   Decree on the Apostolate of the Laity, (Apostolicam Actuositatem).

Freedom   Declaration on Religious Freedom, (Dignitatis Humanae).

Ecumenism   Decree on Ecumenism, (Unitatis Redintegratio).

Easterns   Decree on Eastern Catholic Churches, (Orientalium Ecclesiarum).

Non-Christians Declaration on the Relationship of the Church to Non-Christian Religions, (Nostra Aetate).

Missions Decree on the Church's Missionary Activity, (Ad Gentes).

Communications Decree on the Instruments of Social Communication, (Inter Mirifica).

Education Declaration on Christian Education, (Gravissimum Educationis).

Bishops Decree on the Bishops' Pastoral Office in the Church, (Christus Dominus).

Priests Decree on the Ministry and Life of Priests, (Presbyterorum Ordinis).

Religious Decree on the Appropriate Renewal of the Religious Life, (Perfectae Caritatis).

Seminarians Decree on Priestly Formation, (Optatam Totius).

Part 1
Renewal

PART ONE – RENEWAL

THE REJUVENATION OF CHRISTIAN VITALITY IN MODERN TIMES

The renewal sponsored by Vatican II is intended to stir the spiritual powers of people now, with effects that will reach far into the 21st century and beyond. The first goal proposed by the Council for making the Church-community more dynamic in our time is "to intensify the daily growth of Catholics in Christian living."

When considering this renewal we must ponder responsibly upon what the Church intends to accomplish and what she hopes to prevent. Clearly, the essential purposes of the renewal are pastoral rather than doctrinal. Renewal's first aim is for the rejuvenation of Christian vitality on all levels; its second is a needful adaptation of some traditions and practices within the Church to meet the needs of the present age. It is essential to the vitality of Catholicism that, while adhering to the same basic beliefs, our faith should develop and expand in terms of contemporary requirements. The renewal sought by Vatican II is intended to effect daily growth in Christian living through revitalized faith, enduring hope, and expansive charity. Enthusiasm should be the result, not repression or dejection. Renewal looks toward moving men's minds and hearts in unity and peace to the love and service of God and fellow-man within the current human situation.

Valid renewal does not lie in distortion of doctrine or excess of innovations; nor does it consist in futile questioning of the fundamentals of faith. Rather, renewal is based precisely on the re-affirmation of religious fundamentals in life, with appropriate adaptations proper to the times. Thus, the authorized changes and applications should be accepted with peace of soul, then put into effect with balance of judgment by all involved.

There is much well-founded reason for hope in the world today.

The Church is moving ahead in several aspects. Whole nations are seething with a thirst for a fuller life, genuine freedom, and lasting peace — all of which God must certainly bless. However, true hope must be well-founded, not floundering. We must face up to ills which plague modern society and, as a result, obstruct the effectiveness of Christ's Church in our times. There should not be mere idle condemnations, but helpful solutions for the defects in the world. Furthermore, the Christian community must learn to listen attentively to the secular world and strive to understand its messages with the important undertones which are sometimes pleading, often pathetic, and always profitable to heed before attempting to heal. The Church does not claim to be able to solve all the problems of humanity. Yet, she certainly can guide toward man's well-being in time as well as toward salvation in eternity.

There is urgent need for the leadership and stability which a renewed Christianity can bring to uplift our sad, scared, secularistic societies in modern times. As subjects for discussion, religion and the Church hold a high priority. Nevertheless, as truths to be lived in practical life they are being severely questioned in these times of rather widespread cooling of religious faith. It is no longer exceptional to hear it asked, especially by young adults, "What meaning can God or the Catholic Church or any religion offer for my life? It seems more important to become aware of my own place in today's world, to discover what life's all about, where I'm going and why, and to experience for myself what God or truth may be without any institutional church pointing the way."

This extreme existentialist crisis of religious faith and self-identity reflects the dissatisfaction of many with religion as it is sometimes portrayed to them. They cannot see it as relevant to a progressive life today. A lonely self-centeredness may be discerned in the almost frantic current urge to feel the experiences of life and love solely on a human and secular level, rather than on that of God's norms for human living as presented by Christ, the Lord of life, love and salvation. Due to man's lack of adequate response to God's wise plan for life, religion is far from producing the stability it could and should in many people's lives. The growing disregard for man's past experience, for well-proven structures, for legitimate authority, and for spiritual values in the world, is having ruinous effects on true standards of behavior and is substituting false values which here-and-now demand the free play of gross subjectivism.

Widespread disturbances, caused by social, political, economic, and racial tensions, indicate deep-seated unrest, confusion, and a desire for more freedom for personal and communal decisions. The excesses prevalent in the moral order are evidenced principally in the areas of social injustice and spiritual depression, and by the widespread mis-use of narcotics, sex and alcohol. These are symptoms of an ailing society which decidedly needs the resusitation of rejuvenated Christian vitality.

However, it is precisely the mission assigned by Christ to the Church-community to show others the way from the desert to the promised land. Within the current history of mankind, the living God is profoundly interested in helping His people to have true life more fully. This is the reason He sent His divine Son who established His Church as the Universal Sacrament for the direction and salvation of mankind. The Church understands and offers help with the problems of man today, for she herself is also going through another period of re-evaluation.

In our day, as through past centuries, we can discern the workings of the Holy Spirit, whom Christ has irrevocably sent to guide His people. In the messages of Vatican Council II's call for renewal, that divine voice has again spoken, reminding man that he has not here a lasting city, but must keep renewing his life in the present until he lives finally in the city of God.

Any worthwhile goal requires much effort, self-sacrifice, and discipline for its attainment. Such is required to bring about the spiritual renewal within the Church-community in modern times, beginning with each individual. The subsequent parts of this book will be quite "practical," but without the basis of Part One, the successive parts could hardly stand firm. This is so because self-renewal is the first aim of the Church today, and it constitutes the foundation for a better tomorrow.

The following chapters contain conciliar passages which, if seriously applied to life, will help to bring about the greatly required spiritual renewal. When people earnestly respond to God's love, and live as His people (Chapter I), integrate the secular and the sacred according to His ways (Chapter II), and eliminate the causes of personal and communal sin (Chapter III), man's life will then become truly fulfilled. Its finality will bring an eternity of an even better life together in Christ (Chapter IV). The primary religious activity of man is to know, love and serve God, as it must ever be, and, in the very process of living by God's ways, man thereby fulfills a more truly human life on earth. A rejuvenated Christian vitality is the key to the individual's as well as the world's betterment in modern times.

Chapter I

LIVING AS GOD'S PEOPLE TODAY

For Meaningful Lives

There is always good reason for true hope, since God's love and assistance are ever available. The Lord never abandons His people when they seek His ways in life. He asks, however, that His plan for man's true happiness be sought and followed. God's revealed word offers man the only adequate pattern for a life of real purpose completely consonant with man's nature and goal. To follow God's plan will enrich life now on earth and lead toward an even better life hereafter.

Expressions such as "God's plan", "the Church's structure", "the ten commandments", and "the wisdom of experience" are not intended to restrain or suppress people. When we speak of God's plan for man, it is in the scriptural sense of a dynamic, evolving pattern to help man become truly free and more happy. This can only be achieved according to, not exclusive of, God's norms for man's life. Where is God's design for human happiness discovered? Where better than in sacred Scripture and in His Church-community!

People today are searching avidly to find clearer meaning for their lives. Atheistic and materialistic attitudes and the pressing problems of personal, family and community living are blinding many to the vision of spiritual values. Some Christians even, including Catholics, despite the directing compass of their faith, are being blown off course by the changing winds of modern-day Church life. We must help restore confidence in the guiding star of God's promise to be with His people always, especially in time of need as in contemporary circumstances.

One of the most influential trends in modern times is the philosophy of existentialism, which highly prizes the here-and-now human experience. This movement touches almost every aspect of contemporary life. As with other movements, there is much to be valued in this one, and much to be evaluated in the light of Christian revelation and proven experience.

Secular existentialism shows scant concern for divine revelation because it rejects anything that cannot be experienced personally. In such a personalistic philosophy little is objectively true except what the individual arrives at himself, and the past experiences of mankind have but passing interest, except in an esthetic way. Consequently, authority, whether it derives from traditional sources or from the present structures of society, is looked upon with a skeptical eye. In this respect secular existentialism is basically incompatible with the Christian faith because, instead of seeing divine revelation as a means to true freedom of spirit, it considers it a suppression of one's person. The defects in secular existentialism show up in its demands and protestations for solutions to complex problems right now, based on a particular situation, without consideration of divine or natural laws. It promotes action without reflection, heedless of the wider consequences of its cherished propositions with respect to the likely effects in other people's lives.

Christian existentialism, on the other hand, has a deep concern for current conditions, situations, and the needs of people while it considers also the enduring principles of life in view of the most modern discoveries in psychology and science in the light of revealed truth. It holds, in addition, that the gospels are dynamic and that the Church must keep abreast of the times in all areas of advanced, proven expansions of truth. Christian existentialism weighs matters carefully, examines available data in the light of divine and natural law, considers the rights and welfare of the individual as well as those of the community, while evaluating the effects of a principle or a course of action on the lives of those who will be affected.

Christianity values both the individual with a particular problem, and the welfare of the community. God knows and loves both the individual and the community of His people, and He is most assuredly interested in the situation and salvation of both. To live as a "people", a community dedicated in the same faith to Christ and His cause, requires balancing the welfare of the individual in conjunction with the progress of the total Christian community according to divine revelation. The thorny issues in this regard most frequently involve decisions in the order of morality in which the validity of the individual's proposed action must be related to the consequences pertinent to the whole community of the People of God. In living by the revelation of God, man lives as God's people.

The clearest expression of God's revelation is the Son of Man Himself, Jesus Christ, who has given us both the perfect pattern for meaningful living and the course to salvation. It is the function of Christ's Church-community to guide people through the current difficulties involving life and salvation. Vatican Council II, drawing extensively on sacred Scripture and the wisdom of the Holy Spirit, shows God's plan for His people's happiness and salvation in modern times.

The Church, keenly aware of modern tensions, and, in fulfillment of her mission to mankind, concerns herself deeply with man's problems and the united search for their solutions (Section 1). God is most intimately interested and infinitely concerned with all that pertains to man's life and salvation (Section 2). He calls all people to embrace His ways, become His people, and enjoy His care (Section 3). It is in living as God's people that life in our times, as in any age, can be more fully meaningful.

The central theme throughout this chapter is the Lord's steadfast and loving care for His people's welfare today as always. We must pray with hope that we can respond more fully to His love in complete faith and live more truly as God's people today. It is in response to His love and helpful grace that His revealed norms for our betterment and salvation can be achieved, that life can be beautifully meaningful, and that our world can be better utilized for our improvement and, thereby, to God's praise.

1. THE CURRENT HUMAN CONDITION IS A DEEP CONCERN OF THE CHURCH

A. Searching for Valid Approaches to the Problems of Modern Times

The grass-roots origin of the Vatican II messages came from looking over the surface of the earth and considering the actual circumstances in which men and women, children and youths live in the villages, towns and cities of the world. Consequently, the conciliar passages show deep concern for people suffering in the turmoil and tensions of modern times.

The community of the People of God, the Church, also lives in the midst of life's pressures in the current age. This Church expresses heartfelt desire to be of service to people and she earnestly seeks to share the griefs and anxieties, the joys and sorrows of life with all people. Certainly, the Christian community has significant contributions to offer in the common search for solving contemporary problems. The Church encourages the forward surge of positive thinking and calls on the Lord of all for His timely blessings on all mankind.

To sustain the peoples of the world for truly meaningful living in accord with Scripture, the Church cannot permit stones to be substituted for the bread of God's word. Neither can she stand idly by and watch man's sustenance become merely the weak diet of a secular humanism devoid of God. A life without God starves the human spirit, since people must have the strength that comes from His loving grace.

1. All Aspects of Mankind's Condition Are the Concern of the Christian Community

The joys and the hopes, the griefs and the anxieties of the men of this age, especially those who are poor or in any way afflicted, these too are the joys and hopes, the griefs and anxieties of the followers of Christ. Indeed, nothing genuinely human fails to raise an echo in their hearts. For theirs is a community composed of men. United in Christ, they are led by the Holy Spirit in their journey to the kingdom of their Father and they have welcomed the news of salvation which is meant for every man. That is why this community realizes that it is truly and intimately linked with mankind and its history.

Therefore, the Council focuses its attention on the world of men, the whole human family along with the sum of those realities in the midst of which that family lives. It gazes upon that world which is the theater of man's history, and carries the marks of his energies, his tragedies, and his triumphs; that world which the Christian sees as created and sustained by its Maker's love, fallen indeed into the bondage of sin, yet emancipated now by Christ. He was crucified and rose again to break the stranglehold of personified Evil, so that this world might be fashioned anew according to God's design and reach its fulfillment. *(World, No. 1)*

2. Man's Concern about Himself and the Future in a Fast-Moving World

Though mankind today is struck with wonder at its own discoveries and its power, it often raises anxious questions about the current trend of the world, about the place and role of man in the universe, about the meaning of his individual and collective strivings, and about the ultimate destiny of reality and of humanity. Hence, giving witness and voice to the faith of the whole People of God gathered together by Christ, this council can provide no more eloquent proof of its solidarity with the entire human family with which it is bound up, as well as its respect and love for that family, than by engaging with it in conversation about these various problems. *(World, No. 3)*

3. The Church and Society Seek for Approaches to Man's Problems

The Council brings to mankind light kindled from the gospel, and puts at its disposal those saving resources which the Church herself, under the guidance of the Holy Spirit, receives from her Founder. For the human person deserves to be preserved; human society deserves to be renewed. Hence the pivotal point of our total presentation will be man himself, whole and entire, body and soul, heart and conscience, mind and will.

Therefore, this sacred Synod proclaims the highest destiny of man and champions the godlike seed which has been sown in him. It offers to mankind the honest assistance of the Church in fostering that brotherhood of all men which corresponds to this destiny of theirs. Inspired by no earthly ambition, the Church seeks but a solitary goal: to carry forward the work of Christ Himself under the lead of the befriending Spirit. And Christ entered this world to give witness to the truth, to rescue and not to sit in judgment , to serve and not to be served. *(World, No. 3)*.

4. Amid Man's Anxieties the Church Recalls Stabilizing and Unchanging Truths

Nevertheless, in the face of the modern development of the world, an ever-increasing number of people are raising the most basic questions or recognizing them with a new sharpness: what is man? What is this sense of sorrow, of evil, of death, which continues to exist despite so much progress? What is the purpose of these victories, purchased at so high a cost? What can man offer to society, what can he expect from it? What follows this earthly life?

The Church believes that Christ, who died and was raised up for all, can through His Spirit offer man the light and the strength to measure up to his supreme destiny. Nor has any other name under heaven been given to man by which it is fitting for him to be saved. She likewise holds that in her most benign Lord and Master can be found the key, the focal point, and the goal of all human history.

The Church also maintains that beneath all changes there are many realities which do not change and which have their ultimate foundation in Christ, who is the same yesterday and today, yes and forever. Hence in the light of Christ, the image of the unseen God, the firstborn of every creature, the Council wishes to speak to all men in order to illuminate the mystery of man and to cooperate in finding the solution to the outstanding problems of our time. *(World, No. 10)*

B. Attitudes Regarding Christian Solutions to Problems of the Age

The Christian truly believes that the Holy Spirit whom Christ sent from the Father will help people to find valid answers to modern problems, both religious and secular. When people no longer consider God's ways as relevant to their lives, they multiply confusion as in Babel of old. God promises to help those who turn to Him in time of need. Yet, He has cautioned mankind that life on this earth is temporary and often difficult. Keeping faith with God through times of both stress and ease will prove the man of God.

The right solutions to modern problems require the right approach, namely, respect for divine law, established for man's own true welfare. Only those solutions should be adapted which are in accord with the divine law. The Spirit of Truth will guide people who respect God's law. With His help the community of mankind can establish a more realistic world of practical justice, mutual assistance, and universal peace. The world has much good in it, and Christianity can help improve life if men will heed the voice of their Lord.

5. Answers to Modern Problems Should Be Authentic and Realistic

The People of God believes that it is led by the Spirit of the Lord, who fills the earth. Motivated by this faith, it labors to decipher authentic signs of God's presence and purpose in the happenings, needs, and desires in which this People has a part along with other men of our age. For faith throws a new light on everything, manifests God's design for man's total vocation, and thus directs the mind to solutions which are fully human.

This Council, first of all, wishes to assess in this light those values which are most highly prized today, and to relate them to their divine source. For insofar as they stem from endowments conferred by God on man, these values are exceedingly good. Yet they are often wrenched from their rightful function by the taint in man's heart, and hence stand in need of purification.

What does the Church think of man? What recommendations seem needful for the upbuilding of contemporary society? What is the ultimate significance of human activity throughout the world? People are waiting for an answer to these questions. From the answers it will be increasingly clear that the People of God and the human race in whose midst it lives render service to each other. Thus the mission of the Church will show its religious, and by that very fact, its supremely human character. *(World, No. 11)*

6. Evaluating Modern Man's Achievements and Defects, His Dignity and Destiny

According to the almost unanimous opinion of believers and unbelievers alike, all things on earth should be related to man as their center and crown.

But what is man? About himself he has expressed, and continues to express, many divergent and even contradictory opinions. In these he often exalts himself as the absolute measure of all things or debases himself to the point of despair. The result is doubt and anxiety.

The Church understands these problems. Endowed with light from God, she can offer solutions to them so that man's true situation can be portrayed and his defects explained, while at the same time his dignity and destiny are justly acknowledged.

For sacred Scripture teaches that man was created "to the image of God, " is capable of knowing and loving his Creator, and was appointed by Him as master of all earthly creatures that he might subdue them and use them to God's glory. "What is man that thou art mindful of him or the son of man that thou visitest him? Thou hast made him a little less than the angels, thou hast crowned him with glory and honor: thou hast set him over the works of thy hands, thou hast subjected all things under his feet" (Ps. 8:5-6). *(World, No. 12)*

7. Man's Life Has Its Truest Meaning Through Christ, the Perfect Son of Man

The truth is that only in the mystery of the incarnate Word does the mystery of man take on light. For Adam, the first man, was a figure of Him who was to come, namely, Christ the Lord. Christ, the final Adam, by the revelation of the mystery of the Father and His love, fully reveals man to man himself and makes his supreme calling clear. It is not surprising, then, that in Him all the aforementioned truths find their root and attain their crown.

He who is "the image of the invisible God" (Col. 1:15), is Himself the perfect man. To the sons of Adam He restores the divine likeness which had been disfigured from the first sin onward. Since human nature as He assumed it was not annulled, by that very fact it has been raised up to a divine dignity in our respect too. For by His incarnation the Son of God has united Himself in some fashion with every man. He worked with human hands, He thought with a human mind, acted by human choice, and loved with a human heart. Born of the Virgin Mary, He has truly been made one of us, like us in all things except sin. *(World, No. 22)*

2. GOD IS INTIMATELY INTERESTED TODAY IN MAN'S LIFE AND SALVATION

A. Genuine Human Progress and Salvation Are Essentially Related

There is nothing to fear from becoming a truly religious person. Christian living should enable a person to become more genuinely human and contented while improving his own life and assisting others. The mature Christian will be a good neighbor to the people next door, an example to the local community, and an asset to the world. Earthly progress is not hindered but truly advanced by Christian living which should enliven human beings to produce achievements with temporal and eternal values.

Historically, human society has gained immeasurably from Christian standards on the dignity of all human beings and their freedom to develop themselves and the community in which they live. Christianity, when fully lived, should bring vigor to people's lives and to their works because they see all human progress in the light of bettering the world for man's life and ultimate salvation.

8. There Are Links Between Salvation and True Human Culture

There are many links between the message of salvation and human culture. For God, revealing Himself to His people to the extent of a full manifestation of Himself in His Incarnate Son, has spoken according to the culture proper to different ages.

Living in various circumstances during the course of time, the Church, too, has used in her preaching the discoveries of different cultures to spread and explain the message of Christ to all nations, to probe it and more deeply understand it, and to give it better expression in liturgical celebrations and in the life of the diversified community of the faithful.

But at the same time, the Church, sent to all peoples of every time and place, is not bound exclusively and indissolubly to any race or nation, nor to any particular way of life or any customary pattern of living, ancient or recent. Faithful to her own tradition and at the same time conscious of her universal mission, she can enter into communion with various cultural modes, to her own enrichment and theirs too. *(World, No. 58)*.

9. Man's True Dignity Is Founded in God

Modern man is on the road to a more thorough development of his own personality, and to a growing discovery and vindication of his own rights. Since it has been entrusted to the Church to reveal the mystery of God, who is the ultimate goal of man, she opens up to man at the same time the meaning of his own existence, that is, the innermost truth about himself. The Church truly knows that only God, whom she serves, meets the deepest longings of the human heart, which is never fully satisfied by what this world has to offer.

She also knows that man is constantly worked upon by God's Spirit, and hence can never be altogether indifferent to the problems of religion. The experience of past ages proves this, as do numerous   indications in our own times. For man will always yearn to know, at least in an obscure way, what is the meaning of his life, of his activity, of his death. The very presence of the Church recalls these problems to his mind.

But only God, who created man to His own image and ransomed him from sin, provides a fully adequate answer to these questions. This He does through what He has revealed in Christ His Son, who became man. Whoever follows after Christ, the perfect man, becomes himself more of a man.

Thanks to this belief, the Church can anchor the dignity of human nature against all tides of opinion, for example, those which undervalue the human body or idolize it. By no human law can the personal dignity and liberty of man be so aptly safeguarded as by the gospel of Christ which has been entrusted to the Church. *(World, No. 41)*

10. The Gospel and the Church Foster Human Dignity and Progress

For this gospel announces and proclaims the freedom of the sons of God, and repudiates all the bondage which ultimately results from sin. The gospel has a sacred reverence for the dignity of conscience and its freedom of choice, constantly advises that all human talents be employed in God's service and men's, and, finally, commends all to the charity of all.

All this corresponds with the basic law of the Christian dispensation. For though the same God is Savior and Creator, Lord of human history as well as of salvation history, in the divine arrangement itself the rightful autonomy of the creature, and particularly of man, is not withdrawn. Rather it is re-established in its own dignity and strengthened in it.

Therefore, by virtue of the gospel committed to her, the Church proclaims the rights of man. She acknowledges and greatly esteems the dynamic movements of today by which these rights are everywhere fostered. Yet these movements must be penetrated by the spirit of the gospel and protected against any kind of false autonomy. For we are tempted to think that our personal rights are fully ensured only when we are exempt from every requirement of divine law. But in this way lies not the maintenance of the dignity of the human person, but its annihilation. *(World, No. 41)*

B. Divine Providence for Man Throughout the Past

The theme-song throughout man's history sings of the Lord's care for His people in the needs of every successive generation. This, of course, will be acceptable only to those who believe in divine providence and discern the hand of God within human lives and events. We ponder here mostly God's dealing with "His people" in the scriptural sense of those who acknowledge the Lord, God, in the Judeo-Christian tradition. This does not overlook God's providence, love, and care for those of other civilizations, cultures, ages, and religions. Whenever truth, justice, and charity are practiced, He is praised. Those persons who praise the name of the Lord in good times and in bad are truly the People of God.

It will be helpful to review from holy Scripture God's interest in man's welfare throughout past ages. When we recall God's providence at work in the past we will perceive that His loving concern for His people today is as strong as it has ever been.

11. God Is Intimately Interested in Helping Man

In His goodness and wisdom, God chose to reveal Himself and to make known to us the hidden purpose of His will (cf. Eph. 1:9) by which through Christ, the Word made flesh, man has access to the Father in the Holy Spirit and comes to share in the divine nature (cf. Eph. 2:18; 2 Pet. 1:4). Through this revelation, therefore, the invisible God (cf. Col. 1:15; 1 Tim. 1:17) out of the abundance of His love speaks to men as friends (cf. Ex. 33:11; Jn. 15:14-15) and lives among them (cf. Bar. 3:38), so that He may invite and take them into fellowship with Himself. *(Revelation, No. 2)*

12. God Helps Those Who Try to Serve Him

God, who through the Word creates all things (cf. Jn. 1:3) and keeps them in existence, gives men an enduring witness to Himself in created realities (cf. Rom. 1:19-20). Planning to make known the way of heavenly salvation, He went further and from the start manifested Himself to our first parents. Then after their fall His promise of redemption aroused in them the hope of being saved (cf. Gen. 3:15), and from that time on He ceaselessly kept the human race in His care, in order to give eternal life to those who perseveringly do good in search of salvation (cf. Rom. 2:6-7). *(Revelation, No. 3)*

13. God Has Always Helped His People

In carefully planning and preparing the salvation of the whole human race, the God of supreme love, by a special dispensation, chose for Himself a people to whom He might entrust His promises. First he entered into a covenant with Abraham (cf. Gen. 15:18) and, through Moses, with the people of Israel (cf. Ex. 24:8). To this people which He had acquired for Himself, He so manifested Himself through words and deeds as the one true and living God that

Israel came to know by experience the ways of God with men, and
with God Himself speaking to them through the mouth of the
prophets, Israel daily gained a deeper and clearer understanding of
His ways and made them more widely known among the nations
(cf. Ps. 21:28-29; 95:1-3; Is. 2:1-4; Jer. 3:17). *(Revelation, No. 14)*

14. The Old Covenant of God with His People Is Effective in the New for Today

The principal purpose to which the plan of the Old Covenant
was directed was to prepare for the coming both of Christ, the
universal Redeemer, and of the messianic kingdom, to announce
this coming by prophecy (cf. Lk. 24:44; Jn. 5:39; 1 Pet. 1:10), and
to indicate its meaning through various types (cf. 1 Cor. 10:11).
Now the books of the Old Testament, in accordance with the state
of mankind before the time of salvation established by Christ, reveal
to all men the knowledge of God and of man and the ways in which
God, just and merciful, deals with men. These books, though they
also contain some things which are incomplete and temporary,
nevertheless show us true divine pedagogy. These same books, then,
give expression to a lively sense of God, contain a store of sublime
teachings about God, sound wisdom about human life, and a wonderful treasury of prayers, and in them the mystery of our salvation
is present in a hidden way. Christians should receive them with
reverence. *(Revelation, No. 15)*

C. Scripture Contains God's Plan for Modern Man's Fulfillment

God does not lose interest in the work of His hands; He is never
far removed from those who seek Him. In order to have a life of total
fulfillment and satisfaction we may turn to a variety of experiences
which of themselves may be good, bad or indifferent. Yet, the inner
peace we really seek can come only from our cooperation with God's
word. Man's peace lies in doing the will of God, as presented in His
Son's gospel message and interpreted for our times by those in the
Church whom Christ commissions to speak in His name.

The following brief quotations from Vatican II, are by no means
intended to present God's complete ways for man's happiness. Instead,
they remind us that holy Scripture helps us to spin the fabric of our
lives into a meaningful pattern with the guiding tutorship of the

Church. The gospel of Christ points the way to achieve real self-fulfillment, for He spoke with the power of God not only to His own age but to all the future eras of the earth's existence. Holy Scripture reveals God's plan for life's true happiness here and hereafter, since Christ has brought the fullness of God's revelation to mankind.

15. Christ Brought the Fullness of God's Revelation for Man Today

Then, after speaking in many places and varied ways through the prophets, God "last of all in these days has spoken to us by his son" (Heb. 1:1-2). For he sent His Son, the eternal Word, who enlightens all men, so that He might dwell among men and tell them the innermost realities about God (cf. Jn. 1:1-18). Jesus Christ, therefore, the Word made flesh sent as "a man to men," "speaks the words of God" (Jn. 3:34), and completes the work of salvation which His Father gave Him to do (cf. Jn. 5:36, 17:4). To see Jesus is to see His Father (Jn. 14:9). For this reason Jesus perfected revelation by fulfilling it through His whole work of making Himself present and manifesting Himself: through His words and deeds, His signs and wonders, but especially through His death and glorious resurrection from the dead and final sending of the Spirit of truth. Moreover, He confirmed with divine testimony what revelation proclaimed: that God is with us to free us from the darkness of sin and death, and to raise us up to life eternal.

The Christian dispensation, therefore, as the new and definitive convenant, will never pass away, and we now await no further new public revelation before the glorious manifestation of our Lord Jesus Christ (cf. 1 Tim. 6:14 and Tit. 2:13). *(Revelation, No. 4)*

16. The Gospels Hold Pre-Eminence of God's Revelation for Man

The word of God, which is the power of God for the salvation of all who believe (cf. Rom. 1:16), is set forth and shows its power in a most excellent way in the writings of the New Testament. For when the fullness of time arrived (cf. Gal. 4:4), the Word was made flesh and dwelt among us in the fullness of grace and truth (cf. Jn. 1:14). Christ established the kingdom of God on earth, manifested His Father and Himself by deeds and words, and completed His work by His death, resurrection, and glorious ascension and by the sending of the Holy Spirit. Having been lifted up from the earth, He draws all men to Himself (cf. Jn. 6:68). This mystery had not been manifested to other generations as it was now revealed to His holy apostles and prophets in the Holy Spirit (cf. Eph. 3:4-6. Greek text), so that they might preach the gospel, stir up faith in Jesus, Christ and Lord, and gather the Church together. To these realities, the writings of the New Testament stand as a perpetual and divine witness.

It is common knowledge that among all the Scriptures, even those of the New Testament, the Gospels have a special pre-eminence, and rightly so, for they are the principal witness of the life and teaching of the incarnate Word, our Savior. *(Revelation, No. 17-18)*

17. A Well-Ordered Temporal Life Advances Man's Total Fulfillment

God's plan for the world is that men should work together to restore the temporal sphere of things and to develop it unceasingly.

Many elements make up the temporal order: namely, the good things of life and the prosperity of the family, culture, economic affairs, the arts and professions, political institutions, international relations, and other matters of this kind, as well as their development and progress. All of these not only aid in the attainment of man's ultimate goal but also possess their own intrinsic value. This value has been implanted in them by God, whether they are considered in themselves or as parts of the whole temporal order. "God saw all that he had made, and it was very good" (Gen. 1:31). This natural goodness of theirs takes on a special dignity as a result of their relation to the human person, for whose service they were created. Last of all, it has pleased God to unite all things, both natural and supernatural, in Christ Jesus "that in all things he may have the first place" (Col. 1:18). This destination, however, not only does not deprive the temporal order of its independence, its proper goals, laws, resources, and significance for human welfare but rather perfects the temporal order in its own intrinsic strength and excellence and raises it to the level of man's total vocation upon earth. *(Laity, No. 7)*

D. Man's Response of Faith in God and His Plan for Life

The difference between a distinctly secular outlook on life and a truly spiritual one is faith in God, His words and His presence among His people. Indeed, religious faith is the most reasonable response to life's

movement, events, and goal. Religious faith consists in freely responding to God's love and to what He has revealed as best for us. A faith by
which to live means more than an intellectual assent to God's existence
and dominion. It includes a positive response to God's will motivated
by true love. Faith may be summarized as God revealing and man
responding.

When faith in God's word is strong, the religious person looks
upon life, his fellow-man, and the world of attractive things as related
to the Lord of the universe. To Christians, Christ is the key that un-
locks the door to life's fullest meaning. Faith in Christ as God's fullest
revelation for man's betterment will bring the self-respect and security
that leads to living as God's people today.

18. Man Responds to God by Believing in Him and His Guidance

"The obedience of faith" (Rom. 16:26; cf. 1:5; 2 Cor.
10:5-6) must be given to God who reveals, an obedience by which
man entrusts his whole self freely to God, offering "the full submission of intellect and will to God who reveals," and freely assent-
ing to the truth revealed by Him. *(Revelation, No. 5)*

19. Human Reasoning Experiences God; God's Revelation Helps Man

Through divine revelation, God chose to show forth and communicate Himself and the eternal decisions of His will regarding the
salvation of men. That is to say, He chose "to share those divine
treasures which totally transcend the understanding of the human
mind."

This sacred Synod affirms, "God, the beginning and end of all
things, can be known with certainty from created reality by the
light of human reason" (cf. Rom. 1:20); but the Synod teaches that
it is through His revelation "that those religious truths which are by
their nature accessible to human reason can be known by all men
with ease, with solid certitude, and with no trace of error, even in
the present state of the human race." *(Revelation, No. 6)*

20. Christ Is Man's Way to Temporal Improvement and Eternal Salvaion

While helping the world and receiving many benefits from it,
the Church has a single intention: that God's kingdom may come,

and that the salvation of the whole human race may come to pass. For every benefit which the People of God during its earthly pilgrimage can offer to the human family stems from the fact that the Church is "the universal sacrament of salvation," simultaneously manifesting and exercising the mystery of God's love for man.

For God's Word, by whom all things were made, was Himself made flesh so that as perfect man He might save all men and sum up all things in Himself. The Lord is the goal of human history, the focal point of the longings of history and of civilization, the center of the human race, the joy of every heart, and the answer to all its yearnings. He it is whom the Father raised from the dead, lifted on high, and stationed at His right hand, making Him Judge of the living and the dead. Enlivened and united in His Spirit, we journey toward the consummation of human history, one which fully accords with the counsel of God's love: "To re-establish all things in Christ, both those in the heavens and those on the earth" (Eph. 1:10). *(World, No. 45)*

21. Christ's Paschal Mystery at Work in Those Who Live It

Pressing upon the Christian, to be sure, are the need and the duty to battle against evil through manifold tribulations and even to suffer death. But, linked with the paschal mystery and patterned on the dying Christ, he will hasten forward to resurrection in the strength which comes from hope.

All this holds true not only for Christians, but for all men of good will in whose hearts grace works in an unseen way. For, since Christ died for all men, and since the ultimate vocation of man is in fact one, and divine, we ought to believe that the Holy Spirit in a manner known only to God offers to every man the possibility of being associated with this paschal mystery.

Such is the mystery of man, and it is a great one, as seen by believers in the light of Christian revelation. Through Christ and in Christ, the riddles of sorrow and death grow meaningful. Apart from His gospel, they overwhelm us. Christ has risen, destroying death by His death. He has lavished life upon us so that, as sons in the Son, we can cry out in the Spirit: Abba, Father! *(World, No. 22)*

3. LIVING IN PHASE WITH GOD AS THE COMMUNITY OF HIS PEOPLE

A. God Strengthens the Bond of Faith Among Believers

It is God Himself who fosters among those who respect, love and serve Him a bond so strong and unifying that it forms the community of believers and strengthens them. In Scripture, as in life today, God calls these believing people, "My people."

The Lord God even makes a covenant or promise to be with His people at all times when they strive to serve Him. He sent the Son of Man to fulfill His covenant and save mankind. Christ, the Savior, is now head of the new People of God. These people, united in faith, form the Church of Christ, the community of His people today.

22. God Forms His Community of Believers

At all times and among every people, God has given welcome to whosoever fears Him and does what is right (cf. Acts 10:35). It has pleased God, however, to make men holy and save them not merely as individuals without any mutual bonds, but by making them into a single people, a people which acknowledges Him in truth and serves Him in holiness. He therefore chose the race of Israel as a people unto Himself. With it He set up a covenant. Step by step He taught this people by manifesting in its history both Himself and the decree of His will, and by making it holy unto Himself. All these things, however, were done by way of preparation and as a figure of that new and perfect covenant which was to be ratified in Christ, and of that more luminous revelation which was to be given through God's very Word made flesh. (Church, No.9)

23. Christ Unites the Bond of Faith Among the People of God

Christ instituted this new covenant, that is to say, the new testament, in His blood (cf. 1 Cor. 11:25), by calling together a people made up of Jew and Gentile, making them one, not according to the flesh but in the Spirit.

This was to be the new People of God. For, those who believe in Christ, who are reborn not from a perishable but from an imperishable seed through the Word of the living God (cf. 1 Pet. 1:23), not from the flesh but from water and the Holy Spirit (cf. Jn. 3:5-6), are finally established as "a chosen race, a royal priesthood, a holy nation, a purchased people . . . You who in times past were not a people, but are now the people of God" (1 Pet. 2:9-10). *(Church, No.9)*

24. The Dignity, Freedom, and Goal of the People of God

That messianic people has for its head Christ, "who was delivered up for our sins, and rose again for our justification" (Rom. 4:25), and who now, having won a name which is above all names, reigns in glory in heaven. The heritage of this people are the dignity and freedom of the sons of God, in whose hearts the Holy Spirit dwells as in His temple. Its law is the new commandment to love as Christ loved us (cf. Jn. 13:34). Its goal is the kingdom of God, which has been begun by God Himself on earth, and which is to be further extended until it is brought to perfection by Him at the end of time. Then Christ our life (cf. Col. 3:4), will appear, and "creation itself also will be delivered from its slavery to corruption into the freedom of the glory of the sons of God" (Rom. 8:21). *(Church, No.9)*

25. The People of God Form the Church of Christ

So it is that this messianic people, although it does not actually include all men, and may more than once look like a small flock, is nonetheless a lasting and sure seed of unity, hope, and salvation for the whole human race. Established by Christ as a fellowship of life, charity, and truth, it is also used by Him as an instrument for the redemption of all, and is sent forth into the whole world as the light of the world and the salt of the earth (cf. Mt. 5:13-16).

Israel according to the flesh, which wandered as an exile in the desert, was already called the Church of God (2 Esd. 13:1; cf. Num. 20:4; Dt. 23:1 ff). Likewise the new Israel which, while going forward in this present world, goes in search of a future and abiding city (cf. Heb. 13:14) is also called the Church of Christ (cf. Mt. 16:18). For He has bought it for Himself with His blood (cf. Acts 20:28), has filled it with His Spirit, and provided it with those means which befit it as a visible and social unity. God has gathered together as one all those who in faith look upon Jesus as the author of salvation and the source of unity and peace, and has established them as the Church, that for each and all she may be the visible sacrament of this saving unity. *(Church, No.9)*

B. All Mankind Is Called to Be the People of God

Christ calls all people of every race and condition to enroll in His kingdom of truth, justice, peace and love. His emissaries are commissioned to go forth into every village, city, and nation spreading the good news of salvation in order to help establish with Christ His kingdom in the hearts of all people.

The kingdom Christ wants to establish is both spiritual and visible, comprised of people united in the same religious beliefs. However, the unity of faith leaves intact and even fosters the diversity of valid cultures and customs which exist among the nations of the world.

26. All Mankind Is Invited to Be Counted Among the People of God

All men are called to belong to the new People of God. Wherefore this People, while remaining one and unique, is to be spread throughout the whole world and must exist in all ages, so that the purpose of God's will may be fulfilled. In the beginning God made human nature one. After His children were scattered, He decreed that they should at length be unified again (cf. Jn. 11:52). It was for this reason that God sent His Son, whom He appointed heir of all things (cf. Heb. 1:2), that He might be Teacher, King, and Priest of all, the Head of the new and universal people of the sons of God. For this God finally sent His Son's Spirit as Lord and Lifegiver. He it is who, on behalf of the whole Church and each and every one of those who believe, is the principle of their coming together and remaining together in the teaching of the apostles and in fellowship, in the breaking of bread and in prayers (cf. Acts 2:42, Greek text). *(Church, No.13)*

27. All Nations Can Be United and Blessed as the One People of God

It follows that among all the nations of earth there is but one People of God, which takes its citizens from every race, making them citizens of a kingdom which is of a heavenly and not an earthly nature. For all the faithful scattered throughout the world are in communion with each other in the Holy Spirit, so that "he who occupies the See of Rome knows the people of India are his members." Since the kingdom of Christ is not of this world (cf. Jn. 18:36), the Church or People of God takes nothing away from the temporal welfare of any people by establishing that kingdom. Rather does she foster and take to herself, insofar as they are good, the ability, resources, and customs of each people. Taking them to herself she purifies, strengthens, and ennobles them. The Church in this is mindful that she must harvest with that King to whom the nations were given for an inheritance (cf. Ps. 2:8) and into whose city they bring gifts and presents (cf. Ps. 71[72]:10; Is. 60:4-7; Apoc. 21:24). This characteristic of universality which adorns the People of God is a gift from the Lord Himself. By reason of it, the Catholic Church strives energetically and constantly to bring all humanity with all its riches back to Christ its Head in the unity of His Spirit. *(Church, No.13)*

C. All Sincere People Are Related to Catholic Unity

In the kingdom of Christ there are certainly various levels of response to the call and grace of God among mankind. God has retained to Himself the hidden judgment as to those whom He considers His own, the people of good-will throughout the world. Their number may be larger than men know! There is much hope for all persons who pray pleadingly, "Our Father . . . . "

Catholics believe that Christ, the Lord, has entrusted to them the fullness of His revelation and the surest means for salvation which is to be shared with all peoples of the earth. Only God knows who respond to His call and His grace. Catholics also believe that all people who sincerely strive to serve God, according to their knowledge and acceptance of divine revelation, are related to the unity of the Catholic faith.

28. All Believing People Share in Catholic Unity of the People of God

All men are called to be part of this Catholic unity of the People of God, a unity which is harbinger of the universal peace it promotes. And there belong to it or are related to it in various ways, the Catholic faithful as well as all who believe in Christ, and indeed the whole of mankind. For all men are called to salvation by the grace of God. *(Church, No.13)*

29. Other Christians Share Many Blessings with Catholics

The Church recognizes that in many ways she is linked with those who, being baptized, are honored with the name of Christian, though they do not profess the faith in its entirety or do not preserve unity of communion with the successor of Peter. For there are many who honor sacred Scripture, taking it as a norm of belief and of action, and who show a true religious zeal. They lovingly believe in God the Father Almighty and in Christ, Son of God and Savior. They are consecrated by baptism, through which they are united with Christ. They also recognize and receive other sacraments within their own Churches or ecclesial communities. Many of them rejoice in the episcopate, celebrate the Holy Eucharist, and cultivate devotion toward the Virgin Mother of God. They also share with us in prayer and other spiritual benefits.

Likewise, we can say that in some real way they are joined with us in the Holy Spirit, for to them also He gives His gifts and graces, and is thereby operative among them with His sanctifying power. Some indeed He has strengthened to the extent of the shedding of their blood. In all of Christ's disciples the Spirit arouses the desire to be peacefully united, in the manner determined by Christ, as one flock under one shepherd, and He prompts them to pursue this goal. Mother Church never ceases to pray, hope, and work that they may gain this blessing. She exhorts her sons to purify and renew themselves so that the sign of Christ may shine more brightly over the face of the Church. *(Church, No.15)*

30. God-Respecting People are Related to the People of God

Finally, those who have not yet received the gospel are related in various ways to the People of God. In the first place there is the people to whom the covenants and the promises were given and from whom Christ was born according to the flesh (cf. Rom. 9:4-5). On account of their fathers, this people remains most dear to God, for God does not repent of the gifts He makes nor of the calls He issues (cf. Rom. 11:28-29).

But the plan of salvation also includes those who acknowledge the Creator. In the first place among these there are the Moslems, who, professing to hold the faith of Abraham, along with us adore the one and merciful God, who on the last day will judge mankind. Nor is God Himself far distant from those who in shadows and images seek the unknown God, for it is He who gives to all men life and breath and every other gift (cf. Acts 17:25-28), and who as Savior wills that all men be saved (cf. 1 Tim. 2:4). *(Church, No.16)*

31. All People of Good-Will Can Attain Salvation

Those also can attain to everlasting salvation who through no fault of their own do not know the gospel of Christ or His Church, yet sincerely seek God and, moved by grace, strive by their deeds to do His will as it is known to them through the dictates of conscience. Nor does divine Providence deny the help necessary for salvation to those who, without blame on their part, have not yet arrived at an explicit knowledge of God, but who strive to live a good life, thanks to His grace. Whatever goodness or truth is found among them is looked upon by the Church as a preparation for the gospel. She regards such qualities as given by Him who enlightens all men so that they may finally have life. *(Church, No.16)*

32. The Church Strives to Save Even Hardened Sinners

But rather often men, deceived by the Evil One, have become caught up in futile reasoning and have exchanged the truth of God for a lie, serving the creature rather than the Creator (cf. Rom. 1:21,25). Or some there are who, living and dying in a world without God, are subject to utter hopelessness. Consequently, to promote the glory of God and procure the salvation of all such men, and mindful of the command of the Lord, "Preach the gospel to every creature" (Mk. 16:16), the Church painstakingly fosters her missionary work. *(Church, No.16)*

The concluding reflection of this chapter is that living as God's people always brings the truest meaning to life. As sacred Scripture and the history of man's salvation point out, our main purpose in life is to know, love, and serve our Creator and Savior Who has first loved us. There are blessings attached to following His divine ways for human happiness, which norms are summarized in God's Ten Commandments and implemented in the teaching of Christ's Church. These blessings consist chiefly in personal sanctity, unity of faith, peace among men, and the promise of eternal life. The attainment of these blessings for the individual and for mankind glorifies God, since everything He wills on earth is for man's welfare. In gratitude to our risen Savior, His praise is sung by His people today.

Chapter II

INTEGRATING THE SECULAR AND THE SACRED

Through Wisdom in Our Times

The integration of the secular and the sacred involves bringing into harmony the mundane and the religious aspects of life. The way toward living more meaningful lives as God's people in the world involves the practical aspects of using all things properly in life. This use requires calling upon the natural and divine laws. Here the Church helps greatly, both in private life and in the social order for total human fulfillment. The People of God live and work in a secularistic atmosphere which only infrequently acknowledges the divine norms for man's life and its activities. The Christian Church fosters all true human progress. The world has nothing to lose and much to gain from Vatican II's counsels for the uplifting of man's condition in today's world.

The Church champions the unique worth and destiny of every human being, for God blesses all truly human attributes and achievements as beneficial for the development of man who reflects his Maker's intelligence and design in the world. Moreover, the personal dignity of all people, made in God's image and cherished by Him, must be maintained and fostered in an age which seems intent on excluding the influence of Christianity from the affairs of daily life.

We must distinguish between the secularization of life devoid of God, which degrades human dignity, and the secular world, the temporal order, in which man lives and which he must integrate with the sacred to acquire life's true worth. Indeed, the secular world is the normal sphere to which the Church's members are sent daily by Christ. Intimate dialogue and mutual understanding must be brought about between the Church and the world of secular societies on all levels and in all aspects. Today's thinkers must devise a truly universal medium of communication for open dialogue which is understandable by all, acceptable by all, and applicable to the common problems of mankind. The Christian community must both listen to and learn from secular society. They can both learn from as well as help each other. In this dialogue the voice of the Church is preeminent, while men search together for life's improvement and ultimate fulfillment. The world and all in it is intended by God for man's use.

Secular existentialism looks upon existence as something rather foolish and sarcastically speaks of "the cosmic joke." It may concede the existence of some nebulous "big power" in the universe, even a unifying "it." Yet for its adherents there is no Creator-God, no Revealing-God, little love in life and slight purpose in living except to experience self-fulfillment. The follower of Christ, however, listens to God, loves Him and explores life in the world in a spirit of hopeful improvement. Precisely because the religious man loves God and listens to Him, he becomes a better human being in all practical aspects of life, as he knows himself to be linked with the Father's other children and is aware of their common purpose in life.

To the Christian, the Incarnation of the invisible God's fullest revelation to man is Christ, our Lord. We and the world are His on two counts, since Christ is both God and man, Creator and Redeemer. He is the supreme architect, scientist, and artist, for He works with His word, His grace, and His love. We ally ourselves with His wisdom and His power, because we have first allied ourselves with His love. The Christian moves forward in faith, too close to history to do more than trust the Lord of Salvation. While laboring patiently yet loving mightily, we explore all facets of life excitedly and await Christ's second coming, but not idly.

Wisdom, however, is required to integrate the mundane and the sacred aspects of life for individuals and for mankind. Such wisdom is God's sure-sign for man's arrival at correct decisions, personally and collectively, in his use of created goods and of human means and institutions, in accord with the divine design for human happiness and peace. The gift of wisdom, when sought and received from the Holy Spirit, attracts people to seek truth, goodness, and beauty throughout life. This wisdom is the blessing of knowing how to coordinate the sacred within the secular during life. The needs of modern times require more people of wise perception and steady strength to achieve the peace all men seek. This can come only through proper order in one's life and in society in the light of divine revelation.

The conciliar passages provide guidelines for forging peace in life through the proper integration of man's spiritual and temporal aspirations (Section 1). In fact, the Christian way of life harmoniously motivates its followers to improve their personal and communal lives to the fullest perfection on earth while attaining the perfect integration of temporal and eternal life in God (Section 2).

The Council aids us to resolve the problem of living for two worlds at the same time, the temporal and the eternal. Here we find guidance on how to reconcile our spiritual and material concerns of life. We would do well to beg the Holy Spirit for that gift of true wisdom which inspires us to use properly the faculties of our persons and the good things of life, and to abstain from their misuse. In such a vast undertaking we can thank our Lord for the sure assistance of His Church. Here we learn best how to live in the atmosphere of both the human and the divine, in time for eternity, and in the secular for the sacred.

1. FORGING PEACEFUL LIVING BY
   FOLLOWING GOD'S NORMS IN LIFE

A. Coordinating the Secular
    and the Sacred in Life

Peace in individual lives, as well as among communities or nations, is not easily established and maintained; it must be first forged in the fires of wise choice and then cooled in the waters of right order. Herein lies the function and the fruit of integrating the secular and the sacred in personal, communal, and national life.

Clearly, both the sacred and the secular make indispensable and distinctive contributions to the fullness of human living. Until the day when all will be united with Christ in glory there will, of course, be tension in attaining coordination of the divine and human elements of life. The secular requires the sacred to give meaning and direction to its mundane and transient aspects. Surely, too, as man is constituted in this life, the sacred also needs the secular, as the soul needs the body, as a field of operation and an object of its sanctifying mission. The union of the divine-made-flesh in the Incarnation of Christ uplifts the human and in a real way unites man's endeavors with God's blessing.

33. Wisdom from God Is Required to Avert Disaster in Life

Man judges rightly that by his intellect he surpasses the material universe, for he shares in the light of the divine mind. By relentlessly employing his talents through the ages, he has indeed made progress in the practical sciences, technology, and the liberal arts. In our times he has won superlative victories, especially in his probing of the material world and in subjecting it to himself.

Still he has always searched for more penetrating truths, and finds them. For his intelligence is not confined to observable data alone. It can with genuine certitude attain to reality itself as knowable, though in consequence of sin that certitude is partly obscured and weakened.

The intellectual nature of the human person is perfected by wisdom and needs to be. For wisdom gently attracts the mind of man to a quest and a love for what is true and good. Steeped in wisdom, man passes through visible realities to those which are unseen.

Our era needs such wisdom more than bygone ages if the discoveries made by man are to be further humanized. For the future of the world stands in peril unless wiser men are forthcoming. It should also be pointed out that many nations, poorer in economic goods, are quite rich in wisdom and can offer noteworthy advantages to others.

It is, finally, through the gift of the Holy Spirit that man comes by faith to the contemplation and appreciation of the divine plan. *(World, No.15)*

34. People with Religious Perception Can Integrate Secular with Religious Progress

Because the very plan of salvation requires it, the faithful should learn how to distinguish carefully between those rights and duties which are theirs as members of the Church, and those which they have as members of human society. Let them strive to harmonize the two, remembering that in every temporal affair they must be guided by a Christian conscience. For even in secular affairs there is no human activity which can be withdrawn from God's dominion. In our own time, however, it is most urgent that this distinction and also this harmony should shine forth as radiantly as possible in the practice of the faithful, so that the mission of the Church may correspond more adequately to the special conditions of the world today. For while it must be recognized that the temporal sphere is governed by its own principles, since it is properly concerned with the interests of this world, that ominous doctrine must rightly be rejected which attempts to build a society with no regard whatever for religion, and which attacks and destroys the religious liberty of its citizens. *(Church, No.36)*

35. Learning the Purpose of Created Goods While Acquiring Competence in Life

The faithful, therefore, must learn the deepest meaning and the value of all creation, and how to relate it to the praise of God. They must assist one another to live holier lives even in their daily occupations. In this way the world is permeated by the spirit of Christ and more effectively achieves its purpose in justice, charity, and peace. The laity have the principal role in the universal fulfillment of this purpose.

Therefore, by their competence in secular fields and by their personal activity, elevated from within by the grace of Christ, let them labor vigorously so that by human labor, technical skill, and civic culture created goods may be perfected for the benefit of every last man, according to the design of the Creator and the light of His Word. Let them work to see that created goods are more fittingly distributed among men, and that such goods in their own way lead to general progress in human and Christian liberty. In this manner, through the members of the Church, Christ will progressively illumine the whole of human society with His saving light. *(Church, No.36)*

36. Christians Should Recognize Their Duty to Uplift Society

United on behalf of heavenly values and enriched by them, this family has been "constituted and organized in the world as a society" by Christ, and is equipped with "those means which befit it as a visible and social unity." Thus the Church, at once a visible assembly and a spiritual community, goes forward together with humanity and experiences the same earthly lot which the world does. She serves as a leaven and as a kind of soul for human society as it is to be renewed in Christ and transformed into God's family.

That the earthly and the heavenly city penetrate each other is a fact accessible to faith alone. It remains a mystery of human history, which sin will keep in great disarray until the splendor of

God's sons is fully revealed. Pursuing the saving purpose which is proper to her, the Church not only communicates divine life to men, but in some way casts the reflected light of that life over the entire earth.

This she does most of all by her healing and elevating impact on the dignity of the person, by the way in which she strengthens the seams of human society and imbues the everyday activity of men with a deeper meaning and importance. Thus, through her individual members and her whole community, the Church believes she can contribute greatly toward making the family of man and its history more human. *(World, No.40)*

37. The True Christian Should Foster True Human Progress

This Council exhorts Christians, as citizens of two cities, to strive to discharge their earthly duties conscientiously and in response to the gospel spirit. They are mistaken who, knowing that we have here no abiding city but seek one which is to come, think that they may therefore shirk their earthly responsibilities. For they are forgetting that by the faith itself they are more than ever obliged to measure up to these duties, each according to his proper vocation.

Nor, on the contrary, are they any less wide of the mark who think that religion consists in acts of worship alone and in the discharge of certain moral obligations, and who imagine they can plunge themselves into earthly affairs in such a way as to imply that these are altogether divorced from the religious life. This split between the faith which many profess and their daily lives deserves to be counted among the more serious errors of our age. Long since, the prophets of the Old Testament fought vehemently against this scandal and even more so did Jesus Christ Himself in the New Testament threaten it with grave punishments.

Therefore, let there be no false opposition between professional and social activities on the one part, and religious life on the other. The Christian who neglects his temporal duties neglects his duties toward his neighbor and even God, and jeopardizes his eternal salvation. Christians should rather rejoice that they can follow the example of Christ, who worked as an artisan. In the exercise of all their earthly activities, they can thereby gather their humane, domestic, professional, social, and technical enterprises into one vital synthesis with religious values, under whose supreme direction all things are harmonized unto God's glory. *(World, No.43)*

B. Achieving God's Plan for Order in Man's Life, His Works, and the World

God alone is uncreated. It is He who sets the ultimate purpose for all created beings. Within that purpose, man is entrusted with the whole world and its proper exploration as well as life's improvement in it. It is also in accomplishment of the divine design that man's life, works, and the world find their proper fulfillment and, consequently, their peace.

Man's truest claim to dignity lies precisely in being fashioned in the mold of God's image. It is also man's responsibility and privilege to reflect this image of divinity throughout his entire life, not only to expand and complete his own life but to attain justice and peace among his fellow man.

Entire segments of modern society, especially among young adults, are challenging the validity of discipline in personal conduct, of order in society, and of structure in the Church. These are termed irrelevant to contemporary living. Yet loss of such transcendent values, which constitute the compass points for orderly living, is a chief cause of the modern world's floundering on the rocks of confusion, dissension and chaos.

In following God's ways for human life on earth, man can find the peace he seeks, whatever his attendant external circumstances may be. This must be so because, in all that God ordains, He intends to establish the right order man needs for peace of soul, peace in his works, and peace in his world.

38. Human Rights, Dignity, and Responsibility Regarding Right Order in Life

There is a growing awareness of the exalted dignity proper to the human person, since he stands above all things, and his rights and duties are universal and inviolable. Therefore, there must be made available to all men everything necessary for leading a life truly human, such as food, clothing, and shelter; the right to choose a state of life freely and to found a family, the right to education, to employment, to a good reputation, to respect, to appropriate information, to activity in accord with the upright norm of one's own conscience, to protection of privacy and to rightful freedom in matters religious too.

Hence, the social order and its development must unceasingly work to the benefit of the human person if the disposition of affairs is to be subordinate to the personal realm and not contrariwise, as the Lord indicated when He said that the Sabbath was made for man, and not man for the Sabbath.

This social order requires constant improvement. It must be founded on truth, built on justice, and animated by love; in freedom it should grow every day toward a more humane balance. An improvement in attitudes and widespread changes in society will have to take place if these objectives are to be gained. *(World, No.26)*

39. Evaluating the Use of Created Goods and Human Progress

Through his labors and his native endowments man has ceaselessly striven to better his life. Today, however, especially with the help of science and technology, he has extended his mastery over nearly the whole of nature and continues to do so. Thanks primarily to increased opportunities for many kinds of interchange among nations, the human family is gradually recognizing that it comprises a single world community and is making itself so. Hence many benefits once looked for, especially from heavenly powers, man has now enterprisingly procured for himself.

In the face of these immense efforts which already preoccupy the whole human race, men raise numerous questions among themselves. What is the meaning and value of this feverish activity? How should all these things be used? To the achievement of what goal are the strivings of individuals and societies heading?

The Church guards the heritage of God's Word and draws from it religious and moral principles, without always having at hand the solution to particular problems. She desires thereby to add the light of revealed truth to mankind's store of experience, so that the path which humanity has taken in recent times will not be a dark one. *(World, No.33)*

40. Man's Temporal Progress Unfolds God's Mysterious Design for Man

Throughout the course of the centuries, men have labored to better the circumstances of their lives through a monumental amount of individual and collective effort. To believers, this point is settled: considered in itself, such human activity accords with God's will. For man, created to God's image, received a mandate to subject to himself the earth and all that it contains, and to govern the world with justice and holiness; a mandate to relate himself and the totality of things to Him who was to be acknowledged as the Lord and Creator of all. Thus, by the subjection of all things to man, the name of God would be wonderful in all the earth.

This mandate concerns even the most ordinary everyday activities. For while providing the substance of life for themselves and their families, men and women are performing their activities in a way which appropriately benefits society. They can justly consider that by their labor they are unfolding the Creator's work, consulting the advantages of their brother men, and contributing by their personal industry to the realization in history of the divine plan.

Thus, far from thinking that works produced by man's own talent and energy are in opposition to God's power, and that the rational creature exists as a kind of rival to the Creator, Christians are convinced that the triumphs of the human race are a sign of God's greatness and the flowering of His own mysterious design. For the greater man's power becomes, the farther his individual and community responsibility extends. Hence it is clear that men are not deterred by the Christian message from building up the world, or impelled to neglect the welfare of their fellows. They are, rather, more stringently bound to do these very things. *(World, No.34)*

41. Man Is More Precious for What He Is than for What He Accomplishes

Just as human activity proceeds from man, so it is ordered toward man. For when a man works he not only alters things and society, he develops himself as well. He learns much, he cultivates his resources, he goes outside of himself and beyond himself.

Rightly understood, this kind of growth is of greater value than any external riches which can be garnered. A man is more precious for what he is than for what he has. Similarly, all that men do to obtain greater justice, wider brotherhood, and a more humane ordering of social relationships has greater worth than technical advances. For these advances can supply the material for human progress, but of themselves alone they can never actually bring it about.

Hence, the norm of human activity is this: that in accord with the divine plan and will, it should harmonize with the genuine good of the human race, and allow men as individuals and as members of society to pursue their total vocation and fulfill it. *(World, No.35)*

42. The Human Person Should Be the Object of True Progress

For the aforementioned reasons, the Church recalls to the mind of all that culture must be made to bear on the integral perfection of the human person, and on the good of the community and the whole of society. Therefore the human spirit must be cultivated in such a way that there results a growth in its ability to wonder, to understand, to contemplate, to make personal judgments, and to develop a religious, moral, and social sense.

Because it flows immediately from man's spiritual and social nature, culture has constant need of a just freedom if it is to develop. It also needs the legitimate possibility of exercising its independence according to its own principles. Rightly, therefore, it demands respect and enjoys a certain inviolability, at least as long as the rights of the individual and of the community, whether particular or universal, are preserved within the context of the common good. *(World, No.59)*

43. The Value of Human Accomplishments Derives from Conformity to God's Design

Now, many of our contemporaries seem to fear that a closer bond between human activity and religion will work against the independence of men, of societies, or of the sciences.

If by the autonomy of earthly affairs we mean that created things and societies themselves enjoy their own laws and values which must be gradually deciphered, put to use, and regulated by men, then it is entirely right to demand that autonomy. Such is not merely required by modern man, but harmonizes also with the will of the Creator. For by the very circumstance of their having been created, all things are endowed with their own stability, truth, goodness, proper laws, and order. Man must respect these as he isolates them by the appropriate methods of the individual sciences or arts.

Therefore, if methodical investigation within every branch of learning is carried out in a genuinely scientific manner and in accord with moral norms, it never truly conflicts with faith. For earthly matters and the concerns of faith derive from the same God. Indeed, whoever labors to penetrate the secrets of reality with a humble and steady mind, is, even unawares, being led by the hand of God, who holds all things in existence, and gives them their identity.

Consequently, we cannot but deplore certain habits of mind, sometimes found too among Christians, which do not sufficiently attend to the rightful independence of science. The arguments and controversies which they spark lead many minds to conclude that faith and science are mutually opposed.

But if the expression, the independence of temporal affairs, is taken to mean that created things do not depend on God, and that man can use them without any reference to their Creator, anyone who acknowledges God will see how false such a meaning is. For without the Creator the creature would disappear. For their part, however, all believers of whatever religion have always heard His revealing voice in the discourse of creatures. But when God is forgotten the creature itself grows unintelligible. *(World, No.36)*

44. The Christian Philosophy of Using Created Goods Wisely

Hence if anyone wants to know how this unhappy situation can be overcome, Christians will tell him that all human activity, constantly imperiled by man's pride and deranged self-love, must be purified and perfected by the power of Christ's cross and resurrection. For, redeemed by Christ and made a new creature in the Holy Spirit, man is able to love the things themselves created by God, and ought to do so. He can receive them from God, and respect and reverence them as flowing constantly from the hand of God.

Grateful to his Benefactor for these creatures, using and enjoying them in detachment and liberty of spirit, man is led forward into a true possession of the world, as having nothing, yet possessing all things. "All are yours, and you are Christ's, and Christ is God's" (1 Cor. 3:22-23). *(World, No. 37)*

2. MAN'S LIFE IS PERFECTED TEMPORALLY AND ETERNALLY BY CHRISTIAN LIVING

A. The Church's Teaching on Culture and Religion Benefits Human Living

The word "culture", as used here, includes the gamut of man's needs, both spiritual and temporal. The fulfillment of both is required for a life of full development. Christianity has enriched the culture of society through the inner dynamism of its lofty and practical ideals in men's lives. Inspired by these, men and women have given the fullest outpouring of their lives not only to improve the conditions of the poor and needy, but to produce, as well, the finest of literary and artistic works. Too often, however, some people will embrace the cultural benefits of the Church, while at the same time rejecting her religious aims. Nevertheless, the respect which the Church receives for her aesthetic works tends to lead perceptive persons to look more deeply into her beautiful soul and character, as in a courtship. The consummation comes after the person weds the Church as the bride of Christ, for both her spiritual and cultural beauty.

When the right order of truth is followed, as Vatican II points out, then man's human talents, efforts and accomplishments find proper direction and goals. When Christ's teachings are respected and put into action, man's economic and technological achievements become means to his betterment and sanctification rather than ends in themselves. Christ came to liberate man from injustice, prejudice, selfishness, and ungodliness on earth as well as to redeem man for heaven. Our Savior left for His Church spokesmen empowered by Him to interpret and apply His teachings to the needs of all ages and situations. The Church would like nothing more than to see every person enjoying the fullest benefits of human living while becoming even more alive in Christ.

45. The Significance of True Human Culture and Progress

It is a fact bearing on the very person of man that he can come to an authentic and full humanity only through culture, that is, through the cultivation of natural goods and values. Wherever human life is involved, therefore, nature and culture are quite intimately connected.

The word "culture" in its general sense indicates all those factors by which man refines and unfolds his manifold spiritual and bodily qualities. It means his effort to bring the world itself under his control by his knowledge and his labor. It includes the fact that by improving customs and institutions he renders social life more human both within the family and in the civic community. Finally, it is a feature of culture that throughout the course of time man expresses, communicates, and conserves in his works great spiritual experiences and desires, so that these may be of advantage to the progress of many, even of the whole human family.

Hence it follows that human culture necessarily has a historical and social aspect and that the word "culture" often takes on a sociological and ethnological sense. It is in this sense that we speak of a plurality of cultures.

Various conditions of community living, as well as various patterns for organizing the goods of life, arise from diverse ways of using things, of laboring, of expressing oneself, of practicing religion, of forming customs, of establishing laws and juridical institutions, of advancing the arts and sciences, and of promoting beauty. Thus the customs handed down to it form for each human community its proper patrimony. Thus, too, is fashioned the specific historical environment which enfolds the men of every nation and age and from which they draw the values which permit them to promote human and civic culture. *(World, No.53)*

46. The Modern Age of Human Culture Can Advance through Christian Principles

The living conditions of modern man have been so profoundly changed in their social and cultural dimensions, that we can speak of a new age in human history. Fresh avenues are open, therefore, for the refinement and the wider diffusion of culture. These avenues have been paved by the enormous growth of natural, human, and social sciences, by progress in technology, and by advances in the development and organization of the means by which men communicate with one another.

Hence the culture of today possesses particular characteristics. For example, the so-called exact sciences sharpen critical judgment to a very fine edge. Recent psychological research explains human activity more profoundly. Historical studies make a signal contribution to bringing men to see things in their changeable and evolutionary aspects. Customs and usages are becoming increasingly uniform. Industrialization, urbanization, and other causes of community living create new forms of culture (mass-culture), from which arise new ways of thinking, acting, and making use of leisure. The growth of communication between the various nations and social groups opens more widely to all the treasures of different cultures. *(World, No.54)*

47. The Genuine Christian Humanist Helps to Unite the Human Race in Christ

In every group or nation, there is an ever-increasing number of men and women who are conscious that they themselves are the artisans and the authors of the culture of their community. Throughout the world there is a similar growth in the combined sense of independence and responsibility. Such a development is of paramount importance for the spiritual and moral maturity of the human race. This truth grows clearer as we consider how the world is becoming unified and how we have the duty to build a better world based upon truth and justice. Thus we are witnesses of the birth of a new humanism, one in which man is defined first of all by his responsibility toward his brothers and toward history. *(World, No.55)*

48. God Blesses Human Collaboration for Improving Standards of Living

The possibility now exists of liberating most men from the misery of ignorance. Hence it is a duty most befitting our times that men, especially Christians, should work strenuously on behalf of certain decisions which must be made in the economic and political fields, both nationally and internationally. By these decisions universal recognition and implementation should be given to the right of all men to a human and civic culture favorable to personal dignity and free from any discrimination on the grounds of race, sex, nationality, religious, or social conditions.

Therefore it is necessary to provide every man with a sufficient abundance of cultural benefits, especially those which constitute so-called basic culture. Otherwise, because of illiteracy and a lack of responsible activity, very many will be prevented from collaborating in a truly human manner for the sake of the common good. *(World, No.60)*

49. Women Equally Share All Rights toward Advanced Human Culture

Energetic efforts must also be expended to make everyone conscious of his right to culture and of the duty he has to develop himself culturally and to assist others. For existing conditions of life and of work sometimes thwart the cultural strivings of men and destroy in them the desire for self-improvement. This is especially true of country people and laborers. They need to be provided with working conditions which will not block their human development but rather favor it.

Women are now employed in almost every area of life. It is appropriate that they should be able to assume their full proper role in accordance with their won nature. Everyone should acknowledge and favor the proper and necessary participation of women in cultural life. (World, No.60)

50. The Family and All of Human Society Should Progress in Human Culture

The family is, as it were, the primary mother and nurse of this attitude. There, in an atmosphere of love, children can more easily learn the true structure of reality. There, too, tested forms of human culture impress themselves upon the mind of the developing adolescent in a kind of automatic way.

Opportunities for the same kind of education can also be found in modern society, thanks especially to the increased circulation of books and to the new means of cultural and social communication. All such opportunities can foster a universal culture.

The widespread reduction in working hours, for instance, brings increasing advantages to numerous people. May these leisure hours be properly used for relaxation of spirit and the strengthening of mental and bodily health. Such benefits are available through spontaneous study and activity and through travel, which refines human qualities and enriches men with mutual understanding. These benefits are obtainable too from physical exercise and sports events, which can help to preserve emotional balance, even at the community level, and to establish fraternal relations among men of all conditions, nations, and races.

Hence let Christians work together to animate the cultural expressions and group activities characteristic of our times with a human and a Christian spirit. (World, No.61)

51. The Higher Forms of Human Culture and Art Should Be Fostered

Literature and the arts are also, in their own way, of great importance to the life of the Church. For they strive to probe the unique nature of man, his problems, and his experiences as he struggles to know and perfect both himself and the world. They are preoccupied with revealing man's place in history and in the world, with illustrating his miseries and joys, his needs and strengths, and with foreshadowing a better life for him. Thus they are able to elevate human life as it is expressed in manifold forms, depending on time and place.

Efforts must therefore be made so that those who practice these arts can feel that the Church gives recognition to them in their activities, and so that, enjoying an orderly freedom, they can establish smoother relations with the Christian community. Let the Church also acknowledge new forms of art which are adapted to our age and are in keeping with the characteristics of various nations and regions. Adjusted in their mode of expression and conformed to liturgical requirements, they may be introduced into the sanctuary when they raise the mind to God.

In this way the knowledge of God can be better revealed. Also, the preaching of the gospel can become clearer to man's mind and show its relevance to the conditions of human life. (World, No.62)

B. The Church and Secular Society
Cooperating for Life's Improvement

All over the earth, societies and institutions vie for men's allegiance, time, talents and resources. Most societies have a completely human beginning and orientation; the Church alone has a divine origin and purpose. She operates within the framework of all human societies, is restricted to none, and transcends them all. Her chief function is to sanctify people, when allowed to do so, within all human societies, institutions and endeavors. Historically and numerically, the membership of the Church has been identified, unfortunately, with specific nations and cultures. However, the Church has been sent to all nations and she respects and wishes to be associated with all true human cultures and aspirations. The Church will assist and promote any worthwhile human project for mankind's welfare when these movements are consistent with her divine mission.

Vatican II shows particular concern for the innate freedom of all men to develop and improve their condition, and the common efforts of all mankind to this end are encouraged and blessed. It is a function of the People of God to be concerned for those of their fellow-men who are oppressed and restricted by some civil governments. The

Church wishes to have open communication and relaxed dialogue with all civil authorities, since her mission includes man's total welfare in the secular and the sacred realms, in both of which men of all nations should live and advance in freedom and cooperation.

52. The Church Blesses All That Is Truly Good in Human Society

This Council, therefore, looks with great respect upon all the true, good, and just elements found in the very wide variety of institutions which the human race has established for itself and constantly continues to establish. The Council affirms, moreover, that the Church is willing to assist and promote all these institutions to the extent that such a service depends on her and can be associated with her mission. She has no fiercer desire than that, in pursuit of the welfare of all, she may be able to develop herself freely under any kind of government which grants recognition to the basic rights of person and family and to the demands of the common good. *(World, No.42)*

53. The Various Cultures of Humanity Can Be Enriched by Christianity

Just as it is in the world's interest to acknowledge the Church as a historical reality, and to recognize her good influence, so the Church herself knows how richly she has profited by the history and development of humanity.

Thanks to the experience of past ages, the progress of the sciences, and the treasures hidden in the various forms of human culture, the nature of man himself is more clearly revealed and new roads to truth are opened. These benefits profit the Church, too, for, from the beginning of her history, she has learned to express the message of Christ with the help of the ideas and terminology of various peoples, and has tried to clarify it with the wisdom of philosophers, too.

Her purpose has been to adapt the gospel to the grasp of all as well as to the needs of the learned, insofar as such was appropriate. Indeed, this accommodated preaching of the revealed Word ought to remain the law of all evangelization. For thus each nation develops the ability to express Christ's message in its own way. At the same time, a living exchange is fostered between the Church and the diverse cultures of people. *(World, No.44)*

54. Freedom of Human Investigation Discovers God's Truth in Life

All these considerations demand too, that, within the limits of morality and the general welfare, a man be free to search for the truth, voice his mind, and publicize it; that he be free to practice any art he chooses; and finally that he have appropriate access to information about public affairs.

It is not the function of public authority to determine what the proper nature or forms of human culture should be. It should rather foster the conditions and the means which are capable of promoting cultural life among all citizens and even within the minorities of a nation. Hence in this matter men must insist above all else that culture be not diverted from its own purpose and made to serve political or economic interests. *(World, No.59)*

55. The Church's Transcendent but Real Relationship with Society

Since the Church has a visible and social structure as a sign of her unity in Christ, she can and ought to be enriched by the development of human social life. The reason is not that the constitution given her by Christ is defective, but so that she may understand it more penetratingly, express it better, and adjust it more successfully to our times.

She gratefully understands that in her community life no less than in her individual sons, she receives a variety of helps from men of every rank and condition. For whoever promotes the human community at the family level, culturally, in its economic, social, and political dimensions, both nationally and internationally, such a one, according to God's design, is contributing greatly to the Church community as well, to the extent that it depends on things outside itself. Indeed, the Church admits that she has greatly profited and still profits from the antagonism of those who oppose or persecute her. *(World, No.44)*

56. Effort Is Required to Synthesize Human Knowledge and Relate It to God

Today it is more difficult than ever for a synthesis to be formed of the various branches of knowledge and the arts. For while the mass and the diversity of cultural factors are increasing, there is a decline in the individual man's ability to grasp and unify these elements. Thus the ideal of "the universal man" is disappearing more and more. Nevertheless, it remains each man's duty to preserve a view of the whole human person, a view in which the values of intellect, will, conscience, and fraternity are pre-eminent. These values are all rooted in God the Creator and have been wonderfully restored and elevated in Christ. *(World, No.61)*

57. Interpreting Human Progress in the Light of Christ's Gospel

May the faithful, therefore, live in very close union with the men of their time. Let them strive to understand perfectly their way of thinking and feeling, as expressed in their culture. Let them blend modern science and its theories and the understanding of the most recent discoveries with Christian morality and doctrine. Thus their religious practice and morality can keep pace with their scientific knowledge and with an ever-advancing technology. Thus too they will be able to test and interpret all things in a truly Christian spirit. *(World, No.62)*

We are reminded that human living is enhanced when it reflects God as the designer, sustainer, and ultimate goal of people's lives. In living by God's will lies man's peace. Modern man's acknowledged achievements to date can either destroy him or confirm him in progress. It depends on his regard for the right order of God's truth, justice and love. It is not easy to live out the Christian ideal of service of God and our fellow man; to seek justice and brotherhood for the improvement of secular life while integrating it with spiritual realities. Yet, such is the Christian ideal. It's fulfillment aims toward achieving the coordination of the human and the divine aspects of life with consequent personal and social peace in the world. The angels' message of peace on earth among men of good will called for men of heavenly wisdom to see in the new-born Savior the human as uplifted by the divine and God glorified through the human.

God looks at all that He made and declares it good. The current age, with its intricate complexities, stands in dire need of men and women who are receptive to divine wisdom and attentive to the song of life He has composed for His people so that harmony may be heard from men's lives by the order He has decreed in His universe and in men's lives.

Chapter III

PREVENTING SHATTERED LIVES

Of Personal and Communal Sin

God's love is so vast and all-embracing that it cannot possibly be defined or limited; it can only be experienced and described. Sin, the opposite of true love, may here be better described than defined because its depiction shows that it can shatter human lives. In broad terms, we may call personal sin that which a person himself commits and for which he as an individual is culpable. We designate as communal sin that which the community permits, regardless of who, specifically, may be at fault.

It will not be necessary to go into detail regarding the evil of personal sin, except to recall the individual's share in the price of sin — Christ's death. Certainly, too, the vitality of Christianity depends in great measure on the sinlessness of its individual members.

It will be more beneficial, however, to consider the havoc which communal sin reaps in the lives of people throughout the world because of selfishness, injustice, discord, and unconcern for others. These are wrong situations, and therefore sinful, because they violate man's nature and likewise are contrary to the right order desired by God for those He created.

Sin strains the union God wants with His people, changing harmony to discord in individual lives, in relationships with other people, or in man's orderly interchange with situations in life as they should exist. Sin may be considered as man's deliberate refusal to fulfill his true self-perfection by acting contrary to God's law for his human welfare as an individual or as part of a community. Thus, sin opposes not only God's laws for correct human living but also God's love itself. Sin degrades the dignity God rightfully expects within man, since it withholds him from full union with his Lord. Sin also causes depression within the sinner and produces injustice among men. Wherever injustice exists, so does sin; a situation which cries out for correction because it offends God's norms for peoples' lives. Harm to one's own person or to others belittles the greatest commandment of the God of love.

Sinlessness, the removal of obstacles to complete union with God and others, is certainly a primary goal of the Church. Christians may, and often do, fail. Yet it is not the spiritual potential in Christianity which falters but, rather, the weakness of men and women who fail to live the precepts of our merciful Savior.

It is the mission of the Church to uplift man's life of trial and temptation bringing sanctification out of both and stirring his conscience for the improvement of personal and communal living (Section 1). Efforts must be made to irradicate sin's indignity against God, the human person and a just social order (Section 2). In order that the Council's aims may be realized, the People of God, in current times, must become more aware of the need and benefits of personal and communal renewal (Section 3).

The central point of this chapter is that real sin, regardless of whose fault it may be, works an injustice which we must do our best to correct, whether it be personal sin we commit or communal sin which we, as members of the community, permit. Basically, sin violates the chief commandment of all, the love of God and of our neighbor as ourselves. Even our repentence for sin is a blessing for which to thank God whose endless mercy is most abundant, as is His love.

1. ASPECTS OF MAN'S DIGNITY
AND OF SIN AND CONSCIENCE

A. Man's Dignity as God's Image Requires
Respect and Improvement of Life

It is beneath the dignity of man's destiny, created as an image of God, to claim that sin and degradation in life are inevitable or unconquerable. Possessed of a fallen nature, still man has been redeemed through Christ's great love bringing strength and hope. With God's help, man can truly rise above his weaknesses. He can improve his life's condition. In personal lives, weakness, failure and discouragement are understandable, though they are neither desirable nor beneficial to life. In the social order, injustice cries to heaven because of the anguish it causes in people's lives. The source of human dignity comes from God. Man must, therefore, respect himself and others since God has commanded it for our own welfare.

People who become persistent in evil lose their sense of bearing and destiny and are subject to God's judgment. Those who refuse to serve God and who oppress others will pay the penalty He has decreed, while those who strive to live in true dignity as God's people will profit from the promises of the Lord. To have reverence for God includes having respect for the worth and rights of all people.

58. The Discord of Sin Must Be Resolved for Harmony in Life

Although he was made by God in a state of holiness, from the very dawn of history man abused his liberty, at the urging of personified Evil. Man set himself against God and sought to find fulfillment apart from God. Although he knew God, he did not glorify Him as God, but his senseless mind was darkened and he served the creature rather than the Creator.

What divine revelation makes known to us agrees with experience. Examining his heart, man finds that he has inclinations toward evil too, and is engulfed by manifold ills which cannot come from his good Creator. Often refusing to acknowledge God as his beginning, man has disrupted also his proper relationship to his own ultimate goal. At the same time he became out of harmony with himself, with others and with all created things.

Therefore man is split within himself. As a result, all of human life, whether individual or collective, shows itself to be a dramatic struggle between good and evil, between light and darkness. Indeed, man finds that by himself he is incapable of battling the assaults of evil successfully, so that everyone feels as though he is bound by chains.

But the Lord Himself came to free and strengthen man, renewing him inwardly and casting out that prince of this world (cf. Jn. 12:31) who held him in the bondage of sin. For sin has diminished man, blocking his path to fulfillment.

The call to grandeur and the depths of misery are both a part of human experience. They find their ultimate and simultaneous explanation in the light of God's revelation. *(World, No.13)*

59. Temporal Concerns Must Be Subject to Man's Destiny

In the course of history, temporal things have been foully

abused by serious vices. Affected by original sin, men have frequently fallen into multiple errors concerning the true God, the nature of man, and the principles of the moral law. The result has been the corruption of morals and human institutions and not rarely contempt for the human person himself. In our own time, moreover, those many who have trusted excessively in the advances of the natural sciences and of technology have fallen into an idolatry of temporal things and have become their slaves rather than their masters.

It is the task of the whole Church to labor vigorously so that men may become capable of constructing the temporal order rightly and directing it to God through Christ. Her pastors must clearly state the principles concerning the purpose of creation and the use of temporal things, and must make available the moral and spiritual aids by which the temporal order can be restored in Christ. *(Laity, No.7)*

60. For Interior Peace, Man Must Acknowledge God's Dominion and Laws

Though made of body and soul, man is one. Through his bodily composition he gathers to himself the elements of the material world. Thus they reach their crown through him, and through him raise their voice in free praise of the Creator.

For this reason man is not allowed to despise his bodily life. Rather, he is obliged to regard his body as good and honorable since God has created it and will raise it up on the last day. Nevertheless, wounded by sin, man experiences rebellious stirrings in his body. But the very dignity of man postulates that man glorify God in his body and forbid it to serve the evil inclinations of his heart.

Now, man is not wrong when he regards himself as superior to bodily concerns, and as more than a speck of nature or a nameless constituent of the city of man. For by his interior qualities he outstrips the whole sum of mere things. He finds re-enforcement in this profound insight whenever he enters into his own heart. God, who probes the heart, awaits him there. There he discerns his proper destiny beneath the eyes of God. Thus, when man recognizes in himself a spiritual and immortal soul, he is not being mocked by a deceptive fantasy springing from mere physical or social influences. On the contrary he is getting to the depths of the very truth of the matter. *(World, No.14)*

61. Christian Living Looks to Social as Well as Personal Morality

Profound and rapid changes make it particularly urgent that
no one, ignoring the trend of events or drugged by laziness, content
himself with a merely individualistic morality. It grows increasingly
true that the obligations of justice and love are fulfilled only if each
person, contributing to the common good, according to his own
abilities and the needs of others, also promotes and assists the
public and private institutions dedicated to bettering the conditions
of human life.

Yet there are those who, while professing grand and rather
noble sentiments, nevertheless in reality live always as if they cared
nothing for the needs of society. Many in various places even make
light of social laws and precepts, and do not hesitate to resort to
various frauds and deceptions in avoiding just taxes or other debts
due to society. Others think little of certain norms of social life, for
example those designed for the protection of health, or laws establishing speed limits. They do not even avert to the fact that by such
indifference they imperil their own life and that of others.

Let everyone consider it his sacred obligation to count social
necessities among the primary duties of modern man, and to pay
heed to them. For the more unified the world becomes, the more
plainly do the offices of men extend beyond particular groups and
spread by degrees to the whole world. But this challenge cannot be
met unless individual men and their associations cultivate in themselves the moral and social virtues, and promote them in society.
Thus, with the needed help of divine grace, men who are truly new
and artisans of a new humanity can be forthcoming. *(World, No.30)*

62. The Individual's Dedication Toward Removing Social Disorders

In order for individual men to discharge with greater exactness the obligations of their conscience toward themselves and the
various groups to which they belong, they must be carefully educated to a higher degree of culture through the use of the immense
resources available today to the human race. Above all the education of youth from every social background has to be undertaken,
so that there can be produced not only men and women of refined
talents, but those great-souled persons who are so desperately
required by our times.

Now a man can scarcely arrive at the needed sense of responsibility unless his living conditions allow him to become conscious

of his dignity, and to rise to his destiny by spending himself for God and for others. But human freedom is often crippled when a man falls into extreme poverty, just as it withers when he indulges in too many of life's comforts and imprisons himself in a kind of splendid isolation. Freedom acquires new strength, by contrast, when a man consents to the unavoidable requirements of social life, takes on the manifold demands of human partnership, and commits himself to the service of the human community.

Hence, the will to play one's role in common endeavors should be everywhere encouraged. Praise is due to those national procedures which allow the largest possible number of citizens to participate in public affairs with genuine freedom. Account must be taken, to be sure, of the actual conditions of each people and the vigor required by public authority.

If every citizen is to feel inclined to take part in the activities of the various groups which make up the social body, these must offer advantages which will attract members and dispose them to serve others. We can justly consider that the future of humanity lies in the hands of those who are strong enough to provide coming generations with reasons for living and hoping. *(World, No.31)*

B. Following Right Conscience as the Fulfillment of Human Dignity and Destiny

When the light of God's designs for man's happiness becomes eclipsed by rebellious actions, the darkness of sin overshadows men's lives. The freedom of living rightly comes from following the voice of God, man's inner conscience. There is satisfaction and joy, simple yet profound, in striving to serve God by following one's conscience, perhaps not always successfully but always trying. Even a troubled conscience displays the heart of a person who cares for God's inner law of a man's personal being.

By following one's conscience a person fulfills true human dignity as a child of God. The ultimate destiny of a person likewise depends on God's judgment of how well the individual usually abides by His light of truth within man, as he walks the various paths of life.

63. In Fidelity to Conscience Man Fulfills His Highest Activity in Life

In the depths of his conscience, man detects a law which he does not impose upon himself, but which holds him to obedience.

Always summoning him to love good and avoid evil, the voice of conscience can when necessary speak to his heart more specifically: do this, shun that. For man has in his heart a law written by God. To obey it is the very dignity of man; according to it he will be judged.

Conscience is the most secret core and sanctuary of a man. There he is alone with God, whose voice echoes in his depths. In a wonderful manner conscience reveals that law which is fulfilled by love of God and neighbor. In fidelity to conscience, Christians are joined with the rest of men in the search for truth, and for the genuine solution to the numerous problems which arise in the life of individuals and from social relationships. Hence the more that a correct conscience holds sway, the more persons and groups turn aside from blind choice and strive to be guided by objective norms of morality.

Conscience frequently errs from invincible ignorance without losing its dignity. The same cannot be said of a man who cares but little for truth and goodness, or of a conscience which by degrees grows practically sightless as a result of habitual sin. *(World, No.16)*

64. Moral Goodness Proceeds from Free Service of God, the Judge of All

Only in freedom can man direct himself toward goodness. Our contemporaries make much of this freedom and pursue it eagerly; and rightly so, to be sure. Often, however, they foster it perversely as a license for doing whatever pleases them, even if it is evil.

For its part, authentic freedom is an exceptional sign of the divine image within man. For God has willed that man be left "in the hand of his own counsel" so that he can seek his Creator spontaneously, and come freely to utter and blissful perfection through loyalty to Him. Hence man's dignity demands that he act according to a knowing and free choice. Such a choice is personally motivated and prompted from within. It does not result from blind internal impulse nor from mere external pressure.

Man achieves such dignity when, emancipating himself from all captivity to passion, he pursues his goal in a spontaneous choice of what is good, and procures for himself, through effective and skillful action, apt means to that end. Since man's freedom has been damaged by sin, only by the help of God's grace can he bring such a relationship with God into full flower. Before the judgment seat of

God each man must render an account of his own life, whether he has done good or evil. *(World, No.17)*

65. Christ Invites All to Seek Truth Freely

God calls men to serve Him in spirit and in truth. Hence they are bound in conscience but they stand under no compulsion. God has regard for the dignity of the human person whom He Himself created; man is to be guided by his own judgment and he is to enjoy freedom.

This truth appears at its height in Christ Jesus, in whom God perfectly manifested Himself and His ways with men. Christ is our Master and our Lord. He is also meek and humble of heart. And in attracting and inviting His disciples He acted patiently. He wrought miracles to shed light on His teaching and to establish its truth. But His intention was to rouse faith in His hearers and to confirm them in faith, not to exert coercion upon them.

He did indeed denounce the unbelief of some who listened to Him; but He left vengeance to God in expectation of the day of judgment. When He sent His apostles into the world, He said to them: "He who believes and is baptized shall be saved, but he who does not believe shall be condemned" (Mk. 16:16); but He Himself, noting that cockle had been sown amid the wheat, gave orders that both should be allowed to grow until the harvest time, which will come at the end of the world.

He refused to be a political Messiah, ruling by force; He preferred to call Himself the Son of Man, who came "to serve and to give his life as a ransom for many" (Mk. 10:45). He showed Himself the perfect Servant of God; "a bruised reed he will not break, and a smoking wick he will not quench" (Mt. 12:20). *(Freedom, No.11)*

66. The Freedom of Conscience and the Power of God's Word

Taught by the word and example of Christ, the apostles followed the same way. From the very origins of the Church the disciples of Christ strove to convert men to faith in Christ as the Lord— not, however, by the use of coercion or by devices unworthy of the gospel, but by the power, above all, of the Word of God. Steadfastly they proclaimed to all the plan of God our Savior, "who wishes all men to be saved and to come to the knowledge of the truth" (1 Tim. 2:4). At the same time, however, they showed respect for weaker souls even though these persons were in error.

Thus they made it plain that "every one of us will render an account of himself to God" (Rom. 14:12), and for this reason is bound to obey his conscience. *(Freedom, No.11)*

2. SIN'S VIOLATION OF GOD'S LAWS, THE HUMAN PERSON, AND SOCIAL JUSTICE

A. Respect for Human Beings Requires Their Just and Considerate Treatment

Respect for the person and the potential of others, even the least of Christ's brothers and sisters, is less a virtue than a requirement for membership in the unique kingdom of Christ. Certainly society has a right and duty to punish and attempt to rehabilitate offenders against the common good. Nevertheless, regardless of man's tendency to condemn the faults of others, Christ laid down the norms of forgiveness and kindness toward others as the measure of His pardon and mercy for us. Judgment for sin is God's prerogative in eternity, not man's function in time. Respect for each other as God's children requires just and considerate treatment of one another.

Both as an individual and as a member of the human family, each person must have consideration for the rights, needs, and dignity of other people. From the fact of man's innate dignity as a reflection of his Creator, there flows innumerable practical conclusions requiring respect and concern for others in this highly complex and fast-moving age. Man must move forward together.

67. Social Circumstances Must Provide Man with a Wholesome Atmosphere

Man's social nature makes it evident that the progress of the human person and the advance of society itself hinge on each other. For the beginning, the subject and the goal of all social institutions is and must be the human person, which for its part and by its very nature stands completely in need of social life. This social life is not something added on to man. Hence, through his dealings with others, through reciprocal duties, and through fraternal dialogue he develops all his gifts and is able to rise to his destiny.

But if by this social life the human person is greatly aided in responding to his destiny, even in its religious dimensions, it cannot be denied that men are often diverted from doing good and spurred toward evil by the social circumstances in which they live and are immersed from their birth. To be sure the disturbances which so frequently occur in the social order result in part from the natural tensions of economic, political, and social forms. But at a deeper level they flow from man's pride and selfishness, which contaminate even the social sphere. When the structure of affairs is flawed by the consequences of sin, man, already born with a bent toward evil, finds there new inducements to sin, which cannot be overcome without strenuous efforts and the assistance of grace. *(World, No.25)*

68. Sin Against the Reverence Due to Human Beings

Coming down to practical and particularly urgent consequences, this Council lays stress on reverence for man; everyone must consider his every neighbor without exception as another self, taking into account first of all his life and the means necessary to living it with dignity, so as not to imitate the rich man who had no concern for the poor man Lazarus.

In our times a special obligation binds us to make ourselves the neighbor of absolutely every person, and of actively helping him when he comes across our path, whether he be an old person abandoned by all, a foreign laborer unjustly looked down upon, a refugee, a child born of an unlawful union and wrongly suffering for a sin he did not commit, or a hungry person who disturbs our conscience by recalling the voice of the Lord: "As long as you did it for one of these, the least of my brethren, you did it for me" (Mt. 25:40).

Furthermore, whatever is opposed to life itself, such as any type of murder, genocide, abortion, euthanasia, or willful self-destruction, whatever violates the integrity of the human person, such as mutilation, torments inflicted on body or mind, attempts to coerce the will itself; whatever insults human dignity, such as subhuman living conditions, arbitrary imprisonment, deportation, slavery, prostitution, the selling of women and children; as well as disgraceful working conditions, where men are treated as mere tools for profit, rather than as free and responsible persons; all these things and others of their like are infamies indeed. They poison human society, but they do more harm to those who practice them than those who suffer from the injury. Moreover, they are a supreme dishonor to the Creator. *(World, No.27)*

69. Respect for Others Opens the Door to Honest Dialogue and Love

Respect and love ought to be extended also to those who think or act differently than we do in social, political, and religious matters, too. In fact, the more deeply we come to understand their ways of thinking through such courtesy and love, the more easily will we be able to enter into dialogue with them.

This love and good will, to be sure, must in no way render us indifferent to truth and goodness. Indeed love itself impels the disciples of Christ to speak the saving truth to all men. But it is necessary to distinguish between error, which always merits repudiation, and the person in error, who never loses the dignity of being a person, even when he is flawed by false or inadequate religious notions. God alone is the judge and searcher of hearts; for that reason He forbids us to make judgments about the internal guilt of anyone.

The teaching of Christ even requires that we forgive injuries, and extends the law of love to include every enemy, according to the command of the New Law:· "You have heard that it was said, 'Thou shalt love thy neighbor, and shalt hate thy enemy.' But I say to you, love your enemies, do good to those who hate you, and pray for those who persecute and calumniate you" (Mt. 5:43-44). *(World, No.28)*

70. Any Form of Unjust Discrimination Should Be Abhorent to People

Since all men possess a rational soul and are created in God's likeness, since they have the same nature and origin, have been redeemed by Christ, and enjoy the same divine calling and destiny, the basic equality of all must receive increasingly greater recognition.

True, all men are not alike from the point of view of varying physical power and the diversity of intellectual and moral resources. Nevertheless, with respect to the fundamental rights of the person, every type of discrimination, whether social or cultural, whether based on sex, race, color, social condition, language, or religion, is to be overcome and eradicated as contrary to God's intent. For in truth it must still be regretted that fundamental personal rights are not yet being universally honored. Such is the case of a woman who is denied the right and freedom to choose a husband, to embrace a state of life, or to acquire an education or cultural benefits equal to those recognized for men.

Moreover, although rightful differences exist between men, the equal dignity of persons demands that a more humane and just condition of life be brought about. For excessive economic and social differences between the members of the one human family or population groups cause scandal, and militate against social justice, equity, the dignity of the human person, as well as social and international peace.

Human institutions both private and public, must labor to minister to the dignity and purpose of man. At the same time let them put up a stubborn fight against any kind of slavery, whether social or political, and safeguard the basic rights of man under every political system. Indeed human institutions themselves must be accommodated by degrees to the highest of all realities, spiritual ones, even though meanwhile, a long enough time will be required before they arrive at the desired goal. *(World, No. 29).*

B. Some Central Areas of Communal Sin in the Social Order

Just as the strength of a rope lies in the combined vitality of its strands, so also human society is as strong and stable as the individuals who comprise it. To the degree that individuals permit unjust situations to persist in the social order, the community at large bears responsibility. It also becomes that much weaker. All people are required to assist as best they can in the eradication of community ills which breed disorder.

True temporal progress has for its end the good order of human living. To attain this, the dignity of the human person must be preserved, else the worth of the so-called advances within society are rightly suspect. The soul of the social order is the betterment of man, not the proliferation of things at the expense of human dignity.

71. Injustices Should Be Progressively Rectified in Human Society

Again, we are at a moment in history when the development of economic life could diminish social inequalities if that development were guided and coordinated in a reasonable and human way. Yet all too often it serves only to intensify the inequalities. In some places it even results in a decline in the social status of the weak and in contempt for the poor.

While an enormous mass of people still lack the absolute necessities of life, some, even in less advanced countries, live sumptuously or squander wealth. Luxury and misery rub shoulders. While the few enjoy very great freedom of choice, the many are deprived of almost all possibility of acting on their own initiative and responsibility, and often subsist in living and working conditions unworthy of human beings.

A similar lack of economic and social balance is to be noted between agriculture, industry, and the services, and also between different parts of one and the same country. The contrast between the economically more advanced countries and other countries is becoming more serious day by day, and the very peace of the world can be jeopardized in consequence.

Our contemporaries are coming to feel these inequalities with an ever sharper awareness. For they are thoroughly convinced that the wider technical and economic potential which the modern world enjoys can and should correct this unhappy state of affairs. Hence, numerous reforms are needed at the socio-economic level, along with universal changes in ideas and attitudes. *(World, No. 63)*

72. In the Progress of Science and Technology Man's Dignity Must Be Preserved

No doubt today's progress in science and technology can foster a certain exclusive emphasis on observable data, and an agnosticism about everything else. For the methods of investigation which these sciences use can be wrongly considered as the supreme rule for discovering the whole truth. By virtue of their methods, however, these sciences cannot penetrate to the intimate meaning of things. Yet the danger exists that man, confiding too much in modern discoveries, may even think that he is sufficient unto himself and no longer seek any higher realities.

These unfortunate results, however, do not necessarily follow from the culture of today, nor should they lead us into the temptation of not acknowledging its positive values. For among its values are these: scientific study and strict fidelity toward truth in scientific research, the necessity of working together with others in technical groups, a sense of international solidarity, an ever clearer awareness of the responsibility of experts to aid men and even to protect them, the desire to make the conditions of life more favorable for all, especially for those who are deprived of the opportunity to exercise responsibility or who are culturally poor.

All of these values can provide some preparation for the acceptance of the message of the gospel — a preparation which can be animated with divine love by Him who came to save the world. *(World, No. 57)*

73. The Dignity of Marriage and the Family Must Be Protected in Society

Yet the excellence of this institution is not everywhere reflected with equal brilliance. For polygamy, the plague of divorce, so-called free love, and other disfigurements have an obscuring effect. In addition, married love is too often profaned by excessive self-love, the worship of pleasure, and illicit practices against human generation. Moreover, serious disturbances are caused in families by modern economic conditions, by influences at once social and psychological, and by the demands of civil society. Finally, in certain parts of the world problems resulting from population growth are generating concern.

All these situations have produced anxious consciences. Yet, the power and strength of the institution of marriage and family can also be seen in the fact that time and again, despite the difficulties produced, the profound changes in modern society reveal the true character of this institution in one way or another. *(World, No. 47)*

3. THE NEED AND BENEFITS OF EFFECTIVE RENEWAL TODAY

A. The Call to Repentance and Renewal of the People of God

Freedom from sin is an ideal which only Christ could present. And yet the ultimate goal of Christianity is the sanctification of all mankind for their happiness and God's glorification.

The Church is composed of people who must ever strive for the renewal of their individual lives as well as of the laws and structures which buttress Christianity. The current era is undergoing a profound renewal both from interiorly instigated movements and from exterior pressures of current circumstances.

Without denying the remarkable accomplishments of Christianity throughout past ages, today's People of God openly acknowledge their faults and failings. However, the Church-community invites all men of good will to repentance for defects and to renewal of their lives so that mankind may draw ever closer to the God of all.

74. Church Renewal Is Essentially a Fuller Living of Our Catholic Faith

Every renewal of the Church essentially consists in an increase of fidelity to her own calling. Undoubtedly this explains the dynamism of the movement toward unity.

Christ summons the Church, as she goes her pilgrim way, to that continual reformation of which she always has need, insofar as she is an institution of men here on earth. Therefore, if the influence of events or of the times has led to deficiencies in conduct, in Church discipline, or even in the formulation of doctrine (which must be carefully distinguished from the deposit itself of faith), these should be appropriately rectified at the proper moment.

Church renewal therefore has notable ecumenical importance. Already this renewal is taking place in various spheres of the Church's life: the biblical and liturgical movements, the preaching of the word of God, catechetics, the apostolate of the laity, new forms of religious life and the spirituality of married life, and the Church's social teaching and activity. *(Ecumenism, No. 6)*

75. More Genuine Living of Our Catholic Religion Helps Others and Glorifies Christ

In ecumenical work, Catholics must assuredly be concerned for their separated brethren, praying for them, keeping them informed about the Church, making the first approaches towards them. But their primary duty is to make an honest and careful appraisal of whatever needs to be renewed and achieved in the Catholic household itself, in order that its life may bear witness more loyally and luminously to the teachings and ordinances which have been handed down from Christ through the apostles.

For although the Catholic Church has been endowed with all divinely revealed truth and with all means of grace, her members fail to live by them with all the fervor they should. As a result, the radiance of the Church's face shines less brightly in the eyes of our separated brethren and of the world at large, and the growth of God's kingdom is retarded. Every Catholic must therefore aim at Christian perfection (cf. Jas. 1:4; Rom. 12:1-2) and, each according to his station, play his part so that the Church, which bears in her own body the humility and dying of Jesus (cf. 2 Cor. 4:10; Phil. 2: 5-8), may daily be more purified and renewed, against the day when Christ will present her to Himself in all her glory, without spot or wrinkle (cf. Eph. 5:27). *(Ecumenism, No. 4)*

76. Genuine Renewal Should Remove Defects of Clergy and Laity

Although by the 'power of the Holy Spirit the Church has remained the faithful spouse of her Lord and has never ceased to be the sign of salvation on earth, still she is very well aware that among her members, both clerical and lay, some have been unfaithful to the Spirit of God during the course of many centuries. In the present age, too, it does not escape the Church how great a distance lies between the message she offers and the human failings of those to whom the gospel is entrusted.

Whatever be the judgment of history on these defects, we ought to be conscious of them, and struggle against them energetically, lest they inflict harm on the spread of the gospel. The Church also realizes that in working out her relationship with the world she always has great need of the ripening which comes with the experience of the centuries. Led by the Holy Spirit, Mother Church unceasingly exhorts her sons "to purify and renew themselves so that the sign of Christ can shine more brightly on the face of the Church." *(World, No. 43)*

77. Penance Is Advocated for the Purifying of the People of God

It is important to impress on the minds of the faithful not only the social consequences of sin but also the fact that the real essence of the virtue of penance is hatred for sin as an offence against God; the role of the Church in penitential practices is not to be passed over, and the people must be exhorted to pray for sinners.

During Lent, penance should not be only internal and individual but also external and social. The practice of penance should be fostered according to the possibilities of the present day and of a given area, as well as of individual circumstances. *(Liturgy, No. 109-110)*

B. Helping People to Profit from Renewal of Life

As does Christ, so also His Church stands ever ready to help all people, especially those who try to improve themselves and assist others. Sinlessness is a noble goal and a practical way for profitable living. A lofty ideal may fall short of its mark and yet be worthwhile for the good it accomplishes. Few Christians reach the apex of perfect accomplishment throughout the entire span of their lives; neither do businessmen, artists, athletes or others. Yet ideals must always inspire people to noble deeds, else lower trends will pull men downward toward an unproductive life.

Christianity clings to the ideal of a world of sanctified people, the perfection of which will be realized at last in eternity. Christ will continue to win men and women to nobleness of spirit and its consequent accomplishment. His Church will do the same. She will probe all means to clarify the gospel message for modern man, and will employ every medium to proclaim it. She will tell the ageless truths in contemporary terms, no less than in former ways. She will reflect the Light of the world even when conditions seem darkest. Christ through His Church continues to propose, exemplify, and produce genuine holiness of life.

78. Christ's Church Offers Understanding for the Weaknesses and Needs of People

Christ was sent by the Father "to bring good news to the poor, to heal the contrite of heart" (Lk. 4:18), "to seek and to save what was lost" (Lk. 19:10). Similarly, the Church encompasses with love all those who are afflicted with human weakness. Indeed, she recognizes in the poor and the suffering the likeness of her poor and suffering Founder. She does all she can to relieve their need and in them she strives to serve Christ. While Christ, "holy, innocent, undefiled" (Heb. 7:26) knew nothing of sin (2 Cor. 5:21), but came to expiate only the sins of the people (cf. Heb. 2:17), the Church, embracing sinners in her bosom, is at the same time holy and always in need of being purified, and incessantly pursues the path of penance and renewal. *(Church, No. 8)*

79. The Gospel and the Church Are Pre-Eminent Sources of Man's Renewal

The good news of Christ constantly renews the life and culture of fallen man. It combats and removes the errors and evils resulting from sinful allurements which are a perpetual threat. It never ceases to purify and elevate the morality of peoples. By riches coming from above, it makes fruitful, as it were from within, the spiritual qualities and gifts of every people and of every age. It strengthens, perfects, and restores them in Christ. Thus by the very fulfillment of her own mission the Church stimulates and advances human and civic culture. By her action, even in its liturgical form, she leads men toward interior liberty. *(World, No. 58)*

80. Theology Must Present the Gospel Message in Modern Terminology to Help Humanity

While adhering to the methods and requirements proper to theology, theologians are invited to seek continually for more suitable ways of communicating doctrine to the men of their times. For the deposit of faith or revealed truths are one thing; the manner in which they are formulated without violence to their meaning and significance is another.

In pastoral care, appropriate use must be made not only of theological principles, but also of the findings of the secular sciences, especially of psychology and sociology. Thus the faithful can be brought to live the faith in a more thorough and mature way. *(World, No. 62)*

Because of the dignity of each human person as a reflection of God, a spirit of hope should prevail in every human heart and every area of the world. Respecting the person of each other and treating all fairly and kindly, men together can prevent shattered lives and uplift drooping spirits. With this desire and the help of God we should all respond to the Council's call for individual and community renewal. We should also pray that others will accept the invitation and join us with courage, concern, and care for one another.

Our Lord's grace is available for the improvement and salvation of all mankind. His love is as enduring as His sustained creation, continual mercy, and uplifting power. Every effort to up-root personal sins and communal injustices makes God's norms for human living become more effective, and His presence more unitive on earth until complete union is won in life eternal with the Lord of all.

Chapter IV

LIFE'S FULFILLMENT AND FINALITY

Through Eternal Values

Life's true fulfillment on earth bears immediate relation to its finality in eternity when God's people shall finally attain the fullness of new life. Here lies the ultimate goal of living in the spirit and grace of the risen Christ. People share in this mystery through incorporation in Christ, in the power of His death and resurrection, and with the grace of the Holy Spirit sent by the Father.

Interest in the future life has fascinated mankind from the beginning. We have only to consider the graveyards of history. The tombs and pyramids of Egypt, the catacombs of Rome, and the worn head-stones of countless church-yards all portray man's awareness of another life beyond mortal death. Anticipation of the joys of eternity has been a source of hope and strength to the oppressed and afflicted, just as fear of the life beyond has worried the oppressor and the proud.

Christians can rejoice in, and share with others, the clear teachings of their faith for they know that Christ is mankind's sure Savior. From Him they know much about the basis of heaven's joys, how to obtain them and why the goal is worth the sacrifice to attain it. God has kept the specific details of heaven as His surprise; but He has clearly revealed through Christ, the Savior of all, the way to this paradise of everlasting happiness.

Reflection upon the contents of this chapter answers many of the most fundamental problems harrowing people's minds and hearts today in their search for fulfillment and a worthwhile goal in life. This is an age of glorification of the secular and human, and of emphasis on finding our Lord through our fellow man. While this current emphasis has merit, it should not be implied that life can have its complete meaning and fulfillment in anyone or anything beyond Jesus Christ and the life He has promised.

It would seem that in ages of stronger faith and hope in eternal life, people produce more outstanding accomplishments. This was so with the martyrs in the early Church, with the men and women of heroic character, with the Christian philosophers, theologians and saints, and with the sculptors, artists and writers of the eras of deep faith. Surely the current times would progress faster and produce more, if people would ponder more vividly and consciously the glory of eternal life with God. This might give more motivation and expand man's imagination for solving the pressing problems that seem to be stifling the human spirit in our times. It is amazing how considerations of the transcendental and eternal values can do so much to produce men and women of high development and practical insight for benefiting the practical aspects of life.

As the renewal requested by the Church in our times becomes more effective, more interest will be aroused in transforming the present life on earth, because more men will be consciously enthusiastic in moving toward their eternal salvation (Section 1). Hence, human living should become improved by staunch Christians, men of their times, whose contributions to their present age abound as they work for the life to come (Section 2).

Reflection on the eternal truths presented by Vatican II should stir genuine enthusiasm for Christian living in modern times. We ponder the greatest good news possible; we have been redeemed. Responding to God's love and grace we fully expect to attain an eternity of complete happiness with our Lord and our loved ones. In this spirit of Christian hope the inner person must exclaim, "Thank God!"

1. MAN MOVES TOWARD SALVATION
AND TRANSFORMATION

A. The New Life Which Lies Ahead
With Christ and Loved Ones

It is fascinating to ponder upon the nature of the life to come when the totality of the human person, body and soul, will have been renewed and glorified. From faith in Christ and His promises, His people can look joyfully beyond the degradation of sin and death. By taking hope in Christ and the future resurrection, the Christian can expect to rise up from the grip of death to live again in a glorified state with God and His people.

In the attempt to make religious realities more meaningful in life, current literature may tend to exaggerate the importance of natural self-fulfillment to the detriment of man's spiritual attainment. Certainly in eternal life the blessed will be substantially the same persons they were on earth. However, the form of new life will vastly exceed a mere continuation of natural human existence however improved, for God has spoken of a newer, more exalted life in eternity. It is left to each person to consider what is implied when the conciliar passages speak of a new heaven and a new earth. Nevertheless, the legitimate hope of the Christian is that he will one day be joined with Christ and his loved ones in the heaven of complete truth, peace and happiness.

81. Man and His World Will Be Fulfilled in Christ One Day

We do not know the time for the consummation of the earth and of humanity. Nor do we know how all things will be trans-formed. As deformed by sin, the shape of this world will pass away. But we are taught that God is preparing a new dwelling place and a new earth where justice will abide, and whose blessedness will an-swer and surpass all the longings for peace which spring up in the human heart. *(World, No. 39)*

82. The Church Will Attain Full Perfection in the Glory of Heaven

The Church, to which we are all called in Christ Jesus, and in which we acquire sanctity through the grace of God, will attain her full perfection only in the glory of heaven. Then will come the time of the restoration of all things (Acts 3:21). Then the human race as well as the entire world, which is intimately related to man and achieves its purpose through him, will be perfectly re-established in Christ (cf. Eph. 1:10; Col. 1:20; 2 Pet. 3:10-13). *(World, No. 48)*

83. Christ Is Continually Active, Helping Men Toward Salvation

Christ, having been lifted up from the earth, is drawing all men to Himself (Jn. 12:32, Greek text). Rising from the dead (cf. Rom. 6:9), He sent His life-giving Spirit upon His disciples and through this Spirit has established His body, the Church, as the universal sacrament of salvation. Sitting at the right hand of the Father, He is continually active in the world, leading men to the Church, and through her joining them more closely to Himself and making them partakers of His glorious life by nourishing them with His own body and blood.

Therefore, the promised restoration which we are awaiting has already begun in Christ, is carried forward in the mission of the Holy Spirit, and through Him continues in the Church. There we learn through faith the meaning, too, of our temporal life, as we perform, with hope of good things to come, the task committed to us in this world by the Father, and work out our salvation (cf. Phil. 2:12). *(Church, No. 48)*

84. Through Christ, toward a Newer Life after Death

For God has called man and still calls him so that with his entire being he might be joined to Him in an endless sharing of a divine life beyond all corruption. Christ won this victory when He rose to life, since by His death He freed man from death. Hence to every thoughtful man a solidly established faith provides the answer to his anxiety about what the future holds for him. At the same time faith gives him the power to be united in Christ with his loved ones who have already been snatched away by death. Faith arouses the hope that they have found true life with God. *(World, No. 18)*

B. Lessons Which Death and the Life Hereafter Teach the Living

Contemplation on the new and higher life to come furnishes positive incentive for striving toward its attainment. Thoughts of death, judgment, resurrection and heaven or hell confirm the attraction for Christian living here and now.

Death and the life beyond the grave are understandably of deep concern to mankind. On the outskirts of Cairo tourists stare in wonder at 4,000-year-old pyramids and study the drawings within the tombs for their depiction of ancient ideas about the life beyond. In Moscow silence prevails along the half-mile line of people daily visiting the tombs in red Square. In Jerusalem, Rome, Prague, Uganda, Auriesville, and other places, there are lines of admirers viewing the early catacombs or later spots from which martyrs and saints have gone to their eternal reward. Truly, the life beyond death elicits various forms of awe and reflection. To some, death signifies merely a passage beyond recall to a bleak ending or possibly a blank existence. To the Christian, however, death is the gateway to a higher, better and endless new life in a resurrected way with loved ones for all who have persevered in the love of God. The lessons which death and the life hereafter can teach the living give practical and potent reasons for striving to live a better life now.

85. Death Contains Some of the Deepest Lessons for the Living

It is in the face of death that the riddle of human existence becomes most acute. Not only is man tormented by pain and by the advancing deterioration of his body, but even more so by a dread of perpetual extinction. He rightly follows the intuition of his heart when he abhors and repudiates the absolute ruin and total disappearance of his own person.

Man rebels against death because he bears in himself an eternal seed which cannot be reduced to sheer matter. All the endeavors of technology, though useful in the extreme, cannot calm his anxiety. For a prolongation of biological life is unable to satisfy that desire for a higher life which is inescapably lodged in his breast.

Although the mystery of death utterly beggars the imagination, the Church has been taught by divine revelation, and herself firmly teaches, that man has been created by God for a blissful purpose beyond the reach of earthly misery. In addition, that bodily death from which man would have been immune had he not sinned will be vanquished, according to the Christian faith, when man who was ruined by his own doing is restored to wholeness by an almighty and merciful Savior. *(World, No. 18)*

86. Salvation Is Obtainable by Cooperating with Christ and His Love

Since we know not the day nor the hour, on our Lord's advice we must constantly stand guard. Thus when we have finished the one and only course of our earthly life (cf. Heb. 9:27) we may merit to enter into the marriage feast with Him and to be numbered among the blessed (cf. Mt. 25:31-46). Thus we may not be commanded to go into eternal fire (cf. Mt. 25:41) like the wicked and slothful servant (cf. Mt. 25:26), into the exterior darkness where "there will be the weeping and the gnashing of teeth" (Mt. 22:13; 25:30). For before we reign with the glorious Christ, all of us will be made manifest "before the tribunal of Christ, so that each one may receive what he has won through the body, according to his works, whether good or evil" (2 Cor. 5:10). At the end of the world, "they who have done good shall come forth unto resurrection of life; but those who have done evil unto resurrection of judgment" (Jn. 5:29; cf. Mt. 25:46).

We reckon therefore that "the sufferings of the present time are not worthy to be compared with the glory to come that will be revealed in us" (Rom. 8:18; cf. 2 Tim. 2:11-12). Strong in faith we look for "the blessed hope and glorious coming of our great God and Savior, Jesus Christ" (Tit. 2:13) "who will refashion the body of our lowliness, conforming it to the body of his glory" (Phil. 3:21) and who will come "to be glorified in his saints, and to be marveled at in all those who have believed" (2 Th. 1:10). *(Church, No. 48)*

87. The Expectation of Heaven Should Stimulate Christian Living on Earth

Then, with death overcome, the sons of God will be raised up in Christ. What was sown in weakness and corruption will be clothed with incorruptibility. While charity and its fruits endure, all the creation which God made on man's account will be unchained from the bondage of vanity.

Therefore, while we are warned that it profits a man nothing if he gain the whole world and lose himself, the expectation of a new earth must not weaken but rather stimulate our concern for cultivating this one. For here grows the body of a new human family, a body which even now is able to give some kind of foreshadowing of the new age. *(World, No. 39)*

88. God's People Help Achieve the Renovation of Mankind and of the World

The final age of the world has already come upon us (cf. 1 Cor. 10:11). The renovation of the world has been irrevocably decreed and in this age is already anticipated in some real way. For even now on this earth the Church is marked with a genuine though imperfect holiness. However, until there is a new heaven and a new earth where justice dwells (cf. 2 Pet. 3:13), the pilgrim Church in her sacraments and institutions, which pertain to this present time, takes on the appearance of this passing world. She herself dwells among creatures who groan and travail in pain until now and await the revelation of the sons of God (cf. Rom. 8:19-22).

Joined with Christ in the Church and signed with the Holy Spirit "who is the pledge of our inheritance" (Eph. 1:14), we are truly called sons of God and such we are (cf. 1 Jn. 3:1). But we have not yet appeared with Christ in the state of glory (cf. Col. 3:4), in which we shall be like to God, since we shall see Him as He is (cf. 1 Jn. 3:2). Therefore "while we are in the body, we are exiled from the Lord" (2 Cor. 5:6), and having the first fruits of the Spirit we groan within ourselves (cf. Rom. 8:23) and desire to be with Christ (cf. Phil. 1:23). A common love urges us to live more for Him, who died for us and rose again (cf. 2 Cor. 5:15). We strive therefore to please the Lord in all things (cf. 2 Cor. 5:9). We put on the armor of God that we may be able to stand against the wiles of the devil and resist on the evil day (cf. Eph. 6:11-13). *(Church, No. 48)*.

2. IMPROVING HUMAN LIVING NOW
WHILE STRIVING TO JOIN THE SAINTS

A. Christians Should Enhance Life on Earth as They Aim for Heaven

Inwardly, man moves toward his own perfection and ultimate salvation. As pilgrims on earth men journey toward heaven, the new life which awaits those who love God. In life's journey Christians are expected not only to live full human lives themselves, but to contribute to the common welfare of mankind. It is man's assigned function to honor and serve the Lord while cultivating all aspects of human living for the benefit of the human race whose God is master of the temporal and the eternal.

Christ is Lord of the entire universe of spirit and of matter. The temporal order, wounded in various ways, calls out for the healing of the divine physician. God's vast plan includes the improvement of life in this world for man's own good which is to His glory. Christians are not homeless refugees but pilgrims who enthusiastically progress toward eternal life while striving to improve life on earth as part of their Christian calling.

89. True Earthly Progress Should Assist People to Heaven

Earthly progress must be carefully distinguished from the growth of Christ's kingdom. Nevertheless, to the extent that the former can contribute to the better ordering of human society, it is of vital concern to the kingdom of God.

For after we have obeyed the Lord, and in His Spirit nurtured on earth the values of human dignity, brotherhood and freedom, and indeed all the good fruits of our nature and enterprise, we will find them again, but freed of stain, burnished and transfigured. This will be so when Christ hands over to the Father a kingdom eternal and universal: "a kingdom of truth and life, of holiness and grace, of justice, love, and peace." On this earth that kingdom is already present in mystery. When the Lord returns, it will be brought into full flower. *(World, No. 39)*

90. The Church Helps Form the Family of God on Earth

Coming forth from the eternal Father's love, founded in time by Christ the Redeemer, and made one in the Holy Spirit, the Church has a saving and an eschatological purpose which can be fully attained only in the future world. But she is already present in this world, and is composed of men, that is, of members of the earthly city who have a call to form the family of God's children during the present history of the human race, and to keep increasing it until the Lord returns. *(World, No. 40)*

91. Christians Should Make This World More Human While Aiming For Heaven

Christians, on pilgrimage toward the heavenly city, should seek and savor the things which are above. This duty in no way decreases, but rather increases, the weight of their obligation to work with all men in constructing a more human world. In fact, the mystery of the Christian faith furnished them with excellent incentives and helps toward discharging this duty more energetically and especially toward uncovering the full meaning of this activity, a meaning which gives human culture its eminent place in the integral vocation of man.

For when, by the work of his hands or with the aid of technology, man develops the earth so that it can bear fruit and become a dwelling worthy of the whole human family, and when he consciously takes part in the life of social groups, he carries out the design of God. Manifested at the beginning of time, the divine plan is that man should subdue the earth, bring creation to perfection, and develop himself. When a man so acts he simultaneously obeys the great Christian commandment that he place himself at the service of his brother men. *(World, No. 57)*

B. Benefits From the Union of Those in Heaven with Those on Earth

At the final transformation of this world all will be re-made in a new heaven and a new earth. Then Christ's rightful majesty and glory will show forth for all to behold with unlimited joy or eternal regret. At the present time, Christ is the one mediator, the Supreme Pontifex or bridge-builder, who can unite man's life in time with that of eternity. He also provides that no one is ever completely alone on his journey through life, since, through incorporation in His Mystical Body, the Church, people are spiritually united on earth and with the saints in heaven.

Certainly in heaven people know their loved ones and friends, and are known and loved by them in God. The human faculties of knowing and loving will be expanded to the fullest in the life to come. Sacred Scripture and the Church encourage us to think about our future life with God, to desire the happiness of heaven, and to take inspiration from our Blessed Mother and the saints who await our arrival in our everlasting home of complete happiness. All our efforts to join them will be blessed a hundred-fold by Christ, our Savior, who has promised those who love Him, a welcome that begins "Come blessed . . . ."

92. The Victorious in Heaven Are United with Us on Earth

When the Lord comes in His majesty, and all the angels with Him (cf. Mt. 25:31), death will be destroyed and all things will be subject to Him (cf. 1 Cor. 15:26-27). Meanwhile some of His disciples are exiles on earth. Some have finished with this life and are being purified. Others are in glory, beholding "clearly God Himself triune and one, as He is."

But in various ways and degrees we all partake in the same love for God and neighbor, and all sing the same hymn of glory to our God. For all who belong to Christ, having His Spirit, form one Church and cleave together in Him (cf. Eph. 4:16). Therefore the union of the wayfarers with the brethren to have gone to sleep in the peace of Christ is not in the least interrupted. On the contrary, according to the perennial faith of the Church, it is strengthened through the exchanging of spiritual goods.

For by reason of the fact that those in heaven are more closely united with Christ, they establish the whole Church more firmly in holiness, lend nobility to the worship which the Church offers on earth to God, and in many ways contribute to its greater upbuilding (cf. 1 Cor. 12:12-27). For after they have been received into their heavenly home and are present to the Lord (cf. 2 Cor. 5:8), through Him and with Him and in Him, they do not cease to intercede with the Father for us. Rather they show forth the merits which they won on earth through the one Mediator between God and man, Christ Jesus (cf. 1 Tim. 2:5). There they served God in all things and filled up in their flesh whatever was lacking of the sufferings of Christ on behalf of His body which is the Church (cf. Col. 1:24). Thus by their brotherly interest our weakness is very greatly strengthened. *(Church, No. 49)*

93. Fellowship with the Saints Inspires Christian Living

Now, it is not only by the title of example that we cherish the memory of those in heaven. We do so still more in order that the union of the whole Church may be strengthened in the Spirit by the practice of fraternal charity (cf. Eph. 4:1-6). For just as Christian communion among wayfarers brings us closer to Christ, so our companionship with the saints joins us to Christ, from whom as from their fountain and head issue every grace and the life of God's people itself.

It is supremely fitting, therefore, that we love those friends and fellow heirs of Jesus Christ, who are also our brothers and extraordinary benefactors, that we render due thanks to God for them and "suppliantly invoke them and have recourse to their prayers, their power and help in obtaining benefits from God through His Son, Jesus Christ, our Lord, who is our sole Redeemer and Savior." For by its very nature every genuine testimony of love which we show to those in heaven tends toward and terminates in Christ, who is the "crown of all saints." Through Him it tends toward and terminates in God, who is wonderful in His saints and is magnified in them. *(Church, No. 50)*

94. Union with Those in Heaven Helps One Practice His Faith on Earth

Our union with the Church in heaven is put into effect in its noblest manner when with common rejoicing we celebrate together the praise of the divine Majesty. Then all those from every tribe and tongue and people and nation (cf. Apoc. 5:9) who have been redeemed by the blood of Christ and gathered together into one Church, with one song of praise magnify the one and triune God. Such is especially the case in the sacred liturgy, where the power of the Holy Spirit acts upon us through sacramental signs. Celebrating the Eucharistic sacrifice, therefore, we are most closely united to the worshipping Church in heaven as we join with and venerate the memory first of all of the glorious ever-Virgin Mary, of Blessed Joseph and the blessed apostles and martyrs, and of all the saints. *(Church, No. 50)*

Thus, while God has prepared a marvelous eternal life for us, its attainment by no means excludes His concern for our present condition in temporal life. A person's life becomes fulfilled when human and divine love abound in it. For our lives to attain everlasting love with Christ and our loved ones, the expectation of a glorious new life hereafter helps us to live the present one better. At times during this life, repentence and renewal will be most necessary.

In the connotation of holy Scripture, "heart" stands for the total person; in that full sense, the Sacred Heart of Jesus completely pardons the repentant sinner who begs His forgiveness. It is a tribute to Christ's love to take confidence in His mercy. We can be certain that Christ, as He assures us in His gospels, delights in nothing better than to shepherd His sheep toward His Father's home of eternal peace and happiness.

Summary of Part One – **RENEWAL**

The foregoing chapters dealt with our renewal, both as individuals and as members of the Christian community of believers, to the end that we might become more aware of our Christian vitality and the impelling need for spiritual rejuvenation in our times. This renewal is intended both to uplift life's values for the human spirit and to seek means for correcting current fallacies which would degrade man and entice him from his ultimate goal in life. Vital and ennobling renewal should favorably inspire the lives of people in the world during the era of Vatican II and beyond.

Living as God's people in the course of salvation history will bring more meaning to man's life in these as in any times (Chapter I). To this end, the integration of secular interests with sacred values must be achieved through the use of divine wisdom by following God's norms for correct living (Chapter II). However, lest the grand design of life be shattered by sin, human beings require constant strength from Christ. This spiritual energy is generated from God's grace and from remedial action with respect to the wrongs and injustices we have committed as individuals or permitted as communities Chapter II). The fulfillment of life seeks to reach the peak of perfection in terms of transformation in Christ. From this derives the hope of glorious resurrection after entry into the newer life which awaits those who live the charity of Christ (Chapter IV).

The following passage serves as a capsule-summary of the renewal desired in this Vatican II era, the way to which was presented in the conciliar passages contained throughout Part One.

95. May Renewal Create Deeper Rejuvenation of Christian Vitality in Modern Times

Drawn from the treasures of Church teaching, the proposals of this sacred Synod look to the assistance of every man of our time, whether he believes in God, or does not explicitly recognize Him. Their purpose is to help men gain a sharper insight into their full destiny, so that they can fashion the world more to man's surpassing dignity, search for a brotherhood which is universal and more deeply rooted, and meet the urgencies of our age with a gallant and unified effort born of love.

Undeniably this conciliar program is but a general one in several of its parts — and deliberately so, given the immense variety of situations and forms of human culture in the world. Indeed, while it presents teaching already accepted in the Church, the program will have to be further pursued and amplified, since it often deals with matters in a constant state of development. Still, we have relied on the Word of God and the spirit of the gospel. Hence we entertain the hope that many of our proposals will be able to bring substantial benefit to everyone, especially after they have been adapted to individual nations and mentalities by the faithful, under the guidance of their pastors. *(World, No. 91)*

We have reflected on the renewal envisioned by the Council so that rejuvenation of Christian vitality can be brought to fruition. Part One contained a summary of the history, scope, and goal of man's quest for salvation while bettering his life and his world. We consider next, in Part Two, the consequences of personal and collective renewal which should result in deepening our Christian commitment to Christ and His cause by the service of His people in our times.

Part 2
Commitment

COMMITMENT
A symbol of strength. Man must take
hold of his cross as an integral part in
Salvation. To the right appears the
ancient sign of community among
mankind.

PART TWO – COMMITMENT

THE SERVICE OF CHRIST'S CAUSE BY HIS PEOPLE TODAY

This part reflects the second helpful aim of the Church today. In the words of Vatican II, this goal is "to make more responsive to the requirements of our times those Church observances which are open to adaptation." It is precisely in order that the commitment of Christians today may be more meaningful and relevant to the needs of our times that the Church is making changes and adaptations in certain aspects of its practices, customs, laws, liturgy and administration. Its doctrinal content, of course, must remain unchanged.

Commitment implies more than decision; it means the affirmative response of a person in terms of action to a compelling degree. The commitment of Christians is to Christ and His cause within their own times. More specifically, the Christian dedication is to the sanctification of human life through the service of Christ and the advancement of His kingdom on earth. This basic commitment has been essentially the same during every era of Christianity. Yet, the specifics of its fulfillment necessarily vary according to the particular requirements of each and every age.

It will be the task of future historians to assess the lasting effects of Vatican Council II on both the world and the Church since they are becoming plunged into a new and difficult period of the testing of values. To prepare us, Christ predicted that such times would come upon His flock. Yet, He also promised to stay with His Church during all periods of trial, and He asked that His people keep faith with Him while working out the difficulties of their era. The Christians of earlier periods had to go through their Passover, their Paschal Mystery, their test of faith. As a result, subsequent generations profited by the vitality of religious faith these earlier Christians handed down.

Certain test-periods of Christianity may be discerned throughout past ages, from which today's Christians may justifiably take inspiration. For instance, there was the period from the time of the apostles to the reign of Constantine, during which the Church suffered and struggled for its very existence. Then from the fourth century to the sixteenth, there emerged great thinkers and saints, although the Church also had to pass through eras of doctrinal dispute and to withstand the impact of hordes of barbarian invaders, some of whom were themselves conquered by the Church's truth and beauty. As the sixteenth century progressed there were serious divisions within Christianity, which forced the Church to re-examine herself and tighten her disciplines. For the next two to three centuries Christianity spread, but not without difficulties, as the world opened up vast horizons. Then the eighteenth century brought a skepticism which staggered the faith of many with its blows of exaggerated rationalism, the natural spawner of materialism. Coming to the present era, Christians are again called upon to meet the test of their faith in this age of a new humanism, coupled with the attempt at the complete secularization of human life.

Just as in past ages the People of God were commissioned to uplift the spirit of their times, so also are today's Christians required to renew their commitment to Christ and His cause by the strengthening of their faith. The adaptations proposed by Vatican II are intended to help the faithful take their rightful place in the present situations of life, and to help mankind to profit from Christianity's vitality. Consequently, the gospel message will become more meaningful to modern man by up-dating certain Christian attitudes and practices in the light of our Lord's teachings.

It is a chief function of Christians to be of service to their fellow man, even in a society which is becoming more secular-minded to the neglect of spiritual values. Christianity must help the world to use to true advantage its vast newly acquired potential in such areas as technology, the sciences and the arts. This is becoming more urgent, for mankind is now acquiring awesome powers which can be used for man's improvement or detriment, good or evil, life or death. The Christian can also be of basic service to his fellow man by showing from the truth-shown facts of human life that mankind had better have recourse to love and spiritual values, as opposed to strife and material avarice, if the modern world is to save itself from frustration and decay.

Consequently, the Vatican II passages in the following chapters present matter of vital importance to man in modern times. There is absolutely no substitute for the Savior of mankind, Jesus Christ, whose presence among His people is both mystical and real, spiritual and discernable (Chapter V). Christ's people can uplift today's world through their Christian apostolate (Chapter VI), which implies more than lending a helping hand, since it means saving people from spiritual degradation. However, in order that the signs and events of the times may be assessed correctly, according to the Spirit of Christ (Chapter VII), and valid solutions offered for mankind's true betterment, these times, as all past ages, require nothing more important than individual men and women who are committed to holiness of life. Holy people serve the needs of the world far better than it may realize or be able to comprehend (Chapter VIII). The Christian, committed to Christ and His cause, truly reflects Him who is the hope of the world and its Way, Truth, and Life.

Chapter V

CHRIST'S PRESENCE AMONG HIS PEOPLE

His Kingdom and His Church

Christ's presence among His people proceeds from, and is similar to, the mystery of love; the more that each is experienced the more are men's lives truly fulfilled. The stunning and mysterious reality of Christ's presence flows from the nature and mystery of God in Christ. God's ways are often mysteriously fascinating to man; so is Christ's presence among His people attractively divine.

Indeed, the unseen has intrigued man from the very beginning. To the attraction of mystery is added the reward of discovery. This is true of the mystery and discovery of nature, but far more so of the human mystery of love and the divine mystery of God's friendship for man. When we reflect on the presence of Christ in His kingdom, we are pondering the attributes and works of Almighty God, His divine nearness in the visible and invisible world, and His persuasive love as it operates in human lives.

The awareness of Christ's presence seems particularly necessary in these times, when materialistic attitudes are blunting the edge of man's spiritual perceptions and diverting his higher aspirations. The Christian commitment in the Church must include a re-awakening to the presence of Christ. His people must confirm their faith and their service as members of that Mystical Body of which He is the head. Christ is present with His love and His grace, sanctifying, teaching and guiding the Church of His people.

Consequently, it will be beneficial to ponder the conciliar passages regarding the presence of Christ and His kingdom in the world (Section 1). God's revelation is most complete in Christ, who shares the fullness of His presence through the Catholic expression of the Christian faith (Section 2). Service to God and men is the keynote of membership in Christ's kingdom, as He forcefully instructed His apostles (Section 3). It is for this service also that He shares the powers of His mission with all, including the laity (Section 4).

This chapter emphasizes the presence of Christ, from which we gain strength in our faith, confidence that our hope is well founded, and love which becomes more alive because He is near. Through Christ in our midst, our service of His cause in the world becomes more committed and more peaceful as each of us in Christ's Church strives to fulfill our common function and our aspiration, "Thy Kingdom come . . . ."

1. THE PRESENCE OF CHRIST'S KINGDOM IN THE WORLD

A. The Unfolding Mystery of Christ's Kingdom Among Us

God and the kingdom of his divine Son can never be fully comprehended. Christ's kingdom is an attractive mystery. As with all true love, which is the kingdom's foundation, it constantly unfolds more and more of its satisfying truth, its inspiring goodness and its charming beauty. This kingdom includes matter and spirit, time and space, temporal living and heavenly eternity.

The kingdom of Christ spreads across the world with divine vitality among peoples of all races. Part of the thrill of life on earth, as it will be in the new life in heaven, consists of enjoying the everfascinating mystery of Christ's presence, the evolving completion of His kingdom among us. Vatican II expounds on this mystery, that is this presence, of the kingdom of Christ and of His Church in the world.

96. God the Father Sent His Son to Establish His Kingdom

The Son, therefore, came on a mission from His father. It was in Him, before the foundation of the world, that the Father chose us and predestined us to become adopted sons, for in Him it has pleased the Father to re-establish all things (cf. Eph. 1:4-5 and 10). To carry out the will of the Father, Christ inaugurated the kingdom of heaven on earth and revealed to us the mystery of the Father. By His obedience He brought about redemption. The Church, or, in other words, the kingdom of Christ now present in mystery, grows visible in the world through the power of God. *(Church, No. 3)*

97. The Mystery of the Kingdom of God, His Church

The mystery of the holy Church is manifest in her very foundation, for the Lord Jesus inaugurated her by preaching the good news, that is, the coming of God's kingdom, which, for centuries, had been promised in the Scriptures: "The time is fulfilled, and the kingdom of God is at hand" (Mk. 1:15; cf. Mt. 4:17). In Christ's word, in His works, and in His presence this kingdom reveals itself to men. The word of the Lord is like a seed sown in a field (Mk. 4:14). Those who hear the word with faith and become part of the little flock of Christ (Lk. 12:32) have received the kingdom itself. Then, by its own power the seed sprouts and ripens until harvest time (c. Mk. 4:26-29).

The miracles of Jesus also confirm that the kingdom has already arrived on earth: "If I cast out devils by the finger of God, then the kingdom of God has come upon you" (Lk. 11:20; cf. Mt. 12:28).

Before all things, however, the kingdom is clearly visible in the very person of Christ, Son of God and Son of Man, who came "to serve, and to give his life as a ransom for many" (Mk. 10:45).

When Jesus rose up again after suffering death on the cross for mankind, He manifested that He had been appointed Lord, Messiah, and Priest forever (cf. Acts 2:36; Heb. 5:6; 7:17-21), and He poured out on His disciples the Spirit promised by the Father (cf. Acts 2:33). The Church, consequently equipped with the gifts of her Founder and faithfully guarding His precepts of charity, humility, and self-sacrifice, receives the mission to proclaim and to establish among all peoples the kingdom of Christ and of God. She becomes on earth the initial budding forth of that kingdom. While she slowly grows, the Church strains toward the consummation of the kingdom and, with all her strength, hopes and desires to be united in glory with her Lord. *(Church, No. 5)*

B. The Reality of Christ's Mystical Body, The Church

God's action within the world contains a hidden dynamism which impels the kingdom of Christ to prosper because it concerns peoples' welfare and salvation. Christ is Lord of all, both the visible and the spiritual. His Church is both a community which is visible, and the spiritual presence of the risen Christ who proposes Himself for our acceptance.

The Church, the Mystical Body of Christ, is the universal sacrament of salvation. How fascinating it is to ponder in faith its vast spiritual vitality. The source of this forward-movement comes from the real, dynamic activity of the Holy Spirit whom Christ sends to foster His cause among people. The Church of Christ is a living organism intended to affect people in all phases of living. Consequently, the Church must always keep developing with the movements and events of the times.

Whatever new methods and changes may prove suitable as vehicles for bringing Christ's grace to man, the reality of His Church will remain the same. Hence, in the Church of Vatican II, regardless of the adaptation of traditions, customs, laws, disciplines, liturgical practices, and pastoral accomodations which may evolve, the Church will ever remain dynamically alive, for it is the Mystical Body of Christ on earth.

98. United in Christ' Mystical Body by the Holy Spirit

In the human nature which He united to Himself, the Son of God redeemed man and transformed him into a new creation (cf. Gal. 6:15; 2 Cor. 5:17) by overcoming death through His own death and resurrection. By communicating His Spirit to His brothers, called together from all peoples, Christ made them mystically into His own body.

In that body, the life of Christ is poured into the believers, who, through the sacraments, are united in a hidden and real way to Christ who suffered and was glorified. Through baptism we are formed in the likeness of Christ: "For in one Spirit we were all baptized into one body" (1 Cor. 12:13). In this sacred rite, a union with Christ's death and resurrection is both symbolized and brought about: "For we were buried with him by means of Baptism into death." And if "we have been united with him in the likeness of his death, we shall be so in the likeness of his resurrection also" (Rom. 6:4-5). *(Church, No. 7)*

99. Christ is Head of the Church Which He Guides

The Head of this body is Christ. He is the image of the invisible God and in Him all things came into being. He has priority

over everyone and in Him all things hold together. He is the Head of
that body which is the Church. He is the beginning, the firstborn
from the dead, so that in all things He might have the first place (cf.
Col. 1:15-18). By the greatness of His power He rules the things of
heaven and the things of earth, and with His all-surpassing perfection and activity He fills the whole body with the riches of His glory
(cf. Eph. 1:18-23).

From Him, "the whole body supplied and built up by joints
and ligaments, attains a growth that is of God" (Col. 2:19). He
continually distributes in His body, that is, in the Church, gifts of
ministries through which, by His own power, we serve each other
unto salvation so that, carrying out the truth in love, we may
through all things grow up into Him who is our head (cf. Eph.
4:11-16, Greek text). *(Church, No. 7)*

100. Christ Shares His Holy Spirit to Enliven His People

In order that we may be unceasingly renewed in Him (cf. Eph.
4:23), He has shared with us His Spirit who, existing as one and the
same being in the head and in the members, vivifies, unifies, and
moves the whole body. This He does in such a way that His work
could be compared by the holy Fathers with the function which the
soul fulfills in the human body, whose principle of life the soul is.

Having become the model of a man loving his wife as his own
body, Christ loves the Church as His bride (cf. Eph. 5:25-28). For
her part, the Church is subject to her Head (cf. Eph. 5:22-23). "For
in him dwells all the fullness of the Godhead bodily" (Col. 2:9). He
fills the Church, which is His Body and His fullness, with His divine
gifts (cf. Eph. 1:22-23) so that she may grow and reach all the
fullness of God (cf. Eph. 3:19). *(Church, No. 7)*

101. The Church Works in Humility and Self-Sacrifice

Just as Christ carried out the work of redemption in poverty
and under oppression, so the Church is called to follow the same
path in communicating to men the fruits of salvation. Christ Jesus,
"though He was by nature God ... emptied himself, taking the
nature of a slave" (Phil. 2:6), and "being rich, he became poor" (2
Cor. 8:9) for our sakes. Thus, although the Church needs human
resources to carry out her mission, she is not set up to seek earthly
glory, but to proclaim humility and self-sacrifice, even by her own
example. *(Church, No. 8)*

2. THE CATHOLIC FAITH OFFERS
THE FULLNESS OF CHRIST'S REVELATION

A. The Catholic Church Shares With All
the Surest Means for Salvation

Just as Christ declared that He came to serve and to save the world, so also His people comprise a servant Church for the same reasons. Christ wants the salvation of all mankind. This is the basic point of the divine injunction for men. Toward the accomplishment of Christ's design, the Catholic Church believes and teaches that to her the Lord has entrusted the fullness of His revelation and all the surest means of attaining salvation's blessedness. The authentic Catholic religion must dispense this fullness of God's word to all men until the end of time. This belief by no means implies a crushing triumphalism. To the contrary, this assignment from Christ, both imposes a humbling responsibility and presents an inspiring challenge to Roman Catholics to live and to share their fullness of the faith more completely.

The Church has from Christ the commission to sanctify, teach and guide those who will be attentive to her call and respond to it freely. Knowledgeable non-Catholics realize and respect this tenet of Roman Catholic belief. There could be neither substantial unity among Christians nor, indeed, would there by lasting vitality among the largest percentage of Christians in the world, if Roman Catholics should weaken their conviction or slacken their eagerness to put their beliefs into practice.

It may be on this very point that Christianity as a whole could lessen its effectiveness in the modern world which needs people of religious conviction for steady leadership. Should Catholics, in their misguided love or their misunderstanding of their unique function in the world, diminish their sense of mission through watering down their faith, then they would become quite ineffectual with others whom they wished to serve for Christ. It may be well to notice from which documents of Vatican II the passages in this section derive.

102. Christianity of Today Derives from Apostolic Tradition and Its Development

Therefore the apostles, handing on what they themselves had received, warn the faithful to hold fast to the traditions which they have learned either by word of mouth or by letter (cf. 2 Th. 2:15), and to fight in defense of the faith handed on once and for all (cf. Jude 3). Now what was handed on by the apostles includes everything which contributes to the holiness of life, and the increase in faith of the People of God; and so the Church, in her teaching, life, and worship, perpetuates and hands on to all generations all that she herself is, all that she believes.

This tradition which comes from the apostles develops in the Church with the help of the Holy Spirit. For there is a growth in the understanding of the realities and the words which have been handed down. This happens through the contemplation and study made by believers, who treasure these things in their hearts (cf. Lk. 2:19, 51), through the intimate understanding of the spiritual things they experience, and through the preaching of those who have received through episcopal succession the sure gift of truth. For, as the centuries succeed one another, the Church constantly moves forward toward the fullness of divine truth until the words of God reach their complete fulfillment in her. *(Revelation, No. 8)*

103. The Church Should Be Heard as the Guardian of Religious Truth

In order to be faithful to the divine command, "Make disciples of all nations" (Mt. 28:19), the Catholic Church must work with all urgency and concern "that the Word of God may run and be glorified" (2 Th. 3:1). Hence the Church earnestly begs of her children that, first of all, "supplications, prayers, intercessions, and thanksgivings be made for all men . . . For this is good and agreeable in the sight of God our Savior, who wishes all men to be saved and to come to the knowledge of the truth" (1 Tim. 2:1-4).

In the formation of their consciences, the Christian faithful ought carefully to attend to the sacred and certain doctrine of the Church. The Church is, by the will of Christ, the teacher of the truth. It is her duty to give utterance to, and authoritatively to teach, that Truth which is Christ Himself, and also to declare and confirm by her authority those principles of the moral order which have their origin in human nature itself. Furthermore, let Christians walk in wisdom in the face of those outside, "in the Holy Spirit, in unaffected love, in the word of truth" (2 Cor. 6:6-7). Let them be about their task of spreading the light of life with all confidence and apostolic courage, even to the shedding of their blood.

The disciple is bound by a grave obligation toward Christ his

Master ever more adequately to understand the truth received from Him, faithfully to proclaim it, and vigorously to defend it, never—be it understood—having recourse to means that are incompatible with the spirit of the gospel. At the same time, the charity of Christ urges him to act lovingly, prudently and patiently in his dealings with those who are in error or in ignorance with regard to the faith. All is to be taken into account—the Christian duty to Christ, the lifegiving Word which must be proclaimed, the rights of the human person, and the measure of grace granted by God through Christ to men, who are invited freely to accept and profess the faith. *(Freedom, No.14)*

104. The Surest Way to Blessedness Is Through the Catholic Church

First, this sacred Synod professes its belief that God himself has made known to mankind the way in which men are to serve Him, and thus be saved in Christ and come to blessedness. We believe that this one true religion subsists in the catholic and apostolic Church, to which the Lord Jesus committed the duty of spreading it abroad among all men. Thus He spoke to the apostles: "Go, therefore, and make disciples of all nations, baptizing them in the name of the Father, and of the Son, and of the Holy Spirit, teaching them to observe all that I have commanded you" (Mt. 28:19-20). On their part, all men are bound to seek the truth, especially in what concerns God and His Church, and to embrace the truth they come to know, and to hold fast to it. *(Freedom, No. 1)*

105. The Catholic Church Wants to Share Its Fullness of Means for Salvation

For the Spirit of Christ has not refrained from using them as means of salvation which derive their efficacy from the very fullness of grace and truth entrusted to the Catholic Church.

Nevertheless, our separated brethren, whether considered as individuals or as Communities and Churches, are not blessed with that unity which Jesus Christ wished to bestow on all those whom He has regenerated and vivified into one body and newness of life— that unity which the holy Scriptures and the revered tradition of the Church proclaim. For it is through Christ's Catholic Church alone, which is the all-embracing means of salvation, that the fullness of the means of salvation can be obtained. It was to the apostolic college alone, of which Peter is the head, that we believe our Lord entrusted all the blessings of the New Covenant, in order to establish on earth the one Body of Christ into which all those should be fully incorporated who already belong in any way to God's people. During its pilgrimage on earth, this people though still in its members liable to sin, is growing in Christ and is being gently guided by God, according to His hidden designs, until it happily arrives at the fullness of eternal glory in the heavenly Jerusalem. *(Ecumenism, No. 3)*

106. The Human and Divine Elements of the Catholic Church Help It to Be Visible

Christ, the one Mediator, established and ceaselessly sustains here on earth His holy Church, the community of faith, hope, and charity, as a visible structure. Through her He communicates truth and grace to all. But the society furnished with hierarchical agencies and the Mystical Body of Christ are not to be considered as two realities, nor are the visible assembly and the spiritual community, nor the earthly Church and the Church enriched with heavenly things. Rather they form one interlocked reality which is comprised of a divine and a human element. For this reason, by an excellent analogy, this reality is compared to the mystery of the incarnate Word. Just as the assumed nature inseparably united to the divine Word serves Him as a living instrument of salvation, so, in a similar way, does the communal structure of the Church serve Christ's Spirit, who vivifies it by way of building up the body (cf. Eph. 4:16).

This is the unique Church of Christ which in the Creed we avow as one, holy, catholic, and apostolic. After his Resurrection our Savior handed her over to Peter to be shepherded (Jn. 21:17), commissioning him and the other apostles to propagate and govern her (cf. Mt. 28:18 ff.). Her He erected for all ages as "the pillar and mainstay of the truth" (1 Tim. 3:15). This Church, constituted and organized in the world as a society, subsists in the Catholic Church, which is governed by the successor of Peter and by the bishops in union with that successor, although many elements of sanctification and of truth can be found outside of her visible structure. These elements, however, as gifts properly belonging to the Church of Christ, possess an inner dynamism toward Catholic unity. *(Church, No. 8)*

B. Complete and Loyal Membership
in the Catholic Church

The kingdom of Christ is composed of spiritual and visible elements, namely, the divine grace of Christ and the human response of people to the risen Lord. Response to the call of Christ essentially consists in following Him personally within His Church-community. United in the faith, Catholics strive to make Christ's presence realized by others who may wish to join them and share in the blessings of the Church.

The Catholic Christian community, which necessarily embraces Christ's teaching authority, encourages dynamic growth and the forward movement of theological enquiry. While remaining faithful to the teachings handed down from the apostles, the Church must constantly adapt herself to be relevant to the times in such matters as variations in liturgical rites, adaptations in Church administration, and experimentations in pastoral practices.

Those who want to enjoy complete and loyal membership in the Catholic Church follow the currently developed authentic religious and moral precepts as taught by validly commissioned authority. Certainly, our Lord expects His people to live in the Church of their own day, not in the past. Tradition is not petrified, nor is loyalty to the eternal to be confused with clinging blindly to the past. Having the teaching of the Church to listen to should assist the Christian assume full responsibility for his own actions. The teaching of the Church on moral matters aids him in the formation of his conscience and so become a mature Christian. Ultimately, as every Christian knows, Christ and He alone will be the final judge of the worth of a man's life.

What is true of the Church as the guardian and protector of morals is true also in its own way of the deposit of faith. Here also the Church is the exponent of the faith delivered to the apostles and she has not only the right to teach us, but also the duty to do so. She can add nothing to what she has been taught by the Lord, but as time goes on she can see deeper and deeper into the riches that are hers, and which are given to her for man's salvation. Though it is men who speak, it is the Spirit who enlightens.

Much of the truth which is hers has been promulgated in dogmas. These are statements of God's revealed truth couched, as they must be, in the categories of the culture of the speakers and the hearers. These truths are capable of other formulation for other cultures. Not all Church doctrine need be officially defined. The mind of the Church is the mind of Christ, whether official spokesmen have defined it or not, and those who know this mind have a fuller faith, secure and sound.

Catholics can be truly proud of their heritage, God's gift and they can best show their gratitude for it by striving to live it more fully and to share it with others. For the Catholic believes that his Church contains the fullness of Christ's revelation and is the surest way to salvation since it possesses all the means for the attainment of eternal blessedness.

107. Accepting and Living the Entire Authentic Teaching of the Catholic Church

This sacred Synod turns its attention first to the Catholic faithful. Basing itself upon sacred Scripture and tradition, it teaches that the Church, now sojourning on earth as an exile, is necessary for salvation. For Christ, made present to us in His Body, which is the Church, is the one Mediator and the unique Way of salvation. In explicit terms He Himself affirmed the necessity of faith and baptism (cf. Mk. 16:16; Jn. 3:5) and thereby affirmed also the necessity of the Church, for through baptism as through a door men enter the Church. Whosoever, therefore, knowing that the Catholic Church was made necessary by God through Jesus Christ, would refuse to enter her or to remain in her could not be saved.

They are fully incorporated into the society of the Church who, possessing the Spirit of Christ, accept her entire system and all the means of salvation given to her, and through union with her visible structure are joined to Christ, who rules her through the Supreme Pontiff and the bishops. This joining is effected by the bonds of professed faith, of the sacraments, of ecclesiastical government, and of communion. He is not saved, however, who, though he is part of the body of the Church, does not persevere in charity. He remains indeed in the bosom of the Church, but, as it were, only in a "bodily" manner and not "in his heart." All the sons of the Church should remember that their exalted status is to be attributed not to their own merits but to the special grace of Christ. If they fail moreover to respond to that grace in thought, word, and deed, not only will they not be saved but they will be the more severely judged. *(Church, No. 14)*

108. Assenting to Ordinary Teachings of the Pope and United Bishops

Bishops teaching in communion with the Roman Pontiff, are to be respected by all as witnesses to divine and Catholic truth. In matters of faith and morals, the bishops speak in the name of Christ and the faithful are to accept their teaching and adhere to it with a religious assent of soul. This religious submission of will and of mind must be shown in a special way to the authentic teaching authority of the Roman Pontiff, even when he is not speaking ex cathedra. That is, it must be shown in such a way that his supreme magisterium is acknowledged with reverence, the judgments made by him are sincerely adhered to, according to his manifest mind and will. His mind and will in the matter may be known chiefly either from the character of the documents, from his frequent repetition of the same doctrine, or from his manner of speaking. *(Church, No. 25)*

109. God's Guidance of His People through Consecrated Authorities

But when either the Roman Pontiff or the body of bishops, together with him defines a judgment, they pronounce it in accord with revelation itself. All are obliged to maintain and be ruled by this revelation, which, as written or preserved by tradition, is transmitted in its entirety through the legitimate succession of bishops and especially through the care of the Roman Pontiff himself.

Under the guiding light of the Spirit of truth, revelation is thus religiously preserved and faithfully expounded in the Church. The Roman Pontiff and the bishops, in view of their office and of the importance of the matter, strive painstakingly and by appropriate means to inquire properly into that revelation and to give apt expression to its contents. But they do not allow that there could be any new public revelation pertaining to the divine deposit of faith. *(Church, No. 25)*

3. THE SERVICE BY RELIGIOUS LEADERS IN CHRIST'S CHURCH

A. Bishops' Pastoral Leadership in the Church

Christ Himself is head of His Church. His various members have differing responsibilities within the Church, and one of these is the service of exercising authority. As in past ages, so in present time, awesome burdens lie upon those entrusted by Christ with leadership, specifically our Holy Father, the Pope, and the bishops of the Church. In addition to reviewing the chief functions of service by the hierarchy, the following passages aim at eliciting appropriate respect, allegiance, and affection for the successors of the apostles.

The bishops throughout the world, united with the Bishop of Rome, share in the concern and responsibility for the whole Church in addition to the duties pertinent to their own dioceses. The implications of this collegiality, or union among the bishops, will show its effects in such practical ways as sharing manpower and resources, since the united hierarchy shares responsibility for the welfare of the entire Church. Also, without any detriment to the essential charge and powers entrusted to the successor of St. Peter, this united concern for the whole Church on the part of the bishops will result in wider delegation of responsibility. The formation of councils or conferences of bishops, clergymen, religious and the laity on national, diocesan, and parish levels is intended to produce concerted effort for the furtherance of the Church's aims.

The position of the hierarchy in our times seems to be suffering from various shades of disregard for their leadership among some of the clergy and the laity alike. This lessening of the hierarchy's influence may be due partly to the human situation prevalent throughout the world because of which men clamor for more liberty of personal decision-making and self determination in all areas of society. It may stem in part also, from the usual, though regrettable, excesses which follow upon most far-reaching renewals including the current up-dating of the Church. In any case, whatever newer structures evolve in the Church, the Christian community must be guided by those specially appointed to shepherd the flock of Christ. Herein we consider not so much the hierarchical structure of the Church as we do the pastoral service rendered by Christ's Vicar and the bishops united with the Holy See for sanctification, teaching and guidance.

110. Bishops United with Rome Are Successors of the Apostles

For the nurturing and constant growth of the People of God Christ the Lord instituted in His Church a variety of ministries, which work for the good of the whole body. For those ministers who are endowed with sacred power are servants of their brethren, so that all who are of the People of God, and therefore enjoy a true Christian dignity, can work toward a common goal freely and in an orderly way, and arrive at salvation.

This most sacred Synod, following in the footsteps of the First Vatican Council, teaches and declares with that Council that Jesus Christ, the eternal Shepherd, established His holy Church by sending forth the apostles as He Himself had been sent by the Father (cf. Jn. 20:21). He willed that their successors, namely the bishops, should be shepherds in His Church even to the consummation of the world.

In order that the episcopate itself might be one and undivided, He placed blessed Peter over the other apostles, and instituted in him a permanent and visible source and foundation of unity of faith and fellowship. And all this teaching about the institution, the perpetuity, the force and reason for the sacred primacy of the Roman Pontiff and of his infallible teaching authority, this sacred Synod again proposes to be firmly believed by all the faithful. *(Church, No.18)*

111. The Bishops United with the Pope Care for the Whole Church

The order of bishops is the successor to the college of the apostles in teaching authority and pastoral rule; or, rather, in the episcopal order the apostolic body continues without a break. Together with its head, the Roman Pontiff, and never without this head, the episcopal order is the subject of supreme and full power over the universal Church. But this power can be exercised only with the consent of the Roman Pontiff. For our Lord made Simon Peter alone the rock and keybearer of the Church (cf. Mt. 16:18-19), and appointed him shepherd of the whole flock (cf. Jn. 21:15 ff.).

It is definite, however, that the power of binding and loosing, which was given to Peter (Mt. 16:19), was granted also to the college of apostles, joined with their head (Mt. 18:18; 28:16-20). This college, insofar as it is composed of many, expresses the variety and universality of the People of God, but insofar as it is assembled under one head, it expresses the unity of the flock of Christ. In it, the bishops, faithfully recognizing the primacy and pre-eminence of their head, exercise their own authority for the good of their own faithful, and indeed of the whole Church, with the Holy Spirit constantly strengthening its organic structure and inner harmony. *(Church, No.22)*

112. Bishops Concerned for Their Diocese and the Whole Church

As lawful successors of the apostles and as members of the episcopal college, bishops should always realize that they are linked one to the other, and should show concern for all the churches. For by divine institution and the requirement of their apostolic office, each one in concert with his fellow bishops is responsible for the Church. They should be especially concerned about those parts of the world where the Word of God has not yet been proclaimed or where, chiefly because of the small number of priests, the faithful are in danger of departing from the precepts of the Christian life, and even of losing the faith itself.

Let bishops, therefore, make every effort to have the faithful actively support and promote works of evangelization and the apostolate. Let them strive, moreover, to see to it that suitable sacred ministers as well as assistants, both religious and lay, are prepared for the missions and other areas suffering from a lack of clergy. As far as possible, they should also arrange for some of their own priests to go to such missions or dioceses to exercise the sacred ministry permanently or at least for a set period of time.

Moreover, in administering ecclesiastical assets, bishops should think not only of the needs of their own dioceses, but of other ones as well, for these too are part of the one Church of Christ. Finally, in proportion to their means, bishops should give attention to relieving the disasters which afflict other dioceses and regions. *(Bishops, No. 6)*

113. Teaching Functions of Bishops for Current Needs of People

In exercising their duty of teaching, they should announce the gospel of Christ to men, a task which is eminent among the chief duties of bishops. They should, in the power of the Spirit, summon men to faith or confirm them in a faith already living. They should expound the whole mystery of Christ to them, namely, those truths the ignorance of which is ignorance of Christ. At the same time they should point out the divinely revealed way to give glory to God and thus attain to everlasting bliss.

They should show, moreover, that earthly goods and human institutions structured according to the plan of God the Creator are also related to man's salvation, and therefore can contribute much to the upbuilding of Christ's Body.

Hence let them teach with what seriousness the Church believes these realities should be regarded: the human person with his freedom and bodily life, the family and its unity and stability, the procreation and education of children, civil society with its laws and professions, labor and leisure, the arts and technical inventions, poverty and affluence. Finally, they should set forth the ways by which are to be solved the very grave questions concerning the ownership, increase, and just distribution of material goods, peace and war, and brotherly relations among all peoples. *(Bishops, No.12)*

114. Sanctifying Functions of Bishops for Spiritual Care of People

In fulfilling their duty to sanctify, bishops should be mindful that they have been taken from among men and appointed their representatives before God in order to offer gifts and sacrifices for sins. Bishops enjoy the fullness of the sacrament of orders, and all priests as well as deacons are dependent upon them in the exercise of authority. For the "presbyters" are prudent fellow workers of the episcopal order and are themselves consecrated as true priests of the New Testament, just as deacons are ordained for service and minister to the People of God in communion with the bishop and his presbytery. Therefore bishops are the principal dispensers of the mysteries of God, just as they are the governors, promoters, and guardians of the entire liturgical life in the church committed to them.

Hence, they should constantly exert themselves to have the faithful know and live the paschal mystery more deeply through the Eucharist and thus become a firmly knit body in the solidarity of Christ's love. "Intent upon prayer and the ministry of the word" (Acts 6:4), they should devote their labor to this end, that all those committed to their care may be of one mind in prayer and through the reception of the sacraments may grow in grace and be faithful witnesses to the Lord.

As those who lead others to perfection, bishops should be

diligent in fostering holiness among their clerics, religious, and laity according to the special vocation of each. They should also be mindful of their obligation to give an example of holiness through charity, humility, and simplicity of life. Let them so hallow the churches entrusted to them that the true image of Christ's universal Church may shine forth fully in them. For that reason they should foster priestly and religious vocations as much as possible, and take a special interest in missionary vocations. *(Bishops, No.15)*

115. Guiding Functions of Bishops in the Pastoral Care of People

(a) In exercising his office of father and pastor, a bishop should stand in the midst of his people as one who serves. Let him be a good shepherd who knows his sheep and whose sheep know him. Let him be a true father who excels in the spirit of love and solicitude for all and to whose divinely conferred authority all gratefully submit themselves. Let him so gather and mold the whole family of his flock that everyone, conscious of his own duties, may live and work in the communion of love.

(b) To accomplish these things effectively, a bishop, "ready for every good work" (2 Tim. 2:21) and "enduring all things for the sake of the chosen ones" (2 Tim. 2:10), should arrange his life in such a way as to accommodate it to the needs of the time.

(c) A bishop should always welcome priests with a special love since they assume in part the bishop's duties and cares and carry the weight of them day by day so zealously. He should regard his priests as sons and friends. Thus by his readiness to listen to them and by his trusting familiarity, a bishop can work to promote the whole pastoral work of the entire diocese.

(d) He should be concerned about the spiritual, intellectual, and material condition of his priests, so that they can live holy and pious lives and fulfill their ministry faithfully and fruitfully. For this reason, he should encourage institutes and hold special meetings in which priests can gather from time to time for the performance of lengthier spiritual exercises by way of renewing their lives and for the acquisition of deeper knowledge of ecclesiastical subjects, especially sacred Scripture and theology, the social questions of major importance, and the new methods of pastoral activity. With active mercy a bishop should attend upon priests who are in any sort of danger or who have failed in some respect.

(e) In order to be able to consult more suitably the welfare of the faithful according to the condition of each one, a bishop should strive to become duly acquainted with their needs in the social circumstances in which they live. Hence, he ought to employ suitable methods, especially social research. He should manifest his concern for all, no matter what their age, condition, or nationality, be they natives, strangers, or foreigners. In exercising this pastoral care he should preserve for his faithful the share proper to them in Church affairs; he should also recognize. their duty and right to collaborate actively in the building up of the Mystical Body of Christ.

(f) He should deal lovingly with the separated brethren, urging the faithful also to conduct themselves with great kindness and charity in their regard, and fostering ecumenism as it is understood by the Church. He should also have the welfare of the non-baptized at heart so that upon them too there may shine the charity of Christ Jesus, to whom the bishop is a witness before all men. *(Bishops, No.16)*

116. Adapting Pastoral Services to Needs of People Today

Special concern should be shown for those among the faithful who, on account of their way or condition of life, cannot sufficiently make use of the common and ordinary pastoral services of parish priests or are quite cut off from them. Among this group are very many migrants, exiles and refugees, seamen, airplane personnel, gypsies, and others of this kind. Suitable pastoral methods should also be developed to sustain the spiritual life of those who journey to other lands for a time for the sake of recreation. *(Bishops, No.18)*

B. Priests' Ministering to God's People Today

The interpretation of the gospel-message for modern circumstances comes ultimately from the bishops united with the Vicar of Christ. Local priests, however, usually come in closer pastoral contact with people in the daily applications of Church teachings. As leaders in the Church-community, priests merit from the people they serve, both personal acceptance within the community, and respect, affection, and assistance.

Since the Church is re-evaluating itself in order to be more relevant to current needs, undoubtedly the clergy must do the same. Some of these may encounter rather traumatic experiences in the process. Symptomatic of this deep re-evaluation of the role of the priest in the world today are the numbers who can no longer reconcile within themselves the emerging new structures or the fading of older ones. This temporary upheaval is also evident in the decline of numbers entering seminaries and religious congregations.

Whatever forms the future personal life and public ministry of priests may take, the Church ordains and commissions priests not to preach their own ideas specifically, but to proclaim, in the name of the Church, her complete and authentic message of salvation. We view here some fundamentals of priests' spiritual ministry among the people today, whose careful guidance of the flock of Christ is so essential for the advancement of His Church.

117. The Needs of People Require Clergy Involvement

In fulfilling the office of shepherd, pastors should first take pains to know their own flock. Since they are the servants of all the sheep, they should foster growth in Christian living among the individual faithful and also in families, in associations especially dedicated to the apostolate, and in the whole parish community. Therefore, they should visit homes and schools to the extent that their pastoral work demands. They should pay special attention to adolescents and youth, devote themselves with a paternal love to the poor and the sick, and have a particular concern for workingmen. Finally, they should encourage the faithful to assist in the works of the apostolate. (Bishops, No.30)

118. Priests' Practical Preaching for Contemporary Needs

Toward all men, therefore, priests have the duty of sharing the gospel truth in which they themselves rejoice in the Lord. And so, whether by honorable behavior among the nations they lead them to glorify God, whether by openly preaching they proclaim the mystery of Christ to unbelievers, whether they hand on the Christian faith or explain the Church's teaching, or whether in the light of Christ they strive to deal with contemporary problems, the task of priests is not to teach their own wisdom but God's Word, and to summon all men urgently to conversion and to holiness.

No doubt, priestly preaching is often very difficult in the circumstances of the modern world. If it is to influence the mind of the listener more fruitfully, such preaching must not present God's

Word in a general and abstract fashion only, but it must apply the perennial truth of the gospel to the concrete circumstances of life. *(Priests, No.4)*

119. Priests Strive to Help the Individual's Faith to Maturity

Therefore, as educators in the faith, priests must see to it, either by themselves or through others, that the faithful are led individually in the Holy Spirit to a development of their own vocation as required by the gospel, to a sincere and active charity, and to that freedom with which Christ has made us free. Ceremonies however beautiful, or associations however flourishing, will be of little value if they are not directed toward educating men in the attainment of Christian maturity.

To further this goal, priests should help men see what is required and what is God's will in the great and small events of life. Christians should also be taught that they do not live for themselves alone, but, according to the demands of the new law of charity, every man must administer to others the grace he has received. In this way all will discharge in a Christian manner their duties within the community of men. *(Priests, No.6)*

120. Priests Helping to Build a Christian Community

The office of pastor is not confined to the care of the faithful as individuals, but is also properly extended to the formation of a genuine Christian community. If community spirit is to be duly fostered, it must embrace not only the local Church but the universal Church. The local community should not only promote the care of its own faithful, but filled with a missionary zeal, it should also prepare the way to Christ for all men. To this community in a special way are entrusted catechumens and the newly baptized, who must be gradually educated to recognize and lead a Christian life.

No Christian community, however, can be built up unless it has its basis and center in the celebration of the most Holy Eucharist. Here, therefore, all education in the spirit of community must originate. If this celebration is to be sincere and thorough, it must lead to various works of charity and mutual help, as well as to missionary activity and to different forms of Christian witness.

Moreover, by charity, prayer, example, and works of penance, the Church community exercises a true motherhood toward souls who are to be led to Christ. For this community constitutes an effective instrument by which the path to Christ and to His Church is pointed out and made smooth for unbelievers, and by which the faithful are aroused, nourished, and strengthened for spiritual combat.

In building the Christian community, priests are never to put themselves at the service of any ideology or human faction. Rather, as heralds of the gospel and shepherds of the Church, they must devote themselves to the spiritual growth of the Body of Christ. *(Priests, No.6)*

121. The Clergy Utilizing the Laity's Special Graces and Abilities

Priests must sincerely acknowledge and promote the dignity of the laity and the role which is proper to them in the mission of the Church. They should scrupulously honor that just freedom which is due to everyone in this earthly city. They should listen to the laity willingly, consider their wishes in a fraternal spirit, and recognize their experience and competence in the different areas of human activity, so that together with them they will be able to read the signs of the times.

While testing spirits to see if they be of God, priests should discover with the instinct of faith, acknowledge with joy, and foster with diligence the various humble and exalted charisms of the laity. Among the other gifts of God which are found in abundance among the faithful, those are worthy of special attention which are drawing many to a deeper spiritual life. Priests should also confidently entrust to the laity duties in the service of the Church, allowing them freedom and room for action. In fact, on suitable occasions, they should invite them to undertake works on their own initiative. *(Priests, No.9)*

122. Priests' Leadership for Their People's Improvement

Finally, priests have been placed in the midst of the laity to lead them to the unity of charity, that they may "love one another with fraternal charity, anticipating one another with honor" (Rom. 12:10). It is their task, therefore, to reconcile differences of mentality in such a way that no one will feel himself a stranger in the community of the faithful. Priests are defenders of the common good, with which they are charged in the name of the bishop. At the same time, they are strenuous defenders of the truth, lest the faithful be tossed about by every wind of opinion. To their special concern are committed those who have fallen away from the use of the sacraments, or perhaps even from the faith. As good shepherds, they should not cease from going after them.

Mindful of this Council's directives on ecumenism, let them not forget their brothers who do not enjoy full ecclesiastical communion with us.

Finally, to them are commended all those who do not recognize Christ as their Savior. *(Priests, No.9)*

123. The Laity's Respect, Help, and Care for Their Priests

The Christian faithful, for their part, should realize their obligations toward their priests and with filial love they should follow them as their shepherds and fathers. Likewise sharing their cares, they should help their priests by prayer and work to the extent possible, so that their priests can more readily overcome difficulties and be able to fulfill their duties more fruitfully. *(Priests, No.9)*

C. Adaptation of Seminary Training and of Religious Life to Modern Needs

The adaptations in the way of life and in the form of training currently found in seminaries, novitiates, religious houses of study, and convents convey a strong indication of the newer form of leadership which may be expected in the future. From the ranks of these younger men and women will come the future bishops and priests, nuns and brothers for the Church.

In the seminaries the trend is toward attempting to prepare the future priests for their active role in society which the times will require. As with young adults in universities, the seminarians of today are given more personal freedom of choice and decision, in the attempt to produce the mature priest of personal responsibility in a fast-moving age. Several former means of training and the curriculum of studies are being re-evaluated in the light of contemporary requirements, and liberal adaptations are in effect. Some may consider the form of training in seminaries as changing too radically; others may feel a need for even greater change. However, what is happening in the formation of seminarians and religious is being closely studied with a wise, tender and zealous regard for the future.

The consistent balance of Vatican II is evident in the passages on the renewal of religious life. They call for adaptation to the needs of contemporary times both for the religious themselves and for their apostolic works in the Church. There is a great need for the blessings which derive from the consecrated lives of those who are in religious life and for the benefits their dedication brings to the Church. In addition to the works they produce, the lives of consecration to Christ Jesus by priests and religious give witness to God's loving presence in the world and bring most essential service to the entire Church.

The hundreds of thousands of religious in the various congregations throughout the world are renewing themselves, their manner of life and work, in conjunction with the purpose and in the spirit for which they were founded and are currently approved. Any renewal is to maintain the furtherance of true sanctity. There is not to be a revolt against religious life but a renewal of it, similar to the general rejuvenation within the Church and undertaken for the same purpose of increased effectiveness.

Older priests and religious are witnessing deeply significant changes and adaptations of religious life, its structure, rules, and manner of living. The kind of personality that will emerge as the future religious — less restricted in movement, in the discharge of the apostolate, in the manner of dress, and so forth — will surely be different. There is also every hope that the new religious will be effective for meeting the needs of the times in helping people to get closer to God in their daily lives.

124. Seminarians' Training for Contemporary Needs of People

That pastoral concern which should thoroughly penetrate the entire training of seminarians also requires that they be carefully instructed in those matters which have a special bearing on the sacred ministry, especially catechetics, preaching, liturgical worship, the conferral of the sacraments, works of charity, the duty of seeking out the straying sheep and unbelievers, and other pastoral obligations. Let them receive careful instruction in the art of guiding souls, so that they can lead all sons of the Church, before everything else, to a Christian life which is fully conscious and apostolic, and to a fulfillment of the duties of their state. With equal thoroughness they should learn to assist men and women religious to persevere in the grace of their vocation and to make progress according to the spirit of their various communities.

In general, there should be developed in seminarians the abilities most appropriate for the promotion of dialogue with men, such as a capacity to listen to other people and to open their hearts in a spirit of charity to the various circumstances of human need. *(Seminarians, No.19)*

125. Using Modern Means to Foster Future Priests' Apostolate

Let them be taught to use, in a proper manner and according to the norms of Church authority, the helps which pedagogy, psychology, and sociology can offer. Again, they should be trained with exactness to ignite and fan the apostolic activity of laymen, and to promote the various and more successful forms of the apostolate. They need to be penetrated with that truly Catholic spirit by which they can transcend the borders of their own diocese, nation, or rite, be accustomed to consulting the needs of the whole Church, and be ready in spirit to preach the gospel everywhere. *(Seminarians, No.20)*

126. Renewing the Manner of Life of Religious Today

The appropriate renewal of religious life involves two simultaneous processes: (1) a continuous return to the sources of all Christian life and to the original inspiration behind a given community and (2) an adjustment of the community to the changed conditions of the times. It is according to the following principles that such renewal should go forward under the influence of the Holy Spirit and the guidance of the Church.

a) Since the fundamental norm of the religious life is a following of Christ as proposed by the gospel, such is to be regarded by all communities as their supreme law.

b) It serves the best interests of the Church for communities to have their own special character and purpose. Therefore loyal recognition and safekeeping should be accorded to the spirit of founders, as also to all the particular goals and wholesome traditions which constitute the heritage of each community. *(Religious, No.2)*

127. Adaptations to Modern Needs for Effectiveness of Religious

All communities should participate in the life of the Church. According to its individual character, each should make its own and foster in every possible way the enterprises and objectives of the Church in such fields as these: the scriptural, liturgical, doctrinal, pastoral, ecumenical, missionary, and social.

Communities should promote among their members a suitable awareness of contemporary human conditions and of the needs of the Church. For if their members can combine the burning zeal of an apostle with wise judgments, made in the light of faith, concerning the circumstances of the modern world, they will be able to come to the aid of men more effectively.

Since the religious life is intended above all else to lead those who embrace it to an imitation of Christ and to union with God through the profession of the evangelical counsels, the fact must be honestly faced that even the most desirable changes made on behalf of contemporary needs will fail of their purpose unless a renewal of spirit gives life to them. Indeed such an interior renewal must always be accorded the leading role even in the promotion of exterior works. (*Religious, No.2*)

128. The Religious State of Life Benefits the Entire Church

By the charity to which they lead, the evangelical counsels join their followers to the Church and her mystery in a special way. Since this is so, the spiritual life of these followers should be devoted to the welfare of the whole Church. Thence arises their duty of working to implant and strengthen the kingdom of Christ in souls and to extend that kingdom to every land. This duty is to be discharged to the extent of their capacities and in keeping with the form of their proper vocation. The chosen means may be prayer or active undertakings. It is for this reason that the Church preserves and fosters the special character of her various religious communities.

The profession of the evangelical counsels, then, appears as a sign which can and ought to attract all the members of the Church to an effective and prompt fulfillment of the duties of their Christian vocation. The People of God has no lasting city here below, but looks forward to one which is to come. This being so, the religious state by giving its members greater freedom from earthly cares more adequately manifests to all believers the presence of heavenly goods already possessed here below. (*Church, No.44*)

129. The Life, Works, and Value of Religious Life

Religious should carefully consider that through them, to believers and non-believers alike, the Church truly wishes to give an increasingly clearer revelation of Christ. Through them Christ should be shown contemplating on the mountain, announcing God's kingdom to the multitude, healing the sick and the maimed, turning sinners to wholesome fruit, blessing children, doing good to all, and always obeying the will of the Father who sent Him.

Finally, everyone should realize that the profession of the evangelical counsels, though entailing the renunciation of certain values which undoubtedly merit high esteem, does not detract from a genuine development of the human person. Rather by its very nature it is most beneficial to that development. For the counsels, voluntarily undertaken according to each one's personal vocation, contribute greatly to purification of heart and spiritual liberty. They continually kindle the fervor of charity. As the example of so many saintly founders shows, the counsels are especially able to pattern the Christian man after that manner of virginal and humble life which Christ the Lord elected for Himself, and which His Virgin Mother also chose. *(Church, No.46)*

4. THE LAITY'S FUNCTIONAL ROLE IN THE CHURCH

A. The Laity Cooperate in the Sanctifying Mission of Christ, the Priest

Before we reflect on the laity's cooperation in the sanctifying mission of Christ, the High Priest, it will be helpful to review some considerations regarding the layman's integral role in the Church. As Christians incorporated in Christ, there is no basic distinction between the clergy and the laity, though there is a difference in the function each renders. Although much that is presented by the Council on the Christian's functional vitality pertains to priests and religious as well as to laymen, we will focus here on the role of those designated as the laity.

The functional role of the laity in the Church derives from their union with Christ as Priest, Prophet and King. The emerging layman's position is not due merely to Vatican II's emphasis on their role, nor is it a consequence of a shortage of priests, or the desire of lay people to have more voice in the Church. In Christ's kingdom, all have their proper functions to perform. The Church-community is comprised of old, middle-aged, and young people. There are cardinals and clerks, clergymen and housewives, religious and single dedicated Christians.

Respect is due to all as brothers and sisters of Christ. What ultimately matters is that all fulfill their function for the good of the whole Church. All Christian activity is in some way a sharing in the sanctifying, teaching, and ruling mission of Christ the Priest, Prophet and King.

As sharers in the priesthood of Christ, the laity cooperate in His sanctifying mission to the world. They do this first by striving for their own sanctification, chiefly through participation in the liturgical rites of the Church, and secondly by their example and efforts toward the sanctification of others. The laity can discharge several functions within the liturgy. Furthermore, circumstances may arise, as in mission territories, where select lay men and women assist, with ecclesiastical approval, with certain sacred rites, even distributing Holy Communion when ordained priests are unavailable. In any case, all in the Church who have accepted the risen Christ share in His sanctifying mission as High Priest to the world.

130. The Basic Theology of the Laity's Role in the Church

The term laity is here understood to mean all the faithful except those in holy orders and those in a religious state sanctioned by the Church. These faithful are by baptism made one body with Christ and are established among the People of God. They are in their own way made sharers in the priestly, prophetic, and kingly functions of Christ. They carry out their own part in the mission of the whole Christian people with respect to the Church and the world. *(Church, No.31)*

131. How the Laity Share in the Sanctifying Mission of the Church

Since the supreme and eternal Priest, Christ Jesus, wills to continue His witness and serve through the laity too, He vivifies them in His Spirit and unceasingly urges them on to every good and perfect work.

For besides intimately associating them with His life and His mission, Christ also gives them a share in His priestly function of offering spiritual worship for the glory of God and the salvation of men. For this reason the laity, dedicated to Christ and anointed by the Holy Spirit, are marvelously called and equipped to produce in themselves ever more abundant fruits of the Spirit. For all their works, prayers, and apostolic endeavors, their ordinary married and family life, their daily labor, their mental and physical relaxation, if carried out in the Spirit, and even the hardships of life, if patiently borne — all of these become spiritual sacrifices acceptable to God through Jesus Christ (cf. 1 Pet. 2:5). During the celebration of the Eucharist, these sacrifices are most lovingly offered to the Father along with the Lord's body. Thus, as worshippers whose every deed is holy, the laity consecrate the world itself to God. *(Church, No.34)*

132. Relationship of Clergy and Laity in Christ's Priestly Functions

Though they differ from one another in essence and not only in degree, the common priesthood of the faithful and the ministerial or hierarchical priesthood are nonetheless interrelated. Each of them in its own special way is a participation in the one priesthood of Christ. The ministerial priest, by the sacred power he enjoys, molds and rules the priestly people. Acting in the person of Christ, he brings about the Eucharistic Sacrifice, and offers it to God in the name of all the people. For their part, the faithful join in the offering of the Eucharist by virtue of their royal priesthood. They likewise exercise that priesthood by receiving the sacraments, by prayer and thanksgiving, by the witness of a holy life, and by self-denial and active charity. *(Church, No.10)*

B. The Laity Participate in the Teaching Mission of Christ, the Prophet

Christ sends the Paraclete, the Spirit of Truth, to teach and enlighten receptive people in the ways of accepting salvation. Obviously, the Holy Spirit breathes where He will. The laity share in the blessings of the Spirit for their own welfare as well as to be instruments for furthering the cause of Christ. The mission to go teach all nations the gospel of Christ in order to establish His kingdom applies to lay men and women under, of course, the guidance of the teaching authority approved by Christ. To help spread the "good news" of available salvation is an integral part of the Christian commitment.

The laity's participation in Christ's teaching mission implies greater responsibility for learning the faith in depth so that it may be handed down as the authentic teaching of Christ, the Prophet, in His Church. The laity, as do all God's people, receive their special graces, or charisms, to enable them to fulfill their teaching mission in their families and among their friends, neighbors and associates. Every follower of Christ is called to be a disciple spreading His teachings, each according to the opportunities and means available. Those who teach others the ways of Christ will shine like the stars above.

133. How the Laity Share in the Teaching Mission of the Church

Christ, the great Prophet, who proclaimed the kingdom of His Father by the testimony of His life and the power of His words, continually fulfills His prophetic office until His full glory is revealed. He does this not only through the hierarchy who teach in His name and with His authority, but also through the laity. For that very purpose He made them His witnesses and gave them understanding of the faith and the grace of speech (cf. Acts 2:17-18; Apoc. 19:10), so that the power of the gospel might shine forth in their daily social and family life.

They show themselves to be children of the promise, if, strong in faith and in hope, they make the most of the present time (cf. Eph. 5:16; Col. 4:5), and with patience await the glory that is to come (cf. Rom. 8:25). Let them not, then, hide this hope in the depths of their hearts, but even in the framework of secular life let them express it by a continual turning toward God and by wrestling "against the world-rulers of this darkness, against the spiritual forces of wickedness" (Eph. 6:12). *(Church, No.35)*

134. Manifestations of the Holy Spirit Working within the Laity

The holy People of God shares also in Christ's prophetic office. It spreads abroad a living witness to Him, especially by means of a life of faith and charity and by offering to God a sacrifice of praise, the tribute of lips which give honor to His name (cf. Heb. 13:15). The body of the faithful as a whole, anointed as they are by the Holy One (cf. Jn. 2:20, 27), cannot err in matters of belief. Thanks to a supernatural sense of the faith which characterizes the People of God as a whole, it manifests this unerring quality when, "from the bishops down to the last member of the laity," it shows universal agreement in matters of faith and morals.

For, by this sense of faith which is aroused and sustained by the Spirit of truth, God's people accepts not the word of men but the very Word of God (cf. 1 Th. 2:13). It clings without fail to the faith once delivered to the saints (cf. Jude 3), penetrates it more deeply by accurate insights, and applies it more thoroughly to life. All this it does under the lead of a sacred teaching authority to which it loyally defers.

It is not only through the sacraments and Church ministries that the same Holy Spirit sanctifies and leads the People of God and enriches it with virtues. Allotting His gifts "to everyone according as he will" (1 Cor. 12:11), He distributes special graces among the faithful of every rank. By these gifts He makes them fit and ready to undertake the various tasks or offices advantageous for the renewal and upbuilding of the Church, according to the words of the Apostle: "The manifestation of the Spirit is given to everyone for profit" (1Cor. 12:7). These charismatic gifts, whether they be the most outstanding or the more simple and widely diffused, are to be received with thanksgiving and consolation, for they are exceedingly suitable and useful for the needs of the Church. *(Church, No.12)*

135. The Special Gifts of the Holy Spirit Conferred on the Faithful

For the exercise of this apostolate, the Holy Spirit who sanctifies the People of God through the ministry and the sacraments gives to the faithful special gifts as well (cf. 1 Cor. 12:7), "allotting to everyone according as he will" (1 Cor. 12:11). Thus may the individual, "according to the gift that each has received, administer it to one another" and become "good stewards of the manifold grace of God" (1 Pet. 4:10), and build up thereby the whole body in charity (cf. Eph. 4:16). From the reception of these charisms or gifts, including those which are less dramatic, there arise for each believer the right and duty to use them in the Church and in the world for the good of mankind and for the upbuilding of the Church. In so doing, believers need to enjoy the freedom of the Holy Spirit who "breathes where he wills" (Jn. 3:8). At the same time, they must act in communion with their brothers in Christ, especially with their pastors. The latter must make a judgment about the true nature and proper use of these gifts, not in order to extinguish the Spirit, but to test all things and hold fast to what is good (cf. 1 Th. 5:12, 19, 21). *(Laity, No.3)*

136. The Laity Must Hand Down the Faith, Even Amid Difficulties

Consequently, even when preoccupied with temporal cares, the laity can and must perform eminently valuable work on behalf of bringing the gospel to the world. Some of them do all they can to provide sacred services when sacred ministers are lacking or are blocked by a persecuting regime. Many devote themselves entirely to apostolic work. But all ought to cooperate in the spreading and intensifying of the kingdom of Christ in the world. Therefore, let the laity strive skillfully to acquire a more profound grasp of revealed truth, and insistently beg of God the gift of wisdom. *(Church, No. 35)*

C. The Laity Share in the Ruling Mission of Christ, the King

It would seem, from a perusal of the Acts of the Apostles and from historical and contemporary writings, that there may have been from the beginning and may ever be "traditionalists" and "progressives" in the Christian community. It may be just as well that a wholesome tension exists in the Church, each extreme leveling off the other, that the truth may ultimately emerge, as the Christian community moves forward in its practice of charity. Each group must respect and accept the sincerity of the other in their mutual concern for and loyal interest in all that pertains to Church affairs. The faithful share in the ruling or guiding mission of Christ, the King, and they hold a common concern that His kingdom be rightly ruled so that it may move forward in the world.

There is no question of the laity's right to share, according to their capacity, in all that refers to the proper conduct of Church matters. In fact, the laity's competence in spiritual matters, as well as in concrete secular affairs, must be used for the furtherance of the mission of the whole Church. There are times when lay men and women are obliged to assist in the proper conduct of the Church's mission on all levels, international, national, diocesan and parochial. Laymen and religious as well as the clergy must cooperate for the full functioning of various conferences, councils and all the interests of the Church. The harmonious solution of problems common to all citizens of Christ's kingdom does honor to the Lord and furthers His mission among all mankind.

137. How the Laity Share in the Ruling Mission of the Church

Christ obeyed even at the cost of death, and was therefore raised up by the Father (cf. Phil. 2:8-9). Thus He entered into the glory of His kingdom. To Him all things are made subject until He subjects Himself and all created things to the Father, that God may be all in all (cf. 1 Cor. 15:27-28). Now, Christ has communicated this power of subjection to His disciples that they might be established in royal freedom and that by self-denial and a holy life they might conquer the reign of sin in themselves (cf. Rom. 6:12). Further, He has shared this power so that by serving Him in their fellow men they might through humility and patience lead their brother men to that King whom to serve is to reign.

For the Lord wishes to spread His kingdom by means of the laity also, a kingdom of truth and life, a kingdom of holiness and grace, a kingdom of justice, love, and peace. In this kingdom, creation itself will be delivered out of its slavery to corruption and into the freedom of the glory of the sons of God (cf. Rom. 8:21). Clearly then a great promise and a great mandate are committed to the disciples: "For all are yours, and you are Christ's, and Christ is God's" (1 Cor. 3:23). (Church, No. 36)

138. Some Rights of the Laity in Church Matters

The laity have the right, as do all Christians, to receive in abundance from their sacred pastors the spiritual goods of the Church, especially the assistance of the Word of God and the sacraments. Every layman should openly reveal to them his needs and desires with that freedom and confidence which befits a son of God and a brother in Christ. An individual layman, by reason of the knowledge, competence, or outstanding ability which he may enjoy, is permitted and sometimes even obliged to express his opinion on things which concern the good of the Church. When occasions arise, let this be done through the agencies set up by the Church for this purpose. Let it always be done in truth, in courage, and in prudence, with reverence and charity toward those who by reason of their sacred office represent the person of Christ. (Church, No.37)

139. Cooperation of Clergy and Laity in the Church

Let sacred pastors recognize and promote the dignity as well as the responsibility of the layman in the Church. Let them willingly make use of his prudent advice. Let them confidently assign duties to him in the service of the Church, allowing him freedom and room for action. Further, let them encourage the layman so that he may undertake tasks on his own initiative. Attentively in Christ, let them consider with fatherly love the projects, suggestions, and desires proposed by the laity. Furthermore, let pastors respectfully acknowledge that just freedom which belongs to everyone in this earthly city.

A great many benefits are to be hoped for from this familiar dialogue between the laity and their pastors: in the laity, a strengthened sense of personal responsibility, a renewed enthusiasm, a more ready application of their talents to the projects of their pastors. The latter, for their part, aided by the experience of the laity, can more clearly and more suitably come to decisions regarding spiritual and temporal matters. In this way, the whole Church, strengthened by each one of its members, can more effectively fulfill its mission for the life of the world. *(Church, No.37)*

A brief review of this chapter will call to mind that the Church is God's great mystery. All mankind is to be invited to belong to His flock which Christ Himself tends as its Good Shepherd. The presence of Christ among His people sanctifies, teaches and guides us in the kingdom which He began in time and will complete in eternity. Our Lord calls us through His gospel, through His Holy Spirit and through His Church to respond to Him with love, strength and peace. As His love, so His presence knows no bounds, for He is Lord of time and space, and of the saints in heaven and of mankind on earth.

Chapter VI

CHRIST'S PEOPLE IN ACTION

The Laity's Apostolate

The previous chapter ended with the theology of the laity's function in the Church. This theological background laid the foundation for the super-structure of the active apostolate of lay men and women in the world. Basically, the apostolate means one's entire Christian life of dedication to Christ and His cause. Religion involves the whole man; it is not actually divided into spiritual and secular works. As a man is being composed of soul and body, he is nevertheless, a single unified person and acts as such. To look upon life as unified in the person of Jesus Christ, with His human and divine nature, simplifies the Christian's understanding of the material and spiritual aspects of his role in the world. It is in the Incarnation of Christ that the Word and the world, the sacred and the secular, become united temporally. It is, therefore, in imitation of Christ's Incarnation that the Christian can best fulfill his function in life, as he works to instill the spirit of Christ in the world.

All in the Church share the same mission entrusted by Christ, though their individual talents and state in life differ. The Christian community includes those we designate as the hierarchy, the clergy, the religious, and the laity. All together constitute a single unitive entity while performing diverse functions and discharging a variety of responsibilities. Just as all Christians are called to sanctity of life, they must also share in the apostolate of advancing the cause of Christ throughout their lives. One cannot be a Christian, a member of the Mystical Body, without also having a role in the activity of the Church in her efforts to spread the word of salvation and to acquire new followers of Christ. Christian membership is not simply a passport to eternal life but a commitment to a missionary Church which is destined to expand to the limits of the earth and the end of time. Obviously, the activity of Christ's people includes their inner spirituality as well as their outer good works. Contemplation is a Christian activity as vital to the community as outward activities. Actually, spiritual union with our Lord provides the dynamism for carrying out the Christian apostolate. However, in addition to the strictly spiritual elements of Christianity, it requires outward works in order to expand.

It is undoubtedly the working of the Holy Spirit which is helping the laity become even more conscious of their particular responsibilities as full sharers in the mission of the Church in the modern world. "The developing age of the layman" is an apt expression of a major tenet of the Second Vatican Council. This trend should not be evaluated as a revolt or a threat, but rather as a promising indication of the renewed self-awareness in the whole Church. Possibly too, when increasing numbers of lay men and women take on larger spheres of responsibility in the Church, priests may find themselves even more desperately needed in their unique and specific vocation of handling the spiritual direction and religious guidance of the emerging laymen. In fact, it may be that the more laymen become actively involved in the Church's works the more priests will be required to help support the laity by professional skills in the advancement of the spiritual life. The role of the clergy will become, thereby, even more sharply defined and more urgently needed.

The vast potential of the laity's advancing role in the Church is unmeasurable and it must be more widely developed. For instance, in addition to the obvious apostolates of married people and of those in the religious state, special concentration should be directed toward that numerous, talented, and dedicated group of Christians — the single men and women in the world. There is too much waste of excellent capability among the huge numbers of unmarried adult Christians. Allied with the single are also the college and working youth, the widowed, separated, and retired, in addition to that large group of dedicated seminarians and others. While maintaining constant interest in the Christian family, the Church's pastoral theologians and writers, with the assistance of the unmarried themselves, must devise a theology with a more advanced attitude toward single peoples' commitment to Christ which follows approaches different from those in the religious state. While spirituality is basically the same for all, there are aspects of Christian vitality especially suited to the advancement of the unmarried. The single state, in addition to other ways of life, can be a

unique vocation to serve the Lord and a most useful asset to the whole
Christian community's work in the world.

The word of God, the good-news of available salvation, must
reach into every segment of human society among all nations of the
world. All members of Christ's Mystical Body are called to active participation in the Church's mission (Section 1). The laity are in especially advantageous positions to lend relevant Christian influence in
every area, occupation, and movement within secular society (Section
2). However, in order to be really effective in carrying out the Christian
apostolate in the more complex aspects of current requirements, the
laity need adequate preparation so that their various forms of activity
may be more fruitful (Section 3).

Christ's people in action is an extension of the effects of His
Incarnation and Redemption in the world. All members of the Church
must share in this vital activity. Christ calls upon His own people to
further advance His redemptive work. In these challenging times a vast
and most rewarding mission of service is open to all, especially to those
staunch and self-sacrificing lay men and women who will actively foster
the cause of Christ by their Christian life and works.

1. CHRIST'S PEOPLE EXTEND THE EFFECTS OF HIS INCARNATION IN THE WORLD

A. All Are Called to Vital Activity in Christ's Mystical Body, The Church

Lay men and women, who necessarily live in the midst of the
secular environment, have the fullest opportunity of displaying to
others the relevance of their Christian convictions. The most efficacious
way in which Christians show their active and practical commitment to
Christ is practiced particularly in the work-a-day circumstances of their
lives. The laity's participation in the mission of Christ furthers His cause
throughout the world. In concrete terms, Christ's people in their
apostolic activities are an extension of His Incarnation. Similar to God's
taking on a human nature to save mankind through Christ, the Christian
sees the world as good, and he enters secular life upraising its standards
according to the teachings of Christ and His Church. Since the relationship between the divine and the human, the sacred and the secular, are
united in Christ, therefore the spiritual and temporal vitality of His
church-community is a continuation of our Lord's saving mission in the
world.

Christ desires that His teachings should be applied in all aspects of daily life. This He accomplishes through Christians who are in the world as other Christs; they represent Him among people of all conditions, colors, and cultures in order to make the life of man more filled with God. The historical Incarnation takes on more practical meaning when others see in Christians, men and women who can become engrossed in fostering to the fullest all the affairs of secular life while maintaining a spiritual attitude toward it all. By the Holy Spirit's working in Christians, Christ's incarnational Church continues to be effective through the vital activity of His dedicated people in all phases of Human life.

140. Effects of Christ's Incarnation Continue in the Church's Activity

For this the Church was founded: that by spreading the kingdom of Christ everywhere for the glory of God the Father, she might bring all men to share in Christ's saving redemption; and that through them the whole world might in actual fact be brought into relationship with Him. All activity of the Mystical Body directed to the attainment of this goal is called the apostolate, and the Church carries it on in various ways through all her members. For by its very nature the Christian vocation is also a vocation to the apostolate. No part of the structure of a living body is merely passive but each has a share in the functions as well as in the life of the body. So, too, in the body of Christ, which is the Church, the whole body, "according to the functioning in due measure of each single part, derives its increase" (Eph. 4:16). Indeed, so intimately are the parts linked and interrelated in this body (cf. Eph. 4:16) that the member who fails to make his proper contribution to the development of the Church must be said to be useful neither to the Church nor to himself.

In the Church, there is diversity of service but unity of purpose. Christ conferred on the apostles and their successors the duty of teaching, sanctifying, and ruling in His name and power. But the laity, too, share in the priestly, prophetic, and royal office of Christ and therefore have their own role to play in the mission of the whole People of God in the Church and in the world. *(Laity, No.2)*

141. All Are Called to Participate in the Lay Apostolate

The laity are gathered together in the People of God and make up the Body of Christ under one Head. Whoever they are, they are called upon, as living members, to expend all their energy for the growth of the Church and its continuous sanctification. For this very energy is a gift of the Creator and a blessing of the Redeemer.

The lay apostolate, however, is a participation in the saving mission of the Church itself. Through their baptism and confirmation, all are commissioned to that apostolate by the Lord Himself. Moreover, through the sacraments, especially the Holy Eucharist, there is communicated and nourished that charity toward God and man which is the soul of the entire apostolate. Now, the laity are called in a special way to make the Church present and operative in those places and circumstances where only through them can she become the salt of the earth. Thus every layman, by virtue of the very gifts bestowed upon him, is at the same time a witness and a living instrument of the mission of the Church herself, "according to the measure of Christ's bestowal" (Eph. 4:7).

Besides this apostolate, which pertains to absolutely every Christian, the laity can also be called in various ways to a more direct form of cooperation in the apostolate of the hierarchy. This was the case with certain men and women who assisted Paul the Apostle in the gospel, laboring much in the Lord (cf. Phil. 4:3; Rom. 16:3 ff.). Further, laymen have the capacity to be deputed by the hierarchy to exercise certain church functions for a spiritual purpose.

Upon all the laity, therefore, rests the noble duty of working to extend the divine plan of salvation ever increasingly to all men of each epoch and in every land. Consequently, let every opportunity be given them so that, according to their abilities and the needs of the times, they may zealously participate in the saving work of the Church. *(Church, No. 33)*

142. The Laity's Call to Labor with Christ and Share His Victory

This most sacred Council, then, earnestly entreats in the Lord that all laymen give a glad, generous, and prompt response to the voice of Christ, who is giving them an especially urgent invitation at this moment, and to the impulse of the Holy Spirit. Younger people should feel that this call has been directed to them in particular, and they should respond to it eagerly and magnanimously. Through this holy Synod, the Lord Himself renews His invitation to all the laity to come closer to Him every day, and, recognizing that what is His is also their own (Phil. 2:5), to associate themselves with Him in His saving mission. Once again He sends them into every town and place where He Himself will come (cf. Lk. 10:1). Thus they can show that they are His co-workers in the various forms and methods of the Church's one apostolate, which must be constantly adapted to the new needs of the times. May they always abound in the works of God, knowing that they will not labor in vain when their labor is for Him (cf. 1 Cor. 15:58). *(Laity, No.33)*

B. The Laity's Rightful Role as Members of the Christian Community

All who respond to Christ share in the same mission to the world which He entrusted to His disciples. Functions may and do vary within the Christian community. But the central objective remains the same whether for the clergy or for the laity. No matter what one's rank in the Church, each shares precisely the same dignity of being a Christian with an important function to perform for the Lord. Together, the priests and the laity must fulfill their specific positions with mutual respect, cooperation, and even friendship. Moreover, it is Christ Himself who calls all His people to take action for His cause by fulfilling their rightful role in the Church. Neither should any members take to themselves personal honor in doing God's will except that of greater service of others in the one Lord, the one faith, and one and the same Spirit.

All rights and duties of the laity, as well as of the clergy or religious, derive from Christ the Lord. The practical application of these rights and obligations should be directed and guided by those who are commissioned to do so by Christ in His Church-community. However, lay men and women have not only the right but the obligation to fulfill their role in spreading Christianity by participating in its apostolic activities. In fact, the laity are urged to take their own initiative in discharging their Christian responsibilities. Moreover, while the laity's activity should certainly include assisting their priests, the apostolate of lay men and women is not restricted merely to this area. The laity should neither expect nor wait for an invitation to active participation in apostolic works. Rather, they should search out on their own the areas of Christian activity best suited to their talents and most in need of their efforts.

Although Catholic apostolic activity is by no means confined to working with other Christians, the parish is, nevertheless, the most suitable source out of which to perform good works. Granted that some former parish organizations and societies are becoming obsolete and ineffectual, the parish-community, under whatever newer forms of it that may emerge, should remain the center for the individual's spiritual advancement and the source of his apostolic activities. In order to promote greater unity of effort and to foster the interests of all in the Church's apostolate, parish councils are currently in formation. Regardless of the difficulties to make them become truly effectual, these parish councils, as well as conferences of priests and diocesan confederations, should all be continually fostered so that the Holy Spirit's workings among all the members of the Church may bring out the truth and advance the cause of Christ in modern times.

143. Laity's Rights and Duties to Participate in the Apostolate

The laity derive the right and duty with respect to the apostolate from their union with Christ their Head. Incorporated into Christ's Mystical Body through baptism and strengthened by the power of the Holy Spirit through confirmation, they are assigned to the apostolate by the Lord himself. They are consecrated into a royal priesthood and a holy people (cf. 1 Pet. 2:4-10) in order that they may offer spiritual sacrifices through everything they do, and may witness to Christ throughout the world. For their part, the sacraments, especially the most holy Eucharist, communicate and nourish that charity which is the soul of the entire apostolate.

The apostolate is carried on through the faith, hope, and charity which the Holy Spirit diffuses in the hearts of all members of the Church. Indeed, the law of love, which is the Lord's greatest commandment, impels all the faithful to promote God's glory through the spread of His kingdom and to obtain for all men that eternal life which consists in knowing the only true God and Him whom He sent, Jesus Christ (cf. Jn. 17:3). On all Christians therefore is laid the splendid burden of working to make the divine message of salvation known and accepted by all men throughout the world. *(Laity, No.3)*

144. Practical Participation by the Laity in the Apostolate

As sharers in the role of Christ the Priest, the Prophet, and the King, the laity have an active part to play in the life and activity of the Church. Their activity is so necessary within church communities that without it the apostolate of the pastors is generally unable to achieve its full effectiveness. In the style of the men and women who helped Paul to spread the gospel (cf. Acts 18:18, 26; Rom. 16:3), the laity with the right apostolic attitude supply what is lacking to their brethren, and refresh the spirit of pastors and of the rest of the faithful (cf. 1 Cor. 16:17-18). Strengthened by active participation in the liturgical life of their community, they are eager to do their share in the apostolic works of that community. They lead to the Church people who are perhaps far removed from it, earnestly cooperate in presenting the word of God especially by means of catechetical instruction, and offer their special skills to make the care of souls and the administration of the temporalities of the Church more efficient. *(Laity, No.10)*

145. Cooperation between Laity and Clergy in the Apostolate

Bishops, pastors of parishes, and other priests of both branches of the clergy should keep in mind that the right and duty to exercise the apostolate is common to all the faithful, both clergy and laity, and that the laity also have their own proper roles in building up the Church. For this reason, they should work fraternally with the laity in and for the Church and take special care of the lay persons engaged in apostolic works. *(Laity, No.25)*

2. CHRISTIAN ACTIVITY IS REQUIRED AS RELEVANT FOR THE TIMES

A. The Laity's Opportunities for Uplifting Modern Society

The laity fully share in the mission of Christ and they should serve as priests of the secular order, in order to uplift it, ennoble it, and make all the concerns of mankind presentable to their heavenly Father. The universal Church should serve as a general sacrament for the betterment and salvation of mankind. The more that Christian vitality is diffused in the world, the more Christ's redemptive Incarnation becomes effective for the everlasting happiness of all men, which is the objective of God's design.

The Council does not, indeed it could not, indicate in every detail precisely how the secular order should be Christianized. Rather, once the formed Christian has obtained the spirit of Christ, the outlook of the gospels, and the mind of the Church, he will then through religious instinct know what he is to do in given situations. The apostolic work of the laity, as of others in the Church, involves spreading the gospel message, sanctifying the world, and performing works of charity toward the immediately needful neighbor. This may involve pushing a wheel-chair, teaching Christian doctrine to teen-agers, inviting some orphans to Christmas dinner, visiting abandoned people, assisting addicts, or caring for other needs of one's neighbor. The Christian apostolate in-cludes joining with all others in the worthwhile projects to make the world more truly human through charitable activity, so that God can thereby re-make men in the image of His divine Son.

Lay men and women live continuously in the center of secular life and are called on by their commitment to Christ to strive to sanc-tify their lives in this environment while assisting others on the course of salvation. Secular life is the very sphere, unreachable for the most part by professional religionists, which most requires the influence of the laity to bring Christ's message of love, justice, and peace to the market places, offices, homes, and daily lives of all who will be recep-tive to the Lord's ways.

146. Secular Involvement Enables the Laity to Exert a Christian Influence

A secular quality is proper and special to laymen. It is true that those in holy orders can at times engage in secular activities, and even have a secular profession. But by reason of their particular vocation they are chiefly and professedly ordained to the sacred ministry. Similarly, by their state in life, religious give splendid and striking testimony that the world cannot be transfigured and offered to God without the spirit of the beatitudes.

But the laity, by their very vocation, seek the kingdom of God by engaging in temporal affairs and by ordering them according to the plan of God. They live in the world, that is, in each and in all of the secular professions and occupations. They live in the ordinary circumstances of family and social life, from which the very web of their existence is woven.

They are called there by God so that by exercising their proper function and being led by the spirit of the gospel they can work for the sanctification of the world from within, in the manner of leaven. In this way they can make Christ known to others, especially by the testimony of a life resplendent in faith, hope, and charity. The layman is closely involved in temporal affairs of every sort. It is therefore his special task to illumine and organize these affairs in such a way that they may always start out, develop, and persist according to Christ's mind, to the praise of the Creator and the Redeemer. *(Church, No.31)*

147. The Laity's Initiative Is Required and the Clergy Cannot Solve All Problems

Secular duties and activities belong properly although not exclusively to laymen. Therefore acting as citizens of the world, whether individually or socially, they will observe the laws proper to each discipline, and labor to equip themselves with a genuine expertise in their various fields. They will gladly work with men seeking the same goals. Acknowledging the demands of faith and endowed with its force, they will unhesitatingly devise new enterprises, where they are appropriate, and put them into action.

Laymen should also know that it is generally the function of their well-formed Christian conscience to see that the divine law is inscribed in the life of the earthly city. From priests they may look for spiritual light and nourishment. Let the layman not imagine that his pastors are always such experts, that to every problem which arises, however complicated, they can readily give him a concrete solution, or even that such is their mission. Rather, enlightened by Christian wisdom and giving close attention to the teaching authority of the Church, let the layman take on his own distinctive role. *(World, No.43)*

148. The Laity Penetrate the Temporal Order with the Christian Spirit

Christ's redemptive work, while of itself directed toward the salvation of men, involves also the renewal of the whole temporal order. Hence the mission of the Church is not only to bring to men the message and grace of Christ, but also to penetrate and perfect the temporal sphere with the spirit of the gospel. In fulfilling this mission of the Church, the laity, therefore, exercise their apostolate both in the Church and in the world, in both the spiritual and the temporal orders. These realms, although distinct, are so connected in the one plan of God that He Himself intends in Christ to appropriate the whole universe into a new creation, initially here on earth, fully on the last day. In both orders, the layman, being simultaneously a believer and a citizen, should be constantly led by the same Christian conscience. *(Laity, No.5)*

149. The Motive of Charity Should Inspire All Apostolic Works

While every exercise of the apostolate should take its origin and power from charity, some works by their very nature can become especially vivid expressions of this charity. Christ the Lord wanted these works to be signs of His messianic mission (cf. Mt. 11:4-5).

The greatest commandment in the law is to love God with one's whole heart and one's neighbor as oneself (cf. Mt. 22:37-40). Christ made this commandment of love of neighbor His own and enriched it with a new meaning. For He wanted to identify Himself with His brethren as the object of this love when He said, "As long as you did it for one of these, the least of my brethren, you did it for me" (Mt. 25:40). Taking on human nature, He bound the whole human race to Himself as a family through a certain supernatural solidarity and established charity as the mark of His disciples, saying, "By this will all men know that you are my disciples, if you have love for one another" (Jn. 13:35). *(Laity, No.8)*

150. Charity's Delicacy Respects Those Helped

That the exercise of such charity may rise above any deficiencies in fact and even in appearance, certain fundamentals must be observed. Thus attention is to be paid to the image of God in which our neighbor has been created, and also to Christ the Lord to whom is really offered whatever is given to a needy person. The freedom and dignity of the person being helped should be respected with the utmost delicacy, and the purity of one's charitable intentions should not be stained by a quest for personal advantage or by any thirst for domination. The demands of justice should first be satisfied, lest the giving of what is due in justice be represented as the offering of a charitable gift. Not only the effects but also the causes of various ills must be removed. Help should be given in such a way that the recipients may gradually be freed from dependence on others and become self-sufficient. *(Laity, No.8)*

B. Some Areas for the Laity's Christian Influence

Every area of society is entrusted to the laity for their concern and work of Christianization. In addition to one's personal life, lay peoples' Christian influence encompasses the family, neighbor-relations, daily work, the spheres of the arts, sciences, and the economic, political and international orders.

It would be a misconception to consider the apostolate of lay men and women as some special calling within the Church. To the contrary, all Christians are called by Christ to fulfill the total commission entrusted to all His followers. In this regard the Council's messages call upon all groups of the laity to take on more responsibilities as the needs of the Church in these times require.

For instance, the incalculable talents of women and their rightfully increasing role in the world should certainly be more recognized and enlarged in the Church. The competence and abilities of women must be called upon even more today. Their vital and unique abilities can be especially steadying in this period of change, upheaval, and development. Just as the Church includes but extends far wider than the clergy, it obviously must count upon the women as well as the men to foster deeper insights into the faith, devise newer means of passing it on to the coming generations, and calm the disturbed segments of the community of Christ's people. As with other aspects of vast importance for advancing Christian influence in modern times, that of women should become more pronounced, respected, called upon and listened to, even as the Blessed Mother of Christ helped the apostles in the beginning of the Church. Women's particular qualities and their penetrating abilities to see into the heart of problems must be utilized more fully and they should be given more voice in the forward-movements of the Church in modern times.

Young adult-Christians should also be called upon more explicitly and more practically for their confident and enthusiastic abilities for fostering the works of the Church in the world of today. Despite their obvious defects, youth has an innate idealism and boundless optimism which are of incalculable value for fostering Christ's cause, particularly in these changing times of which they are the ultimate hope of the future. The older Christian, rightly, becomes more cautious, possibly less daring in his outlook. Youth considers mostly the here-and-now of life and enjoys its exploration and experience. In their own way, the young have honest religious convictions and they love God quite hopefully. The period of youth is the time to think noble thoughts, to reach for high goals, and to face up to daring challenges — all of which our times need. It is amazing to what heights of sacrifice and nobility youth is capable of climbing when encouraged and challenged. Lofty ideals attract young people to peaks difficult to conquer by their elders. It would be a shame to obstruct by over-caution and dampening fears today's young Christians whose faith and hope and charity also derive from the Lord. Christ always could, and He still can, bring out the best in young hearts when they are given challenge, hope, and confidence in the present and for the future. The times are critical;Christ's grace is attainable; the youth are available. It is, after all, their Church as well as that of their elders.

There are numerous and varied outlets for apostolic works available for all ages, groups, and types of Christians. If the individual cannot find sufficient sources on his own, then a phone-call to the local chancery, rectory, or headquarters of various organizations may open up areas for involving the commitment of any daring Christian in works of challenge suitable for his capabilities.

151. The Laity's Involvement in Practical Needs of People

At the present time, when the means of communication have grown more rapid, the distances between men have been overcome in a sense, and the inhabitants of the whole world have become like members of a single family, these actions and works have grown much more urgent and extensive. These charitable enterprises can and should reach out to absolutely every person and every need. Wherever there are people in need of food and drink, clothing, housing, medicine, employment, education; wherever men lack the facilities necessary for living a truly human life or are tormented by hardships or poor health, or suffer exile or imprisonment, there Christian charity should seek them out and find them, console them with eager care and relieve them with the gift of help. This obligation is imposed above all upon every prosperous person and nation. *(Laity, No.8)*

152. Family Life Is the Basic Area for the Christian Apostolate

The family has received from God its mission to be the first and vital cell of society. It will fulfill this mission if it shows itself to be the domestic sanctuary of the Church through the mutual affection of its members and the common prayer they offer to God, if the whole family is caught up in the liturgical worship of the Church, and if it provides active hospitality and promotes justice and other good works for the service of all the brethren in need. Among the multiple activities of the family apostolate may be enumerated the following: the adoption of abandoned infants, hospitality to strangers, assistance in the operation of schools, help-ful advice and material assistance for adolescents, help to engaged couples in preparing themselves better for marriage, catechetical work, support of married couples and families involved in material and moral crises, help for the aged not only by providing them with the necessities of life but also by obtaining for them a fair share of the benefits of economic progress. *(Laity, No.11)*

153. Youth's Importance in All Areas of Society Today

Young persons exert very substantial influence on modern society. There has been a complete change in the circumstances of their lives, their mental attitudes, and their relationships with their own families. Frequently they move too quickly into new social and economic conditions. While their social and even their political im-portance is growing from day to day, they seem to be unable to cope adequately with the new burdens imposed upon them.

Their heightened influence in society demands of them a pro-portionately active apostolate. Happily, their natural qualities fit them for this activity. As they become more conscious of their own personality, they are impelled by a zest for life and abounding energies to assume their own responsibility, and they yearn to play their part in social and cultural life. If this zeal is imbued with the spirit of Christ and is inspired by obedience to and love for the shepherds of the Church, it can be expected to be very fruitful. They themselves ought to become the prime and direct apostles of youth, exercising the apostolate among themselves and through themselves and reckoning with the social environment in which they live. *(Laity, No.12)*

C. Forms and Movements of the Laity's Apostolate

Since being a Christian includes, by its very nature, the desire to share the gift of the faith, all Christians should be moved to participate in the salvific mission of Christ through some form of apostolic activity. Each individual should, then, undertake to fulfill his or her apostolate within the circumstances of each one's life and opportunities.

The heart of the individual Christian's apostolate lies in living a life which proclaims the person and principles of Christ in all aspects of his environment. Taking for granted a deep personal spiritual life, every branch of knowledge can foster the Church's mission whether in the fields of business, sociology, communication-arts, politics, education, or the social and physical sciences. All of human life can be turned to spreading the faith. The apostolate is available on one's local level by helping a family in the neighborhood, assisting needy youth, bettering the condition of the racially or economically disadvantaged, and by other works.

Parents of the young may not be able temporarily to extend themselves much beyond the requirements of their growing family. Yet children become impressed by mothers and fathers who somehow expend themselves in helping others beyond their own families. When the young see their parents taking the practice of the faith seriously, they catch this spirit themselves, first through admiration and then by imitation of their parent's apostolic interests.

Depending on the capability, time, and graces of each person, there are various individual apostolates in which people can be most helpful. There are always the poor and uneducated who require assistance. The sick, abandoned, jobless, and frustrated need help. Those with special skills may be able to work for the readjustment of the handicapped and retarded, the narcotic addicts, alcoholics, homosexuals, delinquents, the mentally sick and for those with other problems. Certainly, the teaching of Christian doctrine to youth or to adults will always remain a prime objective requiring capable lay teachers.

In addition to the apostolic endeavors of each individual, the various religious organizations give concerted productiveness for expanding the work of the Church on the parish, diocesan, national, and international levels. The Council obviously had no intention of naming all specific Church-oriented organizations which foster the apostolate. The documents do point out, however, the vast importance of coordinated works, lest the laity's efforts become dissipated and ineffectual. Whatever newer forms of group apostolates may develop, the laity are surely called upon both to help originate more suitable forms for apostolic accomplishment and to take greater initiative within the existing approved societies.

The more gifted people in the Christian community surely have much to offer for the upbuilding of movements within the apostolate of lay men and women. But, however seemingly insignificant the contribution of the less-talented may seem, the Church moves ahead precisely because of the positive action of each and every person expending his utmost efforts for Christ and his neighbor's service.

154. The Individual's Apostolate

The individual apostolate, flowing generously from the well-spring of a truly Christian life (cf. Jn. 4:14), is the origin and condition of the whole lay apostolate, even in its organized expression, and admits of no substitute.

Regardless of circumstance, all lay persons (including those who have no opportunity or possibility for collaboration in associations) are called to this type of apostolate and obliged to engage in it. Such an apostolate is useful at all times and places, but in certain circumstances it is the only one appropriate and feasible.

There are many forms of the apostolate in which the laity build up the Church, sanctify the world, and give it life in Christ.

A particular form of the individual apostolate, as well as a sign especially suited to our times, is the testimony of a layman's entire life as it develops out of faith, hope, and charity. This form manifests Christ living in those who believe in Him. Then by the apostolate of the word, which is utterly necessary under certain circumstances, lay people announce Christ, explain and spread His teaching according to their situation and ability, and faithfully profess it. *(Laity, No.16)*

155. Group Apostolates Foster Coordinated Efforts for Christ

The faithful are called upon to engage in the apostolate as individuals in the varying circumstances of their life. They should remember, nevertheless, that man is naturally social and that it has pleased God to unite those who believe in Christ in the People of God (cf. 1 Pet. 2:5-10) and into one body (cf. 1 Cor. 12:12). Hence the group apostolate of Christian believers happily corresponds to a human and Christian need and at the same time signifies the communion and unity of the Church in Christ, who said, "Where two or three are gathered together for my sake, there am I in the midst of them" (Mt. 18:20).

For this reason the faithful should exercise their apostolate by way of united effort. Let them be apostles both in their family communities and in their parishes and dioceses, which themselves express the community nature of the apostolate, as well as in voluntary groups which they decide to join.

The group apostolate is highly important also because the apostolate must often be implemented through joint action, in both the church communities and various other spheres. For the associations established to carry on the apostolate in common sustain their members, form them for the apostolate, and rightly organize and regulate their apostolic work so that much better results can be expected than if each member were to act on his own. *(Laity, No.18)*

156. Competent Lay Peoples' Special Services Are Needed

Deserving of special honor and commendation in the Church are those lay people, single or married, who devote themselves and their professional skill either permanently or temporarily, to the service of associations and their activities. The Church derives great joy from the fact that every day an increasing number of lay persons offer their personal service to apostolic associations and activities, either within the limits of their own nation or in the international field, or especially in Catholic mission communities and in regions where the Church has only recently been implanted.

The pastors of the Church should gladly and gratefully welcome these lay persons and make sure that their situation meets the demands of justice, equity, and charity to the fullest possible extent, particularly as regards proper support for them and their families. Pastors should also see to it that these lay people enjoy the necessary formation, spiritual consolation, and incentive. *(Laity, No.22)*

3. PREPARATION OF THE LAITY
FOR A FRUITFUL APOSTOLATE

A. Self-Development Benefits
The Apostolate as Well

Developed and balanced persons can best foster the apostolate of the Church. The development of oneself as a human person and as a Christian are both required for greatest effectiveness for Christ's cause, especially as modern society is developing. The more each individual and the total community of Christians obtain a workable knowledge of religion and its practical applications in the various aspects of life, the more the work of the Church can move forward in the world.

In addition to acquiring a sense of being sent by Christ to Christianize available areas according to one's competence, a deliberate preparation for the apostolate is also required. The Christian should strive to improve himself, both for the innate value of personal advancement and especially as a means of furthering the Church's apostolate. Yet, knowledge and other talents are not the only instruments through which God works to establish His kingdom. Certainly, personal sanctity is the chief means. Moreover, whatever abilities the Christian possesses and uses in the various circumstances of his life, each disciple of Christ can assist in advancing His cause.

Certainly the duties of one's own state in life offer adequate opportunities to foster Christianity's goals in the world. The apostolate begins with an outlook on life, a mentality, which sees all in the world as capable of being transformed and uplifted according to Christ's norms as applicable in particular circumstances. Furthermore, one's apostolic interests and outlets take on various forms throughout his span of life. The forms of Christian activity vary with the age, condition, temperament and circumstances of the person involved. In addition, some are more talented than others at organizing while some are more proficient at performing good works in private. Yet each can develop his particular talents with the help of the same Holy Spirit.

In the self-development of Christians, each person should become aware of his particular responsibilities within the whole Church-community and fulfill his own role in it. Spiritual and apostolic advancement also require discernment, lest secular influences become too dominant. This is particularly evident in the presentation of the sensational happenings in the Church, to the neglect of the solid middle-course progress which is taking place. It will be helpful to counterbalance the accounts of religious events by the secular media with the accounts offered in Catholic newspapers, magazines, pamphlets and books. Apostolic works should also improve one's own self-Christianization, since the life of the follower of Christ is an ever maturing, developing, and expanding experience.

157. Basic Needs of Lay People for the Apostolate

To fulfill the mission of the Church in the world, the laity have certain basic needs. They need a life in harmony with their faith, so they can become the light of the world. They need that undeviating honesty which can attract all men to the love of truth and goodness, and finally to the Church and to Christ. They need the kind of fraternal charity which will lead them to share in the living conditions, labors, sorrows, and hope of their brother men, and which will gradually and imperceptibly dispose the hearts of all around them for the saving work of grace. They need a full awareness of their role in building up society, an awareness which will keep them preoccupied with bringing Christian largeheartedness to the fulfillment of their duties, whether family, social, or professional. If laymen can meet all these needs, their behavior will have a penetrating impact, little by little, on the whole circle of their life and labors. *(Laity, No.13)*

158. Personal Holiness Is Essential for an Effective Lay Apostolate

Since Christ in His mission from the Father is the fountain and source of the whole apostolate of the Church, the success of the lay apostolate depends upon the laity's living union with Christ. For the Lord has said, "He who abides in me, and I in him, he bears much fruit: for without me you can do nothing" (Jn. 15:5). This life of intimate union with Christ in the Church is nourished by spiritual aids which are common to all the faithful, especially active participation in the sacred liturgy. These are to be used by the laity in such a way that while properly fulfilling their secular duties in the ordinary conditions of life, they do not disassociate union with Christ from that life. Rather, by performing their work according to God's will they can grow in that union. In this way must the laity make progress in holiness, showing a ready and happy spirit, and trying prudently and patiently to overcome difficulties. Neither family concerns nor other secular affairs should be excluded from their religious program of life. For as the Apostle states, "Whatever you do in word or work, do all in the name of the Lord Jesus Christ, giving thanks to God the Father through him" (Col. 3:17).

Such a life requires a continual exercise of faith, hope, and charity.

Only by the light of faith and by meditation on the word of God can one always and everywhere recognize God in whom "we live, and move, and have our being" (Acts 17:28), seek His will in every event, see Christ in all men whether they be close to us or strangers, and make correct judgments about the true meaning and value of temporal things, both in themselves and in their relation to man's final goal. *(Laity, No.4)*

159. Balanced Lay Apostolate Considers All Factors Involving the Person

The layman's religious program of life should take its special quality from his status as a married man and a family man, or as one who is unmarried or widowed, from his state of health, and from his professional and social activity. He should not cease to develop earnestly the qualities and talents bestowed on him in accord with these conditions of life, and he should make use of the gifts which he has received from the Holy Spirit.

Furthermore, the laity who in pursuit of their vocation have become members of one of the associations or institutes approved by the Church are trying faithfully to adopt the special charac-teristics of the spiritual life which are proper to these as well. They should also hold in high esteem professional skill, family and civic spirit, and the virtues relating to social behavior, namely, honesty, justice, sincerity, kindness, and courage, without which there can be no true Christian life. *(Laity, No.4)*

B. Formation of All Levels for the Laity's Apostolic Works

It is not alone the Christian community's task to erect, single-handed, a completely unified world of justice, peace, and stability. They should, however, serve as a leaven among mankind inculcating the spirit and principles of the gospels into the mentality, laws, and structure of society. They should show others the value of listening to and accepting the teachings of the Church for mankind's true temporal and eternal welfare. In this way, Christian laymen become even more real imitators of Christ as teachers and priests to the modern world.

There is absolutely no more efficacious way of helping the Christian apostolate become solidly beneficial than the formation of a deep spiritual life as the source of all works for Christ. From each one's spiritual life derives the corporate power of the entire Church, with the help of God. Union with Christ, and through Him with others, is the heart of the Christian apostolate. This is the source of all "practical", lasting, and effective Christian works. Consequently, it was inevitable that the Second Vatican Council would point to the basics of Christian formation for the furthering of the Church's goals on all levels and among all groups of her members. Hence the consistent practices for spiritual formation are again underlined, both for the advancement of the faithful's own Christian calling and for the fulfillment of their mission to the world.

Christian formation is a call from Christ to all in His Church — men and women, children and youth, in whatever state and condition of life they are. This formation is a combination of many factors: the grace of God, the sacraments and guidance of the Church, the example of others, as well as the cooperation of each person himself. There is no one definitive process capable of producing the ideal Christian who is holy, dedicated and fully-formed. However, religious retreats of various kinds can be most effective for forming adults and youth in accordance with the spirit of Scripture, the mind of the Church, and the requirements of our times. In addition, individual and group study and discussion bring out facets of apostolic opportunities while awakening lively interest in taking part in what is going on in the Church today. Indeed, the prayerful study of Church documents is an excellent means for growing in the spirit and application of the apostolate in current circumstances.

Formation for apostolic works involves an inner dedication to Christ and His cause throughout one's entire life. This dedication includes a spirit and an attitude which grow and develop, hopefully unto the fullness of the Christian life. It means an ideal of a life of self-giving. The most profound and profitable formation of all is simply to be a convinced and practicing Catholic who becomes involved to the best his time and talents permit in whatever are the needs of the Church-community and of the world in these times. The need is urgent, each one is called, and Christ Himself will help.

160. A Well-Rounded Development Foster's Lay Apostolate

Since laymen share in their own way in the mission of the Church, their apostolic formation takes its special flavor from the distinctively secular quality of the lay state and from its own form of spirituality.

Formation for the apostolate means a certain human and well-rounded formation adapted to the natural abilities and circumstances of each lay person. Well-informed about the modern world, the lay person should be an active member of his own society and be adjusted to its culture.

Above all, however, the lay person should learn to advance the mission of Christ and the Church by basing his life on belief in the divine mystery of creation and redemption, and by being sensitive to the movement of the Holy Spirit, who gives life to the People of God and who would impel all men to love God the Father as well as the world and mankind in Him. This formation should be deemed the basis and condition for every successful apostolate.

In addition to spiritual formation, there is needed solid doctrinal instruction in theology, ethics, and philosophy, instruction adjusted to differences of age, status, and natural talents. The importance of acquiring general culture along with practical and technical training should not be overlooked in the least.

For the cultivation of good human relations, truly human values must be fostered, especially the art of living fraternally with others, cooperating with them, and initiating conversation with them. *(Laity, No.29)*

161. Practical and Prudent Formation of Lay People

Since formation for the apostolate cannot consist in merely theoretical instruction, from the very beginning of their formation the laity should gradually and prudently learn how to view, judge, and do all things in the light of faith as well as to develop and improve themselves and others through action, thereby entering into the energetic service of the Church. This formation, always in need of improvement because of the increasing maturity of the human person and the unfolding of problems, requires an ever deeper knowledge and the adjustment of activities. In the fulfillment of all the demands of formation, the unity and integrity of the human personality must be kept in mind at all times, so that its harmony and balance may be safeguarded and enhanced.

In this way the lay person will throw himself wholly and energetically into the reality of the temporal order and effectively assume his role in conducting its affairs. At the same time, as a living member and witness of the Church, he will make the Church present and active in the midst of temporal affairs. *(Laity, No.29)*

162. Family, Children, and Youth Are to Be Formed for Their Apostolates

Training for the apostolate should start with a child's earliest education. In a special way, however, adolescents and young adults should be initiated into the apostolate and imbued with its spirit. This formation must be perfected throughout their whole lives in keeping with the demands of new responsibilities. It is evident, therefore, that those who have the obligation to provide for Christian education also have the duty to provide for formation in the apostolate.

In the family, parents have the task of training their children from childhood to recognize God's love for all men. Especially by example they should teach them little by little to show concern for the material and spiritual needs of their neighbor. The whole of family life, then, would become a sort of apprenticeship for the apostolate.

Children must also be educated to transcend the family circle, and to open their minds to ecclesiastical and temporal communities. They should be so involved in the local community of the parish that they will acquire a consciousness of being living and active members of the People of God. In their catechetical instructions, their ministry of the word, their direction of souls, and in their other pastoral services, priests should be preoccupied with forming apostles.

Schools, colleges, and other Catholic educational institutions also have the duty to develop a Catholic sense and apostolic activity in young people. If young people lack this formation either because they do not attend these schools or because of any other reason, parents, pastors of souls, and apostolic organizations should attend to it all the more. Teachers and educators, who carry on a distinguished form of the apostolate of the laity by their vocation and office, should be equipped with the learning and pedagogical skill needed for imparting such apostolic training effectively. *(Laity, No.30)*

163. A Balanced, Progressive Formation Enhances Mature Christian Growth

In keeping with their purpose and according to their measure, lay groups and associations dedicated to the apostolate or to other supernatural goals should carefully and persistently promote formation for the apostolate. Frequently these groups are the ordinary vehicle of harmonious formation for the apostolate since they provide doctrinal, spiritual, and practical formation. Their members meet in small groups with their associates or friends, examine the methods and results of their apostolic activity, and measure their daily way of life against the gospel.

Formation of this type must be designed to take into account the whole lay apostolate, which is to be carried on not only among the organized groups themselves but also in all circumstances of a man's life, especially his professional and social life. Indeed, everyone should painstakingly ready himself personally for the apostolate, especially as an adult. For the advance of age brings with it better self-knowledge, thus enabling each person to evaluate more accurately the talents with which God has enriched his soul and to exercise more effectively those charismatic gifts which the Holy Spirit has bestowed on him for the good of his brothers. *(Laity, No.30)*

164. Special Formation for Specialized Apostolates

Some types of the apostolate demand very special formation.

a) When the apostolate is one of making the gospel known and men holy, the laity must be specially formed to engage in conversation with others, believers or non-believers, in order to manifest Christ's message to all men.

Since in our times, variations of materialism are rampant everywhere, even among Catholics, the laity should not only learn doctrine more carefully, especially those main points which are the subjects of controversy, but should also provide the witness of an evangelical life in contrast to all forms of materialism.

b) With respect to the Christian renewal of the temporal order, laymen should be instructed in the true meaning and value of temporal things, both in themselves and in their relation to the total fulfillment of the human person. They should be trained in the right use of things and the organization of institutions, attentive always to the common good as related to the principles of the moral and social teaching of the Church. Laymen should above all learn the principles and conclusions of this social doctrine so as to become capable of doing their part to advance this doctrine and of rightly applying these same principles and conclusions to individual cases.

c) Since the works of charity and mercy afford the most striking testimony of the Christian life, apostolic formation should lead also to the performance of these works so that the faithful may learn from childhood to have compassion for their brothers and to be generous in helping those in need. *(Laity, No.31)*

165. **Higher Studies and Spiritual Retreats Help to Form Vital Lay People**

There already exist many aids for lay persons devoted to the apostolate, namely, study sessions, congresses, periods of recollection, spiritual exercises, frequent meetings, conferences, books, and periodicals. All these are directed toward the acquisition of a deeper knowledge of sacred Scripture and Catholic doctrine, the nourishment of spiritual life, an appreciation of world conditions, and the discovery and development of suitable methods.

These formative aids take into account the various types of the apostolate, according to the milieu in which it is to be exercised. *(Laity, No.32)*

166. Courses in Scripture, Theology, Sociology, Church Documents

For this purpose also, centers or advanced institutes have been erected, and have already proved highly successful.

This most holy Council rejoices over projects of this kind which are already flourishing in certain areas, and it desires that they may be promoted also in other areas where they are needed.

Furthermore, centers of documentation and study not only in theology but also in anthropology, psychology, sociology, and methodology should be established for all fields of the apostolate, for the better development of the natural capacities of laymen and laywomen, whether they be young persons or adults. *(Laity, No.32)*

Christ's people must become interiorly and exteriorly more involved in the works of the Church extending thereby the effects of our Lord's redemptive Incarnation for the benefit of mankind. The Christian action of the laity is the driving force of the Church in these needy modern times. Many people are becoming more and more enchanted with the rampant naturalistic humanism of today. The Christian cannot afford to be idle in these times or the meaning of the Church will be considered even more irrelevant than it is to mounting numbers of people, particularly among the youth of today. There is no time to yearn for the way things were in the past, or to bemoan the fast-moving events of the present, but rather to reach out and do one's part that the cause of Christ in the world will be accepted in the future.

Through the great Council especially, Christ is calling to the lay men and women of today to become involved in the works of the Church as responsible individuals and as members of some group apostolate. Every Christian is to take an active part in this resurgence of apostolic zeal, for each one has something to offer of himself toward the accomplishment of Christian witness in our times. Young people, particularly when they keep their balance and maintain contact with the body of the Church's teaching authority, are urged to take initiative, move out and accomplish their so-vital responsibilities in a world in which they are such an influential part in these days. Staying close to Christ and His Church, there should be no place for stifling fear in the face of these exhilarating times when the cause of Christianity can lead mankind into a new era of hope and advancement, with the help of Christ Jesus.

Chapter VII

DISCERNING THE SPIRIT OF CHRIST

In The Signs of The Times

As though the earth's surface was a vast painting, Vatican II points to the various individual brush-marks that go to make it up, and it asks us to judge them. Are the forces bearing on the world good or evil? Discernment is required to weigh accurately these influences. Once analyzed, the Christian then asks himself how he is to act, and here prudence leads to proper action. Neither the effort taken in discerning the movements and signs of the times, nor the caution dictated by prudence, need impede the initiative of a man. Indeed, discernment and prudence assure a person that he is directing himself wisely, skillfully, and perseveringly, toward acting as Christ would want.

The times exhibit deep and widespread changes on all levels of human life. These swiftly spread throughout the world chiefly by the advanced means of communication. Ours are times of turbulence and crises which spawn tension and confusion. The forces of evil capitalize on agitation and unrest, on distortion of truth and on false solutions to the ills of the world. A balanced spiritual discernment is required in order to judge correctly which movements within the world and the Church may show signs of the working of the Holy Spirit, and which ones may indicate the machinations of evil forces.

Man must acquire a spiritual discernment to read the signs of his times in the light of God's revelation; he must also learn to recognize both the good and evil in his world. Human discernment flows from an alert awareness of the facts of reality as they actually exist. To approach life on the level of the divine, we must strive to have that outlook which was in Christ Jesus, and is currently at work in the world moving in all aspects of human existence actively assisting man to improve himself and his life's condition. The problems of man's world do not derive from his loving God. The evil that exists is allowed to flourish because man encourages or pursues it, upholding Satan's role in human affairs.

If man neglects his spiritual graces and the insights which they bring, and if he refuses to improve the areas of human misery which disfigure God's design — sin, crime, injustice, oppression, war, poverty, ignorance, disease, atheism — then evil will reign where it should not in God's world. But the Spirit of Christ is always near to those who welcome His action within them. God does not operate as Lord without a people; yet men are capable of making themselves a people without a God. Man must labor to discover and experience what is truly godly upon this earth. He must seek to find, in spite of the causes of sin and the chaos of injustice, the infinite movements of his living God who helps him to conquer the corrupting spirit of evil. To obtain the desired peace and progress of humanity, true spiritual discernment must be acquired through prayer, and employed for exploring the ways of good and evil in the art of discerning the workings of both.

In these times of great tension, strong confidence that the spiritual forces for good will ultimately prevail in the contest with evil is a much needed asset. For Christ, our Lord, can and assuredly will, when asked, help us to dispel fear and discouragement, and will replace them with courage and peace. On the other hand, the consorts of Satan deliberately foster lies, extremes, and despair, wherever possible. Failure to acknowledge the presence of evil influences in our day can only multiply our difficulties. Evil thrives most when it is ignored; twisting the truth to its own advantage, it attempts to bring down the lives and the city of man.

The Vatican II quotations are not intended merely as a woeful listing of the ills of mankind, but rather as a profound analysis of the basic causes generating the disturbances in human living throughout the world of our time. Consequently, the conciliar passages analyze the sign, events and needs of the times (Section 1). Outstanding among mankind's problems is the modern rejection of God and indifference toward structured religion (Section 2). Some basic Christian solutions are offered for the needs of these troubled times (Section 3).

The Holy Spirit of Christ is ever among us unfolding the truth and showing the way, no matter how grave the problems may be. The Spirit of truth enables us to see the beauty of life when our human eyes see only the ugliness of its difficulties. He also strengthens the stouthearted to remain steadfast in the cause of good works. Christ predicted that life's difficulties would sometimes become heavy, bearing down like a cross. He also promised to sustain those who, with faith in the nearness of His love and the sureness of His power, continue in the contest with evil.

1. ANALYZING THE SIGNS AND EVENTS OF THE TIMES

A. The Changes, Upheavals and Confusions In the Modern Age

Lasting solutions to problems can only be found when they are seen in a light that exposes their true nature and cause. Nor should reason be pressured into hasty action by the immediacy of need or the intensity of emotions. The changes, imbalances, uncertainties, and crises existing in modern times require for their dissolution, a steady analysis and an unshakable confidence in the all-pervading providence of Almighty God.

Man is passing through a troubled period of re-evaluating his basic goals, his established institutions, and his former standards. This age, like that of adolescence, is afflicted with crises of doubt and development accompanied by growing-pains. Ways of thinking and approaching life, formerly accepted, are being constantly challenged and frequently found, whether validly or invalidly, lacking in relevance for modern living. This holds true inside as well as outside the Church. There appears to be taking place a transition from a relatively static to a more dynamic concept of life, of philosophy, and even of theology. Though it can be disturbing at times, this transition may well result in revealing hidden treasures as truth unfolds more and more of the divine reality established for mankind's welfare by a wise Creator. In this age of technological advancement and expanding leisure there is so much to be accomplished lest differences in ideologies between adults and youth, the wealthy and indigent nations, and the religious and atheistic elements of human society become irreparable — with catastrophic harm to future generations.

To analyze the great problems of the times and to judge them in the light of Christ's revealed truths for true solutions, requires spiritual discernment. Until we learn to read life's signs correctly, uncertainty, confusion, and bewilderment will prevail. We must, through prayer and the grace of the Holy Spirit, distinguish the path pointed out by Christ, from the pit-falls proposed by the powers of darkness. The fruit of this spiritual discernment is prudence which guards against extreme actions. When we have become convinced of the Holy Spirit's guidance, we will discern the fundamental causes of our own and the world's problems, and realize that lasting solutions to them come through Christ and His Church.

167. Scrutinizing the Signs of the Times in the Light of Christ's Gospel

The Church has always had the duty of scrutinizing the signs of the times and of interpreting them in the light of the gospel. Thus, in language intelligible to each generation, she can respond to the perennial questions which men ask about this present life and the life to come, and about the relationship of the one to the other. We must therefore recognize and understand the world in which we live, its expectations, its longings, and its often dramatic characteristics. *(World, No.4)*

168. Deep, Rapid Changes Often Cause Difficulties in Life

Today, the human race is passing through a new stage of its history. Profound and rapid schanges are spreading by degrees around the whole world. Triggered by the intelligence and creative energies of man, these changes recoil upon him, upon his decisions and desires, both individual and collective, and upon his manner of thinking and acting with respect to things and to people. Hence we can already speak of a true social and cultural transformation, one which has repercussions on man's religious life as well.

As happens in any crisis of growth, this transformation has brought serious difficulties in its wake. Thus while man extends his power in every direction, he does not always succeed in subjecting it to his own welfare. Striving to penetrate farther into the deeper recesses of his own mind, he frequently appears more unsure of himself. Gradually and more precisely he lays bare the laws of society, only to be paralyzed by uncertainty about the direction to give it. *(World, No.4)*

169. Imbalances in Society and Conflicts between Ideologies Bring Disturbances

Never has the human race enjoyed such an abundance of wealth, resources, and economic power. Yet a huge proportion of the world's citizens is still tormented by hunger and poverty, while countless numbers suffer from total illiteracy. Never before today has man been so keenly aware of freedom, yet at the same time, new forms of social and psychological slavery make their appearance.

Although the world of today has a very vivid sense of its unity and of how one man depends on another in needful solidarity, it is most grievously torn into opposing camps by conflicting forces. For political, social, economic, racial, and ideological disputes still continue bitterly, and with them the peril of a war which would reduce everything to ashes. True, there is a growing exchange of ideas, but the very words by which key concepts are expressed take on quite different meanings in diverse ideological systems. Finally, man painstakingly searches for a better world, without working with equal zeal for the betterment of his own spirit.

Caught up in such numerous complications, very many of our contemporaries are kept from accurately identifying permanent values and adjusting them properly to fresh discoveries. As a result, buffeted between hope and anxiety and pressing one another with questions about the present course of events, they are burdened down with uneasiness. This same course of events leads men to look for answers. Indeed, it forces them to do so. (World, No. 4)

170. Changing Conditions Deeply Affect Men's Lives and Practice of Religion

Today's spiritual agitation and the changing conditions of life are part of a broader and deeper revolution. As a result of the latter, intellectual formation is ever increasingly based on the mathematical and natural sciences and on those dealing with man himself, while in the practical order the technology which stems from these sciences takes on mounting importance.

This scientific spirit exerts a new kind of impact on the cultural sphere and on modes of thought. Technology is now transforming the face of the earth, and is already trying to master outer space. To a certain extent, the human intellect is also broadening its dominion over time: over the past by means of historical knowledge; over the future by the art of projecting and by planning.

Advances in biology, psychology, and the social sciences not only bring men hope of improved self-knowledge. In conjunction with technical methods, they are also helping men to exert direct influence on the life of social groups. At the same time, the human race is giving ever-increasing thought to forecasting and regulating its own population growth. *(World, No.5)*

171. Transition From a Static to a Dynamic Outlook on Reality Causes Upheavals

History itself speeds along on so rapid a course that an individual person can scarcely keep abreast of it. The destiny of the human community has become all of a piece, where once the various groups of men had a kind of private history of their own. Thus, the human race has passed from a rather static concept of reality to a more dynamic, evolutionary one. In consequence, there has arisen a new series of problems, a series as important as can be, calling for new efforts of analysis and synthesis. *(World, No.5)*

172. Changing Ways of Thinking Affect the World, Especially Youth

A change in attitudes and in human structures frequently calls accepted values into question. This is especially true of young people, who have grown impatient on more than one occasion, and indeed become rebels in their distress. Aware of their own influence in the life of society, they want to assume a role in it sooner. As a result, parents and educators frequently experience greater difficulties day by day in discharging their tasks.

The institutions, laws, and modes of thinking and feeling as handed down from previous generations do not always seem to be well adapted to the contemporary state of affairs. Hence arises an upheaval in the manner and even the norms of behavior. *(World, No.7)*

173. Drastic Changes Frequently Beget Disturbing Contradictions and Imbalances

Because they are coming so rapidly, and often in a disorderly fashion, all these changes beget contradictions and imbalances, or intensify them. Indeed the very fact that men are more conscious than ever of the inequalities in the world has the same effect.

Within the individual person there too often develops an imbalance between an intellect which is modern in practical matters, and a theoretical system of thought which can neither master the sum total of its ideas, nor arrange them adequately into a synthesis. Likewise, an imbalance arises between a concern for practicality and efficiency, and the demands of moral conscience; also, very often, between the conditions of collective existence and the requisites of personal thought, and even of contemplation. Specialization in any human activity can at length deprive a man of a comprehensive view of reality. *(World, No.8)*

174. Distrust between Youth and Adults, Cultures and Nations

As for the family, discord results from demographic, economic, and social pressures, or from difficulties which arise between succeeding generations, or from new social relationships between men and women.

Significant differences crop up too between races and between various kinds of social orders; between wealthy nations and those which are less influential or are needy; finally, between international institutions born of the popular desire for peace, and the ambition to propagate one's own ideology, as well as collective greed existing in nations or other groups.

What results is mutual distrust, enmities, conflicts, and hardships. Of such is man at once the cause and the victim. *(World, No.8)*

B. Secular Humanism Cannot Fill Man's Needs; Religious Faith is Required

Amid the many changing aspects of modern life, some realities remain unchangeable such as man's quest for happiness and God's love for His people. Today, religious faith is undergoing the test of fire that will either purify or destroy it. To advance, yet not break completely from the past, and to engage in renewal, yet not create a schism within the Church — these are two of the major difficulties which must be resolved. The Church must be in the midst of the world; but how deeply involved in the spirit of the world can Christians become and still fulfill their mission to the world? A household divided from within would tend to become weak and eventually fall apart.

Vatican II expressly enjoins Christians to become involved in secular affairs, but, in that process, the Council warns against the complete secularization of man as a perversion of his nature and destiny. Over-emphasis on temporal and worldly affairs necessarily creates disruption in the Christian community. In an age of the advancement of the human condition so blessed by the Church, it would do no lasting good to so extoll the human qualities and secular interests of mankind as to ignore the requirements of man's spirit, his inner and loftier aspirations, requirements, and goals.

175. Today, Religious Faith Is Being Tested For Better or For Worse

Finally, these new conditions have their impact on religion. On the one hand a more critical ability to distinguish religion from a magical view of the world and from the superstitions which still circulate purifies religion and exacts day by day a more personal and explicit adherence to faith. As a result many persons are achieving a more vivid sense of God.

On the other hand, growing numbers of people are abandoning religion in practice. Unlike former days, the denial of God or of religion, or the abandonment of them, are no longer unusual and individual occurrences. For today it is not rare for such decisions to be presented as requirements of scientific progress or of a certain new humanism. In numerous places these views are voiced not only in the teachings of philosophers, but on every side they influence literature, the arts, the interpretation of the humanities and of history, and civil laws themselves. As a consequence, many people are shaken. (World, No. 7)

176. The Removal of Inequalities as a Step toward Stability

Meanwhile, the conviction grows not only that humanity can and should increasingly consolidate its control over creation, but even more, that it devolves on humanity to establish a political, social, and economic order which will to an ever better extent serve man and help individuals as well as groups to affirm and develop the dignity proper to them.

As a result very many persons are quite aggressively demanding those benefits of which with vivid awareness they judge themselves to be deprived either through injustice or unequal distribution. Nations on the road to progress, like those recently made independent, desire to participate in the goods of modern civilization, not only in the political field but also economically, and to play their part freely on the world scene. Still they continually fall behind while very often their dependence on wealthier nations deepens more rapidly, even in the economic sphere.

People hounded by hunger call upon those better off. Where they have not yet won it, women claim for themselves an equity with men before the law and in fact. Laborers and farmers seek not only to provide for the necessities of life but to develop the gifts of their personality by their labors, and indeed to take part in regulating economic, social, political, and cultural life. Now, for the first time in human history, all people are convinced that the benefits of culture ought to be and actually can be extended to everyone. *(World, No.9)*

177. The Potential of the Modern World for Improvement or Virtual Destruction

Still, beneath all these demands lies a deeper and more widespread longing. Persons and societies thirst for a full and free life worthy of man — one in which they can subject to their own welfare all that the modern world can offer them so abundantly. In addition, nations try harder every day to bring about a kind of universal community.

Since all these things are so, the modern world shows itself at once powerful and weak, capable of the noblest deeds or the foulest. Before it lies the path to freedom or to slavery, to progress or retreat, to brotherhood or hatred. Moreover, man is becoming aware that it is his responsibility to guide aright the forces which he has unleashed and which can enslave him or minister to him. That is why he is putting questions to himself. *(World, No.9)*

178. Man's Internal Disorders Are a Source of His Travail

The truth is that the imbalances under which the modern world labors are linked with that more basic imbalance rooted in the heart of man. For in man himself many elements wrestle with one another. Thus, on the one hand, as a creature he experiences his limitations in a multitude of ways. On the other, he feels himself to be boundless in his desires and summoned to a higher life.

Pulled by manifold attractions, he is constantly forced to choose among them and to renounce some. Indeed, as a weak and sinful being, he often does what he would not, and fails to do what he would. Hence he suffers from internal divisions, and from these flow so many and such great discords in society. *(World, No.10)*

179. The Fallacy of Man's Reliance Solely on the Human Devoid of the Divine

No doubt very many whose lives are infected with a practical materialism are blinded against any sharp insight into this kind of dramatic situation. Or else, weighed down by wretchedness, they are prevented from giving the matter any thought.

Thinking that they have found serenity in an interpreation of reality everywhere proposed these days, many look forward to a genuine and total emancipation of humanity wrought solely by human effort. They are convinced that the future rule of man over the earth will satisfy every desire of his heart.

Nor are there lacking men who despair of any meaning to life and praise the boldness of those who think that human existence is devoid of any inherent significance and who strive to confer a total meaning on it by their own ingenuity alone. *(World, No.10)*

2. THE MODERN REJECTION OF GOD AND STRUCTURED RELIGION

A. Understanding the Causes of Atheism and Religious Indifference

The next conciliar extracts deal with the rejection of Christianity and even of any religious values by those who call themselves atheists. There are several reasons why people profess to be non-believers or reject organized religions in our day. Among the causes of this rejection, the Vatican Council tells us kindly but unmistakably, is the poor and sometimes perverted witness of some Christians themselves. At times, our practice has belied our beliefs. Too often our lack of sympathy, our prejudices, bigotry, and moral failings have scarcely revealed the attractiveness of God or won men to His service. On the other hand, Christians have instigated several charitable works, have cooperated in community enterprises, and have shown compassionate understanding for the troubles of others whose lives are quite empty without God or religion.

The Christian does not condemn the person in error; but he must speak out against the fallacies which lead people astray. Our age is plagued by atheism which is growing both in mentality and in practice. Various current movements are alligned with atheism or are tinged with it. The failure to recognize man's vital and intimate link with God derives from a variety of causes. With religious indifference, stemming from an exaggerated and naturalistic humanism, many today become excessively engrossed in earthly concerns and place undue reliance on the physical and social sciences to satisfy life's requirements. This results in dullness of spiritual perception and loss of higher aspirations. When human independence reaches the point of denial of Almighty God's design in the world, man begins to substitute some false god such as material gain, pleasure in life, or more subtle pursuits like probing the "psyche" on a merely natural plane, instead of seeking God and the welfare of one's soul with the help of the supernatural grace of his Creator and Lord.

The fallacies of the age conspire to delude men concerning the rightful place of Almighty God in man's life to the detriment of his own welfare and happiness. The spiritual realities of life assist man to live his temporal life in security and peace, both toward fulfilling his human perfection and attaining his eternal salvation. This latter is, after all, the primary purpose of human life. The Christian must never cease to feel the hunger of loneliness in the lives of non-believers, if he wishes to help them. The followers of Christ are sent among atheists precisely to win them to Christ's way of life, showing non-believers through their Christian lives, His kindness, understanding, patience, and peace, chiefly through practicing the corporal and spiritual works of mercy toward others. Basically, love is to be the action and the proof which wins others to Christ.

180. Varieties of Atheism Result from False Ideas of God and Lack of Faith

An outstanding cause of human dignity lies in man's call to communion with God. From the very circumstance of his origin, man is already invited to converse with God. For man would not exist were he not created by God's love and constantly preserved by it. And he cannot live fully according to truth unless he freely acknowledges that love and devotes himself to his Creator.

Still, many of our contemporaries have never recognized this intimate and vital link with God, or have explicitly rejected it. Thus atheism must be accounted among the most serious problems of this age, and is deserving of closer examination.

The word atheism is applied to phenomena which are quite distinct from one another. For while God is expressly denied by some, others believe that man can assert absolutely nothing about Him. Still others use such a method so to scrutinize the question of

God as to make it seem devoid of meaning. Many, unduly trans-gressing the limits of the positive sciences, contend that everything can be explained by this kind of scientific reasoning alone, or, by contrast, they altogether disallow that there is any absolute truth. Some laud man so extravagantly that their faith in God lapses into a kind of anemia, though they seem more inclined to affirm man than to deny God. Again some form for themselves such a fallacious idea of God that when they repudiate this figment they are by no means rejecting the God of the gospel. Some never get to the point of raising questions about God, since they seem to experi-ence no religious stirrings nor do they see why they should trouble themselves about religion. *(World, No.19)*

181. Practical Atheism Results from Disillusionment, Discourage-ment, and Bad Example

Moreover, atheism results not rarely from a violent protest against the evil in this world, or from the absolute character with which certain human values are unduly invested, and which thereby already accords them the stature of God. Modern civilization itself often complicates the approach to God, not for any essential reason, but because it is excessively engrossed in earthly affairs.

Undeniably, those who willfully shut out God from their hearts and try to dodge religious questions are not following the dictates of their consciences. Hence they are not free of blame.

Yet believers themselves frequently bear some responsibility for this situation. For, taken as a whole, atheism is not a spon-taneous development but stems from a variety of causes, including a critical reaction against religious beliefs, and in some places against the Christian religion in particular. Hence believers can have more than a little to do with the birth of atheism. To the extent that they neglect their own training in the faith, or teach erroneous doctrine, or are deficient in their religious, moral, or social life, they must be said to conceal rather than reveal the authentic face of God and religion. *(World, No.19)*

182. Modern Atheists and Dialectic Materialists Reject Religious Values as Irrelevant

Modern atheism often takes on a systematic expression, which, in addition to other arguments against God, stretches the desire for human independence to such a point that it finds diffi-culties with any kind of dependence on God. Those who profess atheism of this sort maintain that it gives man freedom to be an end unto himself, the sole artisan and creator of his own history. They claim that this freedom cannot be reconciled with the affirmation of a Lord who is author and purpose of all things, or at least that this freedom makes such an affirmation altogether superfluous. The sense of power which modern technical progress generates in man can give color to such a doctrine.

Not to be overlooked among the forms of modern atheism is that which anticipates the liberation of man especially through his economic and social emancipation. This form argues that by its nature religion thwarts such liberation by arousing man's hope for a deceptive future life, thereby diverting him from the constructing of the earthly city. Consequently, when the proponents of this doctrine gain governmental power they vigorously fight against religion. They promote atheism by using those means of pressure which public power has at its disposal. Such is especially the case in the work of educating the young. *(World, No.20)*

B. The Christian Community Shares Its Concern and Dialogue With All

Solutions to the deep and widespread problem of irreligion among many today requires careful and prayerful consideration. Of course, there can be no yielding to the philosophy of atheistic denial of God's existence and prerogatives. But people who call themselves nonbelievers, or who have rejected organized religion, deserve our deepest concern and charity. Many may well not have so much rejected God as He really is, but only as presented and distorted by others. This may be the meaning behind expressions such as, "the death of God." After all, only Christ Himself can tell us what Almighty God is really like in His nature and infinite love. Any solution to the problem of religious disbelief and indifferentism must begin with open and patient dialogue. Its ending will lie in personal example and genuine self-sacrifice for others, dynamically motivated by love. This is fundamentally what Christ told us with regard to our being witnesses to Him in any irreligious society.

183. Religious People Should Strive to Fathom the Causes of the Rejection of Religion

In her loyal devotion to God and men, the Church has already repudiated and cannot cease repudiating, sorrowfully but as firmly as possible, those poisonous doctrines and actions which contradict reason and the common experience of humanity, and dethrone man from his native excellence.

Still, she strives to detect in the atheistic mind the hidden causes for the denial of God. Conscious of how weighty are the questions which atheism raises, and motivated by love for all men, she believes these questions ought to be examined seriously and more profoundly. *(World, No.21)*

184. Recognition of God Is Conducive to Peace and an Ideal Social Order

The Church holds that the recognition of God is in no way hostile to man's dignity, since this dignity is rooted and perfected in God. For man was made an intelligent and free member of society by the God who created him. Even more importantly, man is called as a son to commune with God and to share in His happiness. She further teaches that a hope related to the end of time does not diminish the importance of intervening duties, but rather undergirds the acquittal of them with fresh incentives. By contrast, when a divine substructure and the hope of life eternal are wanting, man's dignity is most grievously lacerated, as current events often attest. The riddles of life and death, of guilt and of grief go unsolved, with the frequent result that men succumb to despair.

Meanwhile, every man remains to himself an unsolved puzzle, however obscurely he may perceive it. For on certain occasions no one can entirely escape the kind of self-questioning mentioned earlier, especially when life's major events take place. To this questioning only God fully and most certainly provides an answer as He summons man to higher knowledge and humbler probing. *(World, No.12)*

185. Genuine Living of Christianity Is a Most Efficacious Means for Converting Atheists

The remedy which must be applied to atheism, however, is to be sought in a proper presentation of the Church's teaching as well as in the integral life of the Church and her members. For it is the function of the Church, led by the Holy Spirit who renews and purifies her ceaselessly, to make God the Father and His Incarnate Son present and in a sense visible.

This result is achieved chiefly by the witness of a living and mature faith, namely, one trained to see difficulties clearly and to master them. Very many martyrs have given luminous witness to this faith and continue to do so. This faith needs to prove its fruitfulness by penetrating the believer's entire life, including its worldly dimensions, and by activating him toward justice and love, especially regarding the needy. What does the most to reveal God's presence, however, is the brotherly charity of the faithful who are united in spirit as they work together for the faith of the gospel and who prove themselves a sign of unity. *(World, No.21)*

186. The Church Wants Sincere and Prudent Dialogue between Believers and Non-believers

While rejecting atheism, root and branch, the Church sincerely professes that all men, believers and unbelievers alike, ought to work for the rightful betterment of this world in which all alike live. Such an ideal cannot be realized, however, apart from sincere and prudent dialogue. Hence the Church protests against the distinction which some state authorities unjustly make between believers and unbelievers, thereby ignoring fundamental rights of the human person. The Church calls for the active liberty of believers to build up in this world God's temple too. She courteously invites atheists to examine the gospel of Christ with an open mind.

Above all the Church knows that her message is in harmony with the most secret desires of the human heart when she champions the dignity of the human vocation, restoring hope to those who have already despaired of anything higher than their present lot. Far from diminishing man, her message brings to his development light, life, and freedom. Apart from this message nothing will avail to fill up the heart of man: "Thou hast made us for Thyself," O Lord, "and our hearts are restless till they rest in Thee." *(World, No.21)*

3. SOME BASIC CHRISTIAN SOLUTIONS FOR TODAY'S NEEDS

A. The Christian Imperative to Offer Vital Answers for Current Problems

The signs of the times and the needs of people today require that the solutions to problems be fundamental and long-lasting, not superficial and temporary. Christianity does not claim to have the cure-all for every ill harassing men's lives. But Christian principles can help us to approach even the most frightening of problems confronting man today with confidence that we are starting at the right place. The Church has been divinely commissioned to help mankind solve its problems in the light of the divine and natural law. Beginning with an honest acknowledgement of man's great potential for happiness, as well as of his tendency to destroy it by wrong-doing, the problems of our times can be solved by the practical application of Christian principles to the immediate problems at hand. Close examination will disclose that at the roots of these problems there invariably lie moral and religious issues.

The Church must speak its own mind on current issues as well as listen to the message which secular society is trying to convey. Christians should strive to understand the mentality, trends and movements within the world, sometimes to learn from them and at other times to refute them. Without intending any connotation of triumphalism, Christianity does have much to offer secular society and it, too, would do well to listen to the Church. Vatican II has repeatedly suggested the mutual advantages to be derived from open dialogue between the Christian-humanist and the secular-humanist mentalities.

Theology must certainly continue to expand and develop, proposing newer applications of doctrine to current situations, because the confrontation of Christian principles with the demands of the modern world is among the most serious problems of the Church and of mankind today. Nevertheless, the sensational popularizing of expressions such as "the new morality", "the new theology", "the new Church", can bewilder many because of their confusing assumptions and implication. The spiritual welfare of people must be kept in mind in the effort to speak with and understand the mentality of those lacking the same religious orientation and terminology. Christians must strive to understand the secular-humanist mentality, without lessening their own spiritual outlook on life. In the search for suitable approaches and practical answers to current problems, Christians must live and spread the gospel precepts. Some basic solutions for today's needs are truth lived in accordance with right conscience, justice toward all persons, trust among men of good-will, helpfulness to the deserving, and sacrificing charity toward all.

187. Laity Should Know Christian Principles and Apply Them to Modern Needs

Since, in this age of ours, new problems are arising and extremely serious errors are gaining currency which tend to undermine the foundations of religion, the moral order, and human society itself, this sacred Synod earnestly exhorts laymen, each according to his natural gifts and learning, to be more diligent in doing their part according to the mind of the Church, to explain and defend Christian principles, and to apply them rightly to the problems of our era. *(Laity, No.6)*

188. The Scriptures Can Teach Modern Man Much from the Experience of the Ages

Sacred Scripture teaches the human family what the experience of the ages confirms: that while human progress is a great advantage to man, it brings with it a strong temptation. For when the order of values is jumbled, and bad is mixed with the good, individuals and groups pay heed solely to their own interests, and not to those of others. Thus it happens that the world ceases to be a place of true brotherhood. In our own day, the magnified power of humanity threatens to destroy the race itself. *(World, No.37)*

189. Acknowledging the Struggle between Man and the Forces of Evil

For a monumental struggle against the powers of darkness pervades the whole history of man. The battle was joined from the very origins of the world and will continue until the last day, as the Lord has attested. Caught in this conflict, man is obliged to wrestle constantly if he is to cling to what is good. Nor can he achieve his own integrity without valiant efforts and the help of God's grace.

That is why Christ's Church, trusting in the design of the Creator, acknowledges that human progress can serve man's true happiness. Yet she cannot help echoing the Apostle's warning: "Be not conformed to this world" (Rom. 12:2). By the world is here meant that spirit of vanity and malice which transforms into an instrument of sin those human energies intended for the service of God and man. *(World, No.37)*

190. Solutions Require Effort, Sincerity, Dialogue, and Prayer

Often enough the Christian view of things will itself suggest some specific solution in certain circumstances. Yet it happens rather frequently, and legitimately so, that with equal sincerity some of the faithful will disagree with others on a given matter.

Even against the intentions of their proponents, however, solutions proposed on one side or another may be easily confused by many people with the gospel message. Hence it is necessary for people to remember that no one is allowed in the aforementioned situations to appropriate the Church's authority for his opinion. They should always try to enlighten one another through honest discussion, preserving mutual charity and caring above all for the common good.

Since they have an active role to play in the whole life of the Church, laymen are not only bound to penetrate the world with a Christian spirit. They are also called to be witnesses to Christ in all things in the midst of human society. *(World, No.43)*

191. Hear, Distinguish, and Interpret the Many Voices of Our Age

The Church requires special help, particularly in our day, when things are changing very rapidly and the ways of thinking are exceedingly various. She must rely on those who live in the world, are versed in different institutions and specialties, and grasp their innermost significance in the eyes of both believers and unbelievers. With the help of the Holy Spirit, it is the task of the entire People of God, especially pastors and theologians, to hear, distinguish, and interpret the many voices of our age, and to judge them in the light of the divine Word. In this way, revealed truth can always be more deeply penetrated, better understood, and set forth to greater advantage. *(World, No.44)*

B. The Needs of the Times Require Unity and Effort of All

Christ's Church-community can offer some cementing principles for the unification of mankind and the solving of its fundamental problems. All people, regardless of their religious convictions, or the lack of them, are children of the same Father. The forces of evil in the world can be checked through the united efforts of all men of good will as required and blessed by God Almighty for the unification of mankind in Him. To foster this unity, man must become aware of the true realities of life and study the reasons for the present condition of the world form a spiritual point of view. He must take upon himself the burdens of the whole world almost as his own, and try to apply practical solutions in the light of the gospels. It is also necessary, amid the confusion in individual lives lives and the upheaval in the world, that the Christian maintain an awareness of the divine presence and assistance.

Christians respond to Christ as being both divine and human and they look upon man's spiritual and material needs as unified in Him, and life's fundamental problems as finding their solutions in following the principles of His gospel. Complete unanimity among all people regarding solutions to the world's problems could hardly be expected. Yet, the more unity that can be achieved among differing approaches and philosophies of life, the closer today's world can come to more lasting solutions to the problems of the times. Concerted effort as a result of closer unity among people can contribute much toward providing stable conditions for more peaceful and secureliving for all.

192. Human Solidarity among All Peoples Is Necessary for Mankind

Among the signs of our times, the irresistibly increasing sense of solidarity among all peoples is especially noteworthy. It is a function of the lay apostolate to promote this awareness zealously and to transform it into a sincere and genuine sense of brotherhood. Furthermore, the laity should be informed about the international field and about the questions and solutions, theoretical as well as practical, which arise in this field, especially with respect to developing nations.

All who work in or give help to foreign nations must remember that relations among peoples should be a genuine fraternal exchange in which each party is at the same time a giver and a receiver. Whether their purpose is international affairs, private business, or leisure, travelling Christians should remember that they are journeying heralds of Christ wherever they go, and should act accordingly. *(Laity, No.14)*

193. Increased Exchanges among Various Cultures Enriches Mankind

In these conditions, it is no wonder that, feeling his responsibility for the progress of culture, man nourishes higher hopes but also looks anxiously upon many contradictions which he will have to resolve:

What must be done to prevent the increased exchanges between cultures, which ought to lead to a true and fruitful dialogue between groups and nations, from disturbing the life of communities, destroying ancestral wisdom, or jeopardizing the uniqueness of each people?

How can the vitality and growth of a new culture be fostered without the loss of living fidelity to the heritage of tradition? This question is especially urgent when a culture resulting from the enormous scientific and technological progress must be harmonized with an education nourished by classical studies as adapted to various traditions. *(World, No. 56.)*

194. All True Human Values Are Blessed by God

But wherever truth and grace are to be found among the nations, as a sort of secret presence of God, this activity frees from all taint of evil and restores to Christ its maker, who overthrows the devil's domain and wards off the manifold malice of vice. And so, whatever good is found to be sown in the hearts and minds of men, or in the rites and cultures peculiar to various peoples, is not lost. More than that, it is healed, ennobled, and perfected for the glory of God, the shame of the demon, and the bliss of men. *(Missions, No.9)*

195. A Great Sign of Help for the Times Would Be the Unity of Christians

Today, in many parts of the world, under the inspiring grace of the Holy Spirit, multiple efforts are being expended through prayer, word, and action to attain that fullness of unity which Jesus Christ desires. This sacred Synod, therefore, exhorts all the Catholic faithful to recognize the signs of the times and to participate skillfully in the work of ecumenism. *(Ecumenism, No.4)*

196. Adult–Youth Divisions Must Be Overcome for Society's Welfare

Adults ought to engage in friendly discussion with young people so that both groups, overcoming the age barrier, can become better acquainted and can share the special benefits each generation has to offer the other. Adults should attract young persons to the apostolate first by good example, and, if the opportunity presents itself, by offering them balanced advice and effective assistance. For their part, young people would be wise to cultivate toward adults respect and trust. Although the young are naturally attracted to new things, they should exercise an intelligent regard for worthwhile traditions. *(Laity, No.12)*

The ability to discern when and in what actions Christ's Holy Spirit may be working seems to become easier the more we welcome Him and listen to His promptings. Discernment is essential for weighing where the Holy Spirit's movements are in action or where the forces of evil may be at work in the world. Extreme, excessive, or imbalanced solutions to problems of today cannot solve the problems of man's welfare, but, rather, only worsen them. Shallow solutions, prejudiced judgments, and irresponsible actions only beget further problems of their own, thus adding chaos rather than effecting harmony. Consequently, to obtain the spirit of discernment enabling us to detect the movements of the Holy Spirit in life, and to have the prudence to act in accord with this discernment, we need spiritual understanding which comes from prayer, thought, and the grace of God.

Even with all the changes and upheavals confronting the world in our days, these can be exciting times of great opportunity. The Christian does not claim that man's life on earth can be without problems, but he does believe that life's bigger conflicts can be resolved when men live by the teachings of the risen Christ. Our Savior has resolved the two biggest of man's problems in any age; death's outcome and sin's degradation. Christ can also help us to resolve the big difficulties of this present age, for He is ever with His people enlightening and strengthening them in His ways, through the Holy Spirit who continues our Lord's work in the world in the contest with evil.

Chapter VIII

THE CONSTANT CHRISTIAN CHALLENGE

The Call to Holiness

The constant challenge to Christians in every age is that of personal response to the call of Christ for holiness of life. The attainment and enjoyment of salvation is a consequence of this sanctity. All are called by Christ Himself to strive for the sanctification of their lives.

The world today needs nothing so vitally as living saints to help it. To strive for sanctity requires almost daily courage in the struggle with stark reality with which men and women of high ideals are confronted. This world has a surplus of people who claim to be "practical", and who like to keep their "feet on the ground." Yet, these progressive times need more people courageous enough to cherish the high ideals required to rise a little above the earth. If it is considered idealistic to reach for the stars of genuine holiness, if it is thought impractical to maintain the effort for arriving at sanctity's threshold, then our times need more people who are motivated by the heavenly idealism Christ inspires.

Whatever further changes and adaptations may come into effect in the Vatican II era, their chief purpose must always be to assist Christians to fulfill their commitment to Christ Himself and to the cause of His Church-community. Our Lord asks for genuine holiness of life, even under the stress of twentieth century living. In terms of function, this holiness consists in doing the will of God as guided by the Church in concrete situations. The heart of holiness consists in loving God above all else and our neighbor as ourselves.

Holiness is as practical for life's time-span as it is essential for an eternity of happiness. To acquire sanctity requires effort. However, the opposite unconcern for sanctity leaves life quite fruitless, like a barren fig-tree. Ultimately, the effort for holiness during life is like breathing; it is essential for healthy living before death arrives.

Man discharges his main function on earth only through sanctification in response to God's love. There are three levels of man's response to God's call. The first, essential for attaining the salvation Christ won for all, is so to live that when we finally die we do so in love and grace, free from serious sin. At the second level we strive to serve Christ more completely, not so much weighing whether a sin is considered as serious or slight, but striving, rather, to love our Lord free of all deliberate sin. A rapid repentance for faults may be a good sign-post along this course. The third level of love corresponds to the highest sanctity. It consists in so living that we accept all of life's trials as hidden treasures of blessing, the more to imitate our Savior who suffered and gave His entire life for love of us. Holiness, at whatever level or degree, remains basically our response of love to Him who first loved us.

The Vatican II passages point out the ingredients of seasoned holiness and how this may be acquired. Anybody capable of loving God and his fellow man can reach the goal of holiness in life, to which all men are called. Christ and His Church will assist everyone to deepen his commitment to holiness (Section 1). The example of those who give greater dedication to Christ is an ennobling inspiration to the whole Christian community (Section 2). We are helped to keep or to restore the health of our souls by the many sacramental and other means offered by the Church. In addition, Christ's Blessed Mother has been given special prerogatives to enable those devoted to her to strengthen their following of her divine Son (Section 3).

The Vatican II passages in this chapter encourage all, even the fainthearted, reminding everyone that salvation is attainable by anyone who really wants it, regardless of external circumstances. Christ has called us all to genuine holiness in our lives and He constantly assists us throughout this essential endeavor. What other men have done before, men can do today. The saints and the noble lives of good people should inspire our spirits to strive with enthusiasm for sanctity of life, as a fascinating quest. Holiness is indispensible for living a good Christian life. Our Blessed Mother can be of inestimable assistance in our following of Christ during our life's quest for holiness.

1. THE ORDINARY COMMITMENT OF
CHRISTIANS TO UNION WITH CHRIST

A. Christ and His Church Assist
All to Acquire Holiness

No commitment of a person and his life to our Lord can be looked upon as merely "ordinary." Every Christian is called to be an extraordinary person in the world for Christ. Hence, ordinary dedication means the minimal though beautiful response to the call we all receive for holiness of life. This term also implies the use of the ordinary means for personal Christian living — the Eucharistic sacrifice, the sacraments, private prayer, self-sacrifice, personal virtue — as well as participation in the community life of the Church. Truly, Christ and His Church assist all to acquire holiness.

Personal union with Christ is the beginning and the end of holiness, for He in His Church-community is the surest way to this consummation. Through His Church, Christ offers all the means to acquire sanctity, since He is present in His word, in all rites of the liturgy, and whenever His people join in prayer or perform good works in His name.

Love of God and of one another are defined by Christ as the cardinal or hinge commandments of Christianity. Charity, then, sums up the whole Christian way of life. Our Lord invites and inspires each of us, individually, to unite in this love for Him in a community bound together by this tie of unique charity.

197. The Church Helps People Attain Holiness and Salvation

Faith teaches that the Church, whose mystery is being set forth by this sacred Synod, is holy in a way which can never fail. For Christ, the Son of God, who with the Father and the Spirit is praised as being "alone holy," loved the Church as His Bride, delivering Himself up for her. This He did that He might sanctify her (cf. Eph. 5:25-26). He united her to Himself as His own body and crowned her with the gift of the Holy Spirit, for God's glory. Therefore in the Church, everyone belonging to the hierarchy, or being cared for by it, is called to holiness, according to the saying of the Apostle: "For this is the will of God, your sanctification" (1 Th. 4:3; cf. Eph. 1:4).

Now, this holiness of the Church is unceasingly manifested, as it ought to be, through those fruits of grace that the Spirit produces in the faithful. It is expressed in multiple ways by those individuals who, in their walk of life, strive for the perfection of charity, and thereby help others to grow. In a particularly appropriate way this holiness shines out in the practice of the counsels customarily called "evangelical." Under the influence of the Holy Spirit, the practice of these counsels is undertaken by many Christians, either privately or in some Church-approved situation or state, and produces in the world, as produce it should, a shining witness and model of holiness. *(Church, No.39)*

198. Christ Preached Holiness of Life for All

The Lord Jesus, the divine Teacher and Model of all perfection, preached holiness of life to each and every one of His disciples, regardless of their situation: "You therefore are to be perfect, even as your heavenly Father is perfect" (Mt. 5:48). He Himself stands as the Author and Finisher of this holiness of life. For He sent the Holy Spirit upon all men that He might inspire them from within to love God with their whole heart and their whole soul, with all their mind and all their strength (cf. Mk. 12:30) and that they might love one another as Christ loved them (cf. Jn. 13:34; 15:12). *(Church, No.40)*

199. Christ's Followers Are Helped to Holiness Which Benefits Life

The followers of Christ are called by God, not according to their accomplishments, but according to His own purpose and grace. They are justified in the Lord Jesus, and through baptism sought in faith they truly become sons of God and sharers in the divine nature. In this way they are really made holy. Then, too, by God's gifts they must hold on to and complete in their lives this holiness which they have received. They are warned by the Apostle to live "as becomes saints" (Eph. 5:3), and to put on "as God's chosen ones, holy and beloved, a heart of mercy, kindness, humility, meekness, patience" (Col. 3:12), and to possess the fruits of the Spirit unto holiness (cf. Gal. 5:22; Rom. 6:22). Since we all truly offend in many things (cf. Jas. 3:2), we all need God's mercy continuously and must daily pray: "Forgive us our debts" (Mt. 6:12).

Thus it is evident to everyone that all the faithful of Christ of whatever rank or status are called to the fullness of the Christian life and to the perfection of charity. By this holiness a more human way of life is promoted even in this earthly society. In order that the faithful may reach this perfection, they must use their strength according as they have received it, as a gift from Christ. In this way they can follow in His footsteps and mold themselves in His image, seeking the will of the Father in all things, devoting themselves with all their being to the glory of God and the service of their neighbor. In this way too, the holiness of the People of God will grow into an abundant harvest of good, as is brilliantly proved by the lives of so many saints in Church history. *(Church, No.40)*

B. Everyone, In All Circumstances, Is Called to Sanctity of Life

We are all called to sanctification of life and we become united together in this holy enterprise by the indwelling of the Holy Spirit. This calling includes everyone, regardless of the particular circumstances of life. We are called to be holy as individuals belonging to the community of Christ's people, His Church. This holiness is not confined to a set pattern or limited to ancient days, to monasteries, or only to extraordinary people. Rather, holiness means living with lively faith, hope, and love, attainable by everyone, in any walk of life, and in every circumstance, provided God's grace is accepted.

Genuine holiness lies open to people in all age-brackets, situations, careers, and vocations. Sanctity is basically one and the same for housewife, electrical engineer, priest, nun, or student. Holiness shows itself in striving to fulfill the will of God from the motive of love in the practical aspects of daily living. Marriage and single life, routine work, serving as a priest or religious, as well as times of sickness, of hardship or well-being — these are all proper conditions or states in life, and they provide the ground in which the seeds of holiness can grow.

Most people who strive for sanctity, though they may not constantly maintain it, consider themselves somewhat like the breast-beating publican, the prodigal son, or the renewed Magdalene of the gospels. All of these received praise from Christ after their repentence and renewal. There may well be more genuine sanctity in the world than most of us realize or acknowledge!

200. All Are Called to One and the Same Holiness

In the various types and duties of life, one and the same holiness is cultivated by all who are moved by the Spirit of God, and who obey the voice of the Father, worshipping God the Father in spirit and in truth. These souls follow the poor Christ, the humble and cross-bearing Christ, in order to be made worthy of being partakers in His glory. Every person should walk unhesitatingly according to his own personal gifts and duties in the path of a living faith which arouses hopes and works through charity. *(Church, No.41)*

201. Holiness within Marriage and By Single People

Married couples and Christian parents should follow their own proper path to holiness by faithful love, sustaining one another in grace throughout the entire length of their lives. They should imbue their offspring, lovingly welcomed from God, with Christian truths and evangelical virtues. For this they can offer all men an example of unwearying and generous love, build up the brotherhood of charity, and stand as witnesses to and cooperators in the fruitfulness of holy Mother Church. By such lives, they signify and share in that very love with which Christ loved His Bride and because of which He delivered Himself up on her behalf. A like example, but one given in a different way, is that offered by widows and single people, who are able to make great contributions toward holiness and apostolic endeavor in the Church. *(Church, No.41)*

202. Sanctification of Daily Work

Finally, laborers, whose work is often toilsome, should by their human exertions try to perfect themselves, aid their fellow citizens, and raise all of society, and even creation itself, to a better mode of existence. By their lively charity, joyous hope, and sharing of one another's burdens, let them also truly imitate Christ, who roughened His hands with carpenter's tools, and who in union with His Father is always at work for the salvation of all men. By their daily work itself laborers can achieve greater apostolic sanctity. *(Church, No.41)*

203. Sanctifying Conditions of Hardship, Sickness, Sorrow, and Poverty

Those who are oppressed by poverty, infirmity, sickness, or various other hardships, as well as those who suffer persecution for justice' sake — may they all know that in a special way they are united with the suffering Christ for the salvation of the world. The

Lord called them blessed in His gospel. They are those whom "the God of all grace, who has called us unto his eternal glory in Christ Jesus, will himself, after we have suffered a little while, perfect, strengthen, and establish" (1 Pet. 5:10). *(Church, No.41)*

204. Holiness Can Be Obtained within Any Situation

All of Christ's faithful, therefore, whatever be the conditions, duties, and circumstances of their lives, will grow in holiness day by day through these very situations, if they accept all of them with faith from the hand of their heavenly Father, and if they cooperate with the divine will by showing every man through their earthly activities the love with which God has loved the world. *(Church, No.41)*

205. The Chief Means for Nurturing Holiness

"God is love, and he who abides in love abides in God, and God in him" (1 Jn. 4:16). God pours out His love into our hearts through the Holy Spirit, who has been given to us (cf. Rom. 5:5). Thus the first and most necessary gift is that charity by which we love God above all things and our neighbor because of God. If that love, as good seed, is to grow and bring forth fruit in the soul, each one of the faithful must willingly hear the Word of God and with the help of His grace act to fulfill His will.

Each must share frequently in the sacraments, the Eucharist especially, and in liturgical rites. Each must apply himself constantly to prayer, self-denial, active brotherly service and the exercise of all the virtues. For charity, as the bond of perfection and the fulfillment of the law (cf. Col. 3:14; Rom. 13:10), rules over all the means of attaining holiness, gives life to them, and makes them work. Hence it is the love of God and of neighbor which points out the true disciple of Christ. *(Church, No.42)*

206. Guiding Our Affections toward the Attainment of Holiness

All of Christ's followers, therefore, are invited and bound to pursue holiness and the perfect fulfillment of their proper state. Hence, let them all see that they guide their affections rightly. Otherwise, they will be thwarted in the search for perfect charity by the way they use earthly possessions and by a fondness for riches which goes against the gospel spirit of poverty. The Apostle has sounded the warning: let those who make use of this world not get bogged down in it, for the structure of this world is passing away (cf. 1 Cor. 7:31, Greek text). *(Church, No.42)*

2. SPECIAL COMMITMENT CALLS FOR GREATER DEDICATION TO CHRIST

A. Christians Particularly Dedicated to Christ's Cause

We admire human beings who, in a spirit of self-sacrifice, have made discoveries beneficial to mankind, or who have produced creative works ennobling to the human spirit. We are inspired by people who have lived up to the demands of their convictions. Heroines like the deaf, speechless and blind Helen Keller with her vast accomplishments, heroes like the far-traveling St. Francis Xavier with his efforts to conquer the Far East for Christ, help us to strive more heroically toward noble achievements during our own lives. Although most of us may seem to contribute little to the world, our efforts can still have the greatest value in God's eyes. In the quest for holiness, the cumulative effects of our efforts during the years bring us nearer and nearer to victory.

Those who would be perfect in following Christ and spreading His kingdom must go beyond the ordinary response to His call. In brief, those specially dedicated to Christ follow the beatitudes and the evangelical counsels, the demands of which are endurable only to the highest love and sacrifice. Thus do dedicated people such as the ailing husband, the patient mother, the sacrificing daughter, the striving youth, the alert nun, and the laboring missionary, press forward for Christ and with His help.

207. Self-Sacrificing Charity Shows True Holiness

In the pilgrimage of this life, hidden with Christ in God and free from enslavement to wealth, they aspire to those riches which remain forever, and generously dedicate their entire selves to spreading God's kingdom and to fashioning and perfecting the sphere of earthly things according to the spirit of Christ. Among the struggles of this life, they find strength in hope, convinced that "the sufferings of the present time are not worthy to be compared with the glory to come that will be revealed in us" (Rom. 8:18).

Impelled by the divine charity, they do good to all men, especially to those of the household of the faith (cf. Gal. 6:10), laying aside "all malice and all deceit and pretense, and envy, and all slander" (1 Pet. 2:1), and thereby they draw men to Christ. This charity of God, which "is poured forth in our hearts by the Holy Spirit who has been given to us" (Rom. 5:5), enables the laity to express the true spirit of the beatitudes in their lives. Following Jesus who was poor, they are neither depressed by the lack of temporal goods nor puffed up by their abundance. Imitating Christ who was humble, they have no obsession for empty honors (cf. Gal. 5:26) but seek to please God rather than men, ever ready to leave all things for Christ's sake (cf. Lk. 14:26) and to suffer persecution for justice' sake (cf. Mt. 5:10). For they remember the words of the Lord, "If anyone wishes to come after me, let him deny himself, and take up his cross, and follow me" (Mt. 16:24). Promoting Christian friendship among themselves, they help one another in any kind of necessity. *(Laity, No.4)*

208. Christ's Mission is Advanced through Dedicated People

The mission of the Church, therefore, is fulfilled by that activity which makes her fully present to all men and nations. She undertakes this activity in obedience to Christ's command and in response to the grace and love of the Holy Spirit. Thus, by the example of her life and by her preaching, by the sacraments and other means of grace, she can lead them to the faith, the freedom, and the peace of Christ. Thus there lies open before them a free and trustworthy road to full participation in the mystery of Christ.

This mission is a continuing one. In the course of history it unfolds the mission of Christ Himself, who was sent to preach the gospel to the poor. Hence, prompted by the Holy Spirit, the Church must walk the same road which Christ walked: a road of poverty and obedience, of service and self-sacrifice to the death, from which death He came forth a victor by His resurrection. For this did all the apostles walk in hope. On behalf of Christ's body, which is the Church, they supplied what was wanting of the sufferings of Christ by their own many trials and sufferings (cf. Col. 1:24). Often, too, the blood of Christians was like a seed. *(Missions, No.5)*

209. Complete Dedication to Christ Reflects Him to Others

As an innocent lamb He merited life for us by the free shedding of His own blood. In Him God reconciled us to Himself and among ourselves. From bondage to the devil and sin, He delivered us, so that each one of us can say with the Apostle: The Son of God "loved me and gave himself up for me" (Gal. 2:20). By suffering for us He not only provided us with an example for our imitation. He blazed a trail, and if we follow it, life and death are made holy and take on a new meaning.

The Christian man, conformed to the likeness of that Son who is the firstborn of many brothers, receives "the firstfruits of the Spirit" (Rom. 8:23) by which he becomes capable of discharging the new law of love. Through this Spirit, who is "the pledge of our inheritance" (Eph. 1:14), the whole man is renewed from within, even to the achievement of "the redemption of the body" (Rom. 8:23): "If the Spirit of him who raised Jesus from the death dwells in you, then he who raised Jesus Christ from the dead will also bring to life your mortal bodies because of his Spirit who dwells in you" (Rom. 8:11). *(World, No.22)*

210. Heroism Is Required Today as in the Past

There is a very urgent need for this individual apostolate in places where the freedom of the Church is seriously restricted. In exceedingly trying circumstances, the laity do what they can to take the place of priests, risking their freedom and sometimes their lives to teach Christian doctrine to those around them, to train them in a religious way of life and in a Catholic mentality, to lead them to receive the sacraments frequently, and to develop their piety, especially toward the Eucharist. This most sacred Synod heartily thanks God for continuing in our times to raise up lay persons of heroic fortitude in the midst of persecutions, and it embraces them with fatherly affection and gratitude. *(Laity, No.17)*

B. What the Saints Have Done
We Can Do to Some Degree

The saints are rather practical people who work hard at the business of life and its sanctification. However, they become saints not exclusively by means of external accomplishments. It is their inner qualities of soul which make them saints, particularly the intensity of the love with which they seek and follow God's ways in their lives and works.

Although various religious practices and devotions are unquestionably essential for the acquisition of sanctity, the multiplication of them as mere practices has little pertinence to the core of sanctity. Whatever religious practices are adopted in particular instances, they should bear some relevance to the sacred liturgy. Nevertheless, people who sincerely strive for holiness of life need not be worried that they may, perhaps, wake up one day to find that their long, hard efforts were misdirected. God looks at motives in people's hearts as well as at actual accomplishments in their lives. He reads the heart as much as the mind and more than the lips. He certainly considers effort and good intentions more than mistakes. Anyone who really wants to be holy can achieve this goal. Its soul is good love; its breath is good will; its life is good works.

The following of the quest for holiness includes fulfillment of our ordinary duties. Some of these may involve us in cleaning a drain pipe, washing the inevitable dishes, driving a car in the rain to pick up the unconcerned teen-agers, going to confession, reading holy Scripture, preparing a lecture, and so forth.

The conciliar passages outline the nature of true sanctification of life and the means for acquiring it. Sanctity of life means striving for virtue while avoiding or repenting for sin in the movement toward salvation's victory. A life of holiness includes the appreciation and enjoyment of life's simple pleasures, according to each one's taste as oriented by a conscious and informed Christian conscience.

Sanctity is perfectly in harmony with enjoying a baby's first lurdle-lurdle words, singing and dancing together, listening to classical music or to jazz, riding a horse or having a picnic, watching a ball-game with a glass of cool beer in hand, and such simple pleasures. Sanctity actually helps to humanize life to a higher degree. The lawyer preparing a brief, the nun grading the examinations of her students, the mother coaxing her child to go to bed, the military chaplain bouncing along in a jeep, the aspirant writer pounding a typewriter, the young people exchanging news bits, glances and giggles — all these may well be occasions on which the divine sense of humor takes delight and blesses His children, when their hearts are right with His.

People throughout past ages whom we favor now as saints had to overcome their own difficulties. We have ours, no less valuable. Whatever personal circumstances confront us, they supply opportunities for advancing in sanctity. The same Christ is calling us in our life-time; the same Church is helping us to respond wholeheartedly; the same constant Christian challenge to holiness invites our full dedication.

211. The Heroic Martyrs Are United with Us in Christ

The Church has always believed that the apostles, and Christ's martyrs who had given the supreme witness of faith and charity by the shedding of their blood, are quite closely joined with us in Christ. She has always venerated them with special devotion, together with the Blessed Virgin Mary and the holy angels. The Church too has devoutly implored the aid of their intercession. To these were soon added those who had imitated Christ's virginity and poverty more exactly, and finally others whom the outstanding practice of the Christian virtues and the divine charisms recommended to the pious devotion and imitation of the faithful. *(Church, No.50)*

212. Holiness of Life Can Be Lived Today as in the Past

For when we look at the lives of those who have faithfully followed Christ, we are inspired with a new reason for seeking the city which is to come (Heb. 13:14; 11:10). At the same time we are shown a most safe path by which, among the vicissitudes of this world and in keeping with the state in life and condition proper to each of us, we will be able to arrive at perfect union with Christ, that is, holiness. In the lives of those who shared in our humanity and yet were transformed into especially successful images of Christ (cf. 2 Cor. 3:18), God vividly manifests to men His presence and His face. He speaks to us in them, and gives us a sign of His kingdom, to which we are powerfully drawn, surrounded as we are by so many witnesses (cf. Heb. 12:1), and having such an argument for the truth of the gospel. *(Church, No.50)*

213. Inspiration from Authentic Devotion to Saints

Let the faithful be taught, therefore, that the authentic cult of the saints consists not so much in the multiplying of external acts, but rather in the intensity of our active love. By such love, for our own greater good and that of the Church, we seek from the saints "example in their way of life, fellowship in their communion, and aid by their intercession." At the same time, let the people be instructed that our communion with those in heaven, provided that it is understood in the more adequate light of faith, in no way weakens, but conversely, more thoroughly enriches the supreme worship we give to God the Father, through Christ, in the Spirit. *(Church, No.51)*

3. FOLLOWING CHRIST, WITH THE HELP OF HIS BLESSED MOTHER

A. The Prerogatives of the Mother of Jesus Enable Her to Help People

No one can attain holiness completely by himself. Without God's grace we can not become holy; with it, there is no limit. God does not ask a person to sanctify his life without assistance. He encourages us to call on the help of others. We Catholics believe that, besides our union with other people on earth, we are also united with people in heaven. The great prerogatives and power of the Mother of Christ for helping us respond to her divine Son's call aid us to follow our Lord better by conquering fear.

The quest for sanctity of life can be, admittedly, frightening at times. Yet a life without striving for goodness is a wasted one. Holiness, like love, can be at times evasive and illusive. There can even be lapses, falls, and disgust, followed later by advancement in the spiritual life. Abraham and David lapsed; Peter and Thomas fell; Theresa and Ignatius at times became disgusted. Who can measure the discouragements planted by the forces of evil in the pathway to sanctity? Yet, all of these rose up from their slumps, charged ahead with renewed courage, and scaled the heights of sanctity. Everyone experiences difficulties in the struggle for real and lasting holiness of life.

The Blessed Mother of Jesus has exceptional privileges befitting her exalted place in the divine plan for man's encouragement. In addition to the spiritual assistance our Lady offers to those who seek her help, she lends graciousness and a calming assurance that all still will be well with those who strive to follow her divine Son.

214. Christ, Our Savior, Gave an Exalted Position to His Blessed Mother

We have but one Mediator, as we know from the words of the Apostle: "For there is one God, and one Mediator between God and men, himself man, Christ Jesus, who gave himself a ransom for all"

(1 Tim. 2:5-6). The maternal duty of Mary toward men in no way obscures or diminishes this unique mediation of Christ, but rather shows its power. For all the saving influences of the Blessed Virgin on men originate, not from some inner necessity, but from the divine pleasure. They flow forth from the superabundance of the merits of Christ, rest on His mediation, depend entirely on it, and draw all their power from it. In no way do they impede the immediate union of the faithful with Christ. Rather, they foster this union. *(Church, No.60)*

215. The Excellence and Holiness of the Virgin Mary

In the most holy Virgin the Church has already reached that perfection whereby she exists without spot or wrinkle (cf. Eph. 5:27). Yet the followers of Christ still strive to increase in holiness by conquering sin. And so they raise their eyes to Mary who shines forth to the whole community of the elect as a model of the virtues. Devotedly meditating on her and contemplating her in the light of the Word made man, the Church with reverence enters more intimately into the supreme mystery of the Incarnation and becomes ever increasingly like her Spouse.

For Mary figured profoundly in the history of salvation and in a certain way unites and mirrors within herself the central truths of the faith. Hence when she is being preached and venerated, she summons the faithful to her Son and His sacrifice, and to love for the Father. Seeking after the glory of Christ, the Church becomes more like her exalted model, and continually progresses in faith, hope, and charity, searching out and doing the will of God in all things. Hence the Church in her apostolic work also rightly looks to her who brought forth Christ, conceived by the Holy Spirit and born of the Virgin, so that through the Church Christ may be born and grow in the hearts of the faithful also. The Virgin Mary in her own life lived an example of that maternal love by which all should be fittingly animated who cooperate in the apostolic mission of the Church on behalf of the rebirth of men. *(Church, No.65)*

B. True Devotion to Our Lady Fosters Holiness in Serving Christ

It is apparent that strong devotion to our Lady helped to produce staunch Christians during the ages of firm religious faith. In her lifetime on earth, the Mother of Jesus helped her Son's cause by sustaining the apostles in the earliest days of Christianity. Just as the inspiration of the Blessed Mother helped martyrs, confessors, and doctors of the Church, as well as the less outstanding of the faithful in ages past, so in modern times her influence in the Christian community can help to foster deeper commitment to following Christ in holiness.

Our heavenly Mother assists us in these times of tension, just as she has ever done since Christianity began. Today's preachers, teachers, parents, writers, and all others are urged to foster genuine devotion to the Mother of Christ whose firsthand knowledge of authentic Christianity and her power at the throne of God can aid this age of renewal.

Whatever forms of devotion to our Lady are practiced, they should be related to Christ the Savior, as in the sacred liturgy. Obviously, devotion to Mary increases service of her divine Son. Mere emotional practices do not constitute true devotion to Mary. The Blessed Mother of Christ is the one human being who best cooperated with God's will and His grace. She above any sainted person can help us to understand and practice the gospel of Christ in the modern world. True devotion to our Lady must not be allowed to lessen in our times. Christ bequeathed His own Blessed Mother to us for the nurturing of our faith in the living of Christianity.

216. Mary Helps Us Know and Serve Christ and His Church Better

Mary was involved in the mysteries of Christ. As the most holy Mother of God she was, after her Son, exalted by divine grace above all angels and men. Hence the Church appropriately honors her with special reverence. Indeed, from most ancient times the Blessed Virgin has been venerated under the title of "God-bearer." In all perils and needs, the faithful have fled prayerfully to her protection. Especially after the Council of Ephesus the cult of the People of God toward Mary wonderfully increased in veneration and love, in invocation and imitation, according to her own prophetic words: "All generations shall call me blessed; because He who is mighty has done great things for me" (Lk. 1:48).

As it has always existed in the Church, this cult is altogether special. Still, it differs essentially from the cult of adoration which is offered to the Incarnate World, as well as to the Father and Holy Spirit. Yet devotion to Mary is most favorable to this supreme cult. The Church has endorsed many forms of piety toward the Mother of God, provided that they were within the limits of sound and orthodox doctrine. These forms have varied according to the circumstances of time and place and have reflected the diversity of native characteristics and temperament among the faithful. While honoring Christ's Mother, these devotions cause her Son to be rightly known, loved, and glorified, and all His commands observed. Through Him all things have their being (cf. Col. 1:15-16) and in Him "it has pleased [the eternal Father] that . . . all his fullness should dwell" (Col. 1:19). *(Church, No.66)*

217. True Devotion to Mary Helps us Serve Christ with Deeper Commitment

This most holy Synod deliberately teaches this Catholic doctrine. At the same time, it admonishes all the sons of the Church that the cult, especially the liturgical cult, of the Blessed Virgin, be generously fostered. It charges that practices and exercises of devotion toward her be treasured as recommended by the teaching authority of the Church in the course of centuries, and that those decrees issued in earlier times regarding the veneration of images of Christ, the Blessed Virgin, and the saints, be religiously observed.

But this Synod earnestly exhorts theologians and preachers of the divine word that in treating of the unique dignity of the Mother of God, they carefully and equally avoid the falsity of exaggeration on the one hand, and the excess of narrow-mindedness on the other. Pursuing the study of sacred Scripture, the holy Fathers, the doctors, and liturgies of the Church, and under the guidance of the Church's teaching authority, let them rightly explain the offices and privileges of the Blessed Virgin which are always related to Christ, the Source of all truth, sanctity, and piety.

Let them painstakingly guard against any word or deed which could lead separated brethren or anyone else into error regarding the true doctrine of the Church. Let the faithful remember moreover that true devotion consists neither in fruitless and passing emotion, nor in a certain vain credulity. Rather, it proceeds from true faith, by which we are led to know the excellence of the Mother of God, and are moved to a filial love toward our mother and to the imitation of her virtues. *(Church, No.67)*

218. Devotion to the Mother of Our Savior Can Help the Human Family

It gives great joy and comfort to this most holy Synod that among the separated brethren, too, there are those who give due honor to the Mother of our Lord and Savior. This is especially so among the Easterners, who with ardent emotion and devout mind concur in reverencing the Mother of God, ever Virgin.

Let the entire body of the faithful pour forth persevering prayer to the Mother of God and Mother of men. Let them implore that she who aided the beginnings of the Church by her prayers may now, exalted as she is in heaven above all the saints and angels, intercede with her Son in the fellowship of all the saints. May she do so until all the peoples of the human family, whether they are honored with the name of Christian or whether they still do not know their Savior, are happily gathered together in peace and harmony into the one People of God, for the Glory of the Most Holy and Undivided Trinity. *(Church, No.69)*

The great Council has encouraged us to continue striving for a fuller and more fruitful commitment to the constant Christian challenge to holiness of life. This is the call of our loving Savior who was like us in every way, except for sin. His strengthening grace remains always with us, particularly when we try harder to return His love for us.

Holiness is a strong, indeed, almost a frightening word. Yet, we must feel proud, not ashamed or afraid of it. Our commitment allows for nothing less. Much depends on our determination, drawn from the virtue of hope, to be holy even as we are human. Our Blessed Mother was both human and holy. She can help us to follow her divine Son who had both a divine and human nature. Since Christ is with us what can stop us, for are we not His people?

Summary of Part Two – COMMITMENT

Part Two took up the challenge of full commitment to the service of Christ's cause by His people, Christ is actively present in the world, especially through His Church, His people whom He calls upon to help fulfill His mission today (Chapter V). Just as Christ's divinity operated through His humanity, so His Church-community continues the effects of His Incarnation through the various apostolic activities of Christians in the world (Chapter VI). Moreover, in order that Christ's Mystical Body might not be hampered in its vital mission, accurate discernment

186 EXPLORING VATICAN II

of influences is required. This demands a keen awareness of the forces of good and evil that work in the world, and the necessity to discern the workings of each (Chapter VII). All are called to genuine holiness of life as the verifying sign for productive activity by Christians committed to Christ's cause, as the Blessed Virgin Mary exemplified (Chapter VIII).

The following passage, epitomizing Part Two, stresses the mission of the Church-community and the commitment required to foster Christ's cause by His people.

219. May Our Commitment Cause Fuller Service of Christ by His People Today

Christ is the light of all nations. Hence this most sacred Synod, which has been gathered in the Holy Spirit, eagerly desires to shed on all men that radiance of His which brightens the countenance of the Church. This it will do by proclaiming the gospel to every creature (cf. Mk. 16:15).

By her relationship with Christ, the Church is a kind of sacrament or sign of intimate union with God, and of the unity of all mankind. She is also an instrument for the achievement of such union and unity. For this reason, following in the path laid out by its predecessors, this Council wishes to set forth more precisely to the faithful and to the entire world the nature and encompassing mission of the Church. The conditions of this age lend special urgency to the Church's task of bringing all men to full union with Christ, since mankind today is joined together more closely than ever before by social, technical, and cultural bonds. *(Church, No.1)*

When the Christian has responded to Christ's call to the service of His cause, his commitment becomes more full, mature, and sanctified. Throughout Part Two we pondered the kingdom of Christ and our function in it in contemporary times. Commitment to Christ leads toward closer union with our fellow man in the service of our Savior, as Part Three will offer for our reflection.

Part 3
Unity

UNITY
This is the symbol of man's effort and
ability to touch one another in friendship. Together with the ancient sign
depicting friendship between men the
three-armed triangle formed in the
center represents God: triune and one.

PART THREE – UNITY

THE RELEVANCE OF ECUMENISM
AND THE LITURGY IN OUR AGE

One of the most ardent desires of the Church today is for an intensified effort toward stronger unity among the followers of Christ. As Vatican II states it, we are "to nurture whatever can contribute to the unity of all who believe in Christ." Hence, ecumenism as the movement toward unity among Christians, and the sacred liturgy as our participation in the effects of Christ's paschal mystery, are particularly relevant for establishing this unity. Through the liturgy Christians draw strength from our Lord for deeper unity with Him and with one another. This is an era filled with startling changes and developing structures. Unity with one another in Christ is essential so that the emerging new order can give promise of great hope for the Christian community for the future.

The truth must bind men together. Yet the search for truth should not make people become over-bearing toward one another, nor should charity become over-looked in this search. Truth and charity must accompany one another. When charity is not present, truth can become domineering, haughty, and even crushing. When charity lacks the foundation of truth, the supposed love tends to flounder and die out. Consequently, those who wish to impart truth should speak it softly, present it gently, and apply it kindly to others. Charity must clothe the truth in attractive garments or it will not appeal to people.

Greater unity is required, first of all, within the Catholic Church. Catholics these days must exert personal restraint in order to prevent division through mutual accusations or exaggerated criticism of another's position on certain issues within the Church. There is much work to be done without wasting time on unfounded condemnations which further separate Christ's well-intentioned people one from another. Whatever actions seem necessary to be taken, Christ alone has the right to judge the motives of anyone. When people who are united in the one faith and moved by the same Holy Spirit over-react to each other's religious ideas, it causes needless exhaustion and senseless contention, which weaken the bond of unity in the household of the faith. These are times in which all religions are undergoing severe scrutiny and re-evaluation. But at least religious interest is far more desirable than deadening indifference. Much good can ultimately blossom from digging at the roots in the search for modern applications of the basic religious truths. Patient tolerance and kindly understanding are among the gifts of the Holy Spirit in the Church's heritage. Truth is not so passive that it can stay dormant for long; it emerges in due time and with good taste.

The Council acknowledges the spirit of religious liberty and openness of spirit as everyone's prerogative. Christ has promised to stay with His people throughout their works for His cause. Hence, no one Christian need feel compelled to fret excessively over the Church-community. Unless there is certain knowledge to the contrary, it is better to consider the other person as equally sincere in love of the faith. Together, all can explore the facets of truth that lie within the great mystery which ever envelopes the Church of Christ.

The movement toward an intensified love for God and neighbor finds its completion in union with both, for charity tends to unite. Indeed, love contains a certain reflective or contemplative element which both relaxes and strengthens. However, the present age appears more in need of the dynamic actions which love also produces. These result in strengthening the bonds of brotherly unity among fellow men and in experiencing intimately the active participation of close union with our Lord in the liturgical rites of the Church.

People in the present age feel a grave need to be closely united with one another. They are seeking for deep, significant, and warm manifestations of mutual love for one another. This frequently happens when tensions increase, as they do in the current period. It is particularly true among the younger generation. This is evident in their craving to relate meaningfully with one another, such as in folk Masses and other liturgical events in which their active, personal participation must be deeply felt or else they consider these rites quite empty. In their search for fuller external expressions of unity and love, the younger generation also reach out to help others. For instance, among young Christians there is an increasing sympathy for others such as the poor, the colored, the disadvantaged, the weak, and all people in need. These trends produce increased involvement in Christian social actions which is good in itself and which oftentimes furthers the unity so needed in today's world.

The young should be gently encouraged, on the other hand, to acquire an intimate sense of their personal union with Christ Himself, and through Him with one another. Extreme humanism by itself can hardly last when the initial fires of emotional enthusiasm wane. Human fellowship can be deeply rewarding, yet hurtfully disappointing. But when mutual love is founded on a real union with Christ, young people should be allowed to enjoy the deep and enriching experiences of meaningful love and friendship. The world needs love, and the present generation has much of it to give. May Christ bless them in their search for deeper love, for stronger unity, and for more lasting peace in the new times ahead!

Because of the Church's divine origin, long experience, and world-wide extension, she may well be the best suited to help bring unity from among the divergent nations, cultures, movements, philosophies and theologies of modern mankind. The Mystical Body of Christ, the Church, is the only human-divine organism which has long experienced the pains of growth such as the world is experiencing in current times. Consequently, the Church's efforts to assist mankind toward greater unity is most worthy of serious consideration.

During His life on earth, and especially near the time of His redemptive death, Christ pleaded — as He does through the Church today — for the unity of all peoples. His followers are asked to lead the way toward this ecumenical unity (Chapter IX). Christ's death, resurrection, ascension, and His sending of the Holy Spirit continue to produce their sanctifying results in men's lives today. By Christ's active presence in the world and man's participation in liturgical rites, the effects of His paschal mystery become more alive and effective through the sacred liturgy (Chapter X). The relevance of ecumenism and the liturgy for our times can scarcely be estimated, since their power and worth for uniting people in Christ reach to the Father of all mankind.

Chapter IX

CHRIST'S DEATH—PLEA FOR UNITY

Among His People Everywhere

Throughout His life on earth and especially during His sacred passion-time, our Lord pleaded for unity among His followers. He even compared such unity to that which He Himself enjoys with the Father. The epitome of Christianity is contained in the unifying love of God's children for one another and for the same heavenly Father. This unity has, indeed, become a modern-day imperative, for the alternative is division, and as a consequence the splintering of the Christian faith and its unitive influence in the world.

The extension of true brotherly love does not require truth to reconcile itself with falsehood, or principles to yield to expediency. Such love rather prescinds from error in a gracious respect for other persons and it invites dialogue in the face of differences. While complete unity among men will certainly not be achieved until the final resurrection, nevertheless, every effort should be made toward the best possible unification of mankind. Christians must lead the way in the movement toward unity, so essential in modern times and so blessed by Christ.

Religious convictions contain the most sensitive issues regarding the excitement of the emotions and consequent contention with others. However, disunity among Christians disrupts the household of Christ, confuses the wavering, and scandalizes the non-believer. It also disgusts young people who understandably become disillusioned by the bootless and fruitless arguments they see taking place among their elder Christian brethren.

Although the movement toward Christian unity derives from inner sources, such as the will of Christ, the fact remains that people today are weary of divisions and contentions and they look to religion to lead the way toward the unification of mankind. When so many opposing ideologies, cultures, and economic and political systems are dividing humanity, many people rightly expect religion to supply the cohesive force for the unity and solidarity of the world. If Christians do not become more united among themselves and with other God-respecting people, then the secularistic forces in the world may further lose respect for all organized religions. In the name of God His people must make every effort to become more united both as a sign to the world of the common fatherhood of God and as a force for the stability and security of humanity.

Re-echoing the voice of the Master, the Council gives high priority to the fostering of Christian unity (Section 1). In practical terms, the conciliar passages outline the requirements for the advancement of this unity among the Christian denominations (Section 2). It should not be overlooked that the various Christian rites, in union with the See of Peter, share fully in all benefits of the faith with the larger Latin rite (Section 3). In addition, greater union must be achieved among what are designated as Churches not in full union with the Catholic Church.

Since Christ has set the unity of His followers as the outstanding sign of their interior charity, the various Christian denominations stand somewhat embarrassed before the world until they become more united in Him. It is not for Christian soldiers to divide the Church of Christ like a garment. Closer Christian unity can be achieved when deeper appreciation of its necessity results in greater unison of mind and heart and good works among all the followers of Christ.

1. THE FOSTERING OF CHRISTIAN UNITY, OR ECUMENISM

A. Christianity Calls For Unity Among the Followers of Christ

Christ's gospel-message delineates the principles of truth, justice and love for fostering unity among His followers. Without these bases, Christian promotion of unity would have little prospect of success. Of course the unifying processes among Christians could not justifiably exact repudiation of doctrine. Rather they call for a tolerance of differences and a true respect for persons with differing beliefs.

All followers of Christ must show that good-will which brings people together through the cohesive force of love, a chief facet of which is tolerance. The call for unity among Christians contains the essential notes of change of heart, of openness of mind, and of human respect for others. Ecumenism moves into action through honest self-appraisal; it is furthered by open dialogue; it reaches fruition in trust and love, and the mutual benefits these bestow. Catholics, in particular, are asked to lead the way to friendly dialogue with others who as brothers share in the same sources of grace and truth entrusted to the Catholic Church. Consequently, the staunch Catholic-Christian should, prudently and humbly, be the first to understand and befriend others. The Holy Spirit prompts all to seek unity, but especially those who profess their belief in Christ.

220. Reviewing Some Basic Circumstances for Unity among Christians

Promoting the restoration of unity among all Christians is one of the chief concerns of the Second Sacred Ecumenical Synod of the Vatican. The Church established by Christ the Lord is, indeed, one and unique. Yet many Christian communions present themselves to men as the true heritage of Jesus Christ. To be sure, all proclaim themselves to be disciples of the Lord, but their convictions clash and their paths diverge, as though Christ Himself were divided (cf. 1 Cor. 1:13). Without doubt, this discord openly contradicts the will of Christ, provides a stumbling block to the world, and inflicts damage on the most holy cause of proclaiming the good news to every creature.

Nevertheless, the Lord of Ages wisely and patiently follows out the plan of His grace on behalf of us sinners. In recent times He has begun to bestow more generously upon divided Christians remorse over their divisions and a longing for unity. *(Ecumenism, No.1)*

221. The Common Impulse for Unity in Christ

Everywhere, large numbers have felt the impulse of this grace, and among our separated brethren also there increases from day to day a movement, fostered by the grace of the Holy Spirit, for the restoration of unity among all Christians. Taking part in this movement, which is called ecumenical, are those who invoke the Triune God and confess Jesus as Lord and Savior. They join in not merely as individuals but also as members of the corporate groups in which they have heard the gospel, and which each regards as his Church and, indeed, God's. And yet, almost everyone, though in different ways, longs that there may be one visible Church of God, a Church truly universal and sent forth to the whole world that the world may be converted to the gospel and so be saved, to the glory of God.

This sacred Synod, therefore, gladly notes all these factors. It has already declared its teaching on the Church, and now, moved by a desire for the restoration of unity among all the followers of Christ, it wishes to set before all Catholics certain helps, pathways, and methods by which they too can respond to this divine summons and grace. *(Ecumenism, No.1)*

222. Love Is the Basis for Unity in Christ

What has revealed the love of God among us is that the only-begotten Son of God has been sent by the Father into the world, so that, being made man, the Son might by His redemption of the entire human race give new life to it and unify it (cf. 1 Jn. 4:9; Col. 1:18-20; Jn. 11:52). Before offering Himself up as a spotless victim upon the altar of the cross, He prayed to His Father for those who believe: "That all may be one even as thou, Father, in me, and I in thee; that they also may be one in us, that the world may believe that thou hast sent me" (Jn. 17:21). In His Church He instituted the wonderful sacrament of the Eucharist by which the unity of the Church is both signified and brought about. He gave His followers a new commandment of mutual love (cf. Jn. 13:34), and promised the Spirit, their Advocate (cf. Jn. 16:7), who, as Lord and life-giver, would abide with them forever. *(Ecumenism, No.2)*

223. Christ's Gospel Teachings Call for Unity in Him

It is through the faithful preaching of the gospel by the apostles and their successors — the bishops with Peter's successor at their head — through their administration of the sacraments, and through their loving exercise of authority, that Jesus Christ wishes His people to increase under the influence of the Holy Spirit. Thereby too, He perfects His people's fellowship in unity: in the confession of one faith, in the common celebration of divine worship, and in the fraternal harmony of the family of God.

The Church, then, God's only flock, like a standard lifted high for the nations to see (cf. Is. 11:10-12), ministers the gospel of peace to all mankind (cf. Eph. 2:17-18, in conjunction with Mk.

16:15), as she makes her pilgrim way in hope toward her goal, the fatherland above (cf. 1 Pet. 1:3-9).

This is the sacred mystery of the unity of the Church, in Christ and through Christ, with the Holy Spirit energizing a variety of functions. The highest exemplar and source of this mystery is the unity, in the Trinity of Persons, of one God, the Father and the Son in the Holy Spirit. *(Ecumenism, No.2)*

224. Reviewing the History of Christianity Toward Unity

From her very beginnings there arose in this one and only Church of God certain rifts (cf. 1 Cor. 11:18-19; Gal. 1:6-9; 1 Jn. 2:18-19), which the apostle strongly censures as damnable (cf. 1 Cor. 1:11 ff.; 11:22). But in subsequent centuries more widespread disagreements appeared and quite large Communities became separated from full communion with the Catholic Church – developments for which, at times, men of both sides were to blame. However, one cannot impute the sin of separation to those who at present are born into these Communities and are instilled therein with Christ's faith. The Catholic Church accepts them with respect and affection as brothers. For men who believe in Christ and have been properly baptized are brought into a certain, though imperfect, communion with the Catholic Church. Undoubtedly, the differences that exist in varying degrees between them and the Catholic Church – whether in doctrine and sometimes in discipline, or concerning the structure of the Church – do indeed create many and sometimes serious obstacles to full ecclesiastical communion. These the ecumenical movement is striving to overcome. Nevertheless, all those justified by faith through baptism are incorporated into Christ. They therefore have a right to be honored by the title of Christian, and are properly regarded as brothers in the Lord by the sons of the Catholic Church. *(Ecumenism, No.3)*

225. The Many Elements of Agreement among Christian Churches

Moreover some, even very many, of the most significant elements of endowments which together go to build up and give life to the Church herself can exist outside the visible boundaries of the Catholic Church: the written word of God; the life of grace; faith, hope, and charity, along with other interior gifts of the Holy Spirit and visible elements. All of these, which come from Christ and lead back to Him, belong by right to the one Church of Christ.

The brethren divided from us also carry out many of the sacred actions of the Christian religion. Undoubtedly, in ways that vary according to the condition of each Church or Community, these actions can truly engender a life of grace, and can be rightly described as capable of providing access to the community of salvation.

It follows that these separated Churches and Communities, though we believe they suffer from defects already mentioned, have by no means been deprived of significance and importance in the mystery of salvation. For the Spirit of Christ has not refrained from using them as means of salvation which derive their efficacy from the very fullness of grace and truth entrusted to the Catholic Church. *(Ecumenism, No.3)*

B. Conditions in the World
Require the Unity of Mankind

Christianity contains the inner dynamism from the Holy Spirit which can greatly assist human society toward solidarity of mind, heart, interest, and effort for improving the human condition in modern circumstances. Man's personal fulfillment and social nature require the security and stability resulting from community of interest and concern for one another.

Realizing these truths concerning human nature and the human condition in the world today, the Christian community must live its way of life by striving to be more strongly bound together itself. This will assist mankind to share in the beneficent effects of unity regardless of cultural, racial, political, economic, social or even religious differences and affiliations.

226. Man's Social Nature Impels toward Unity

Man's social nature makes it evident that the progress of the human person and the advance of society itself hinge on each other. For the beginning, the subject and the goal of all social institutions is and must be the human person, which for its part and by its very nature stands completely in need of social life. This social life is not something added on to man. Hence, through his dealings with others, through reciprocal duties, and through fraternal dialogue he develops all his gifts and is able to rise to his destiny.

Among those social ties which man needs for his development

some, like the family and political community, relate with greater immediacy to his innermost nature. Others originate rather from his free decision. In our era, for various reasons, reciprocal ties and mutual dependencies increase day by day and give rise to a variety of associations and organizations, both public and private. This development, which is called socialization, while certainly not without its dangers, brings with it many advantages with respect to consolidating and increasing the qualities of the human person, and safeguarding his rights. *(World, No.25)*

227. The Human Family Is Aided toward Unity by Christ and the Church

The union of the human family is greatly fortified and fulfilled by the unity, founded on Christ, of the family of God's sons.

Christ, to be sure, gave His Church no proper mission in the political, economic, or social order. The purpose which He set before her is a religious one. But out of this religious mission itself come a function, a light, and an energy which can serve to structure and consolidate the human community according to the divine law. As a matter of fact, when circumstances of time and place create the need, she can and indeed should initiate activities on behalf of all men. This is particularly true of activities designed for the needy, such as the works of mercy and similar undertakings.

The Church further recognizes that worthy elements are found in today's social movements, especially an evolution toward unity, a process of wholesome socialization and of association in civic and economic realms. For the promotion of unity belongs to the innermost nature of the Church, since she is, "by her relationship with Christ, both a sacramental sign and an instrument of intimate union with God, and of the unity of all mankind." *(World, No.42)*

228. The Church Unifies People of Various Cultures

Thus she shows the world that an authentic union, social and external, results from a union of minds and hearts, namely, from that faith and charity by which her own unity is unbreakably rooted in the Holy Spirit. For the force which the Church can inject into the modern society of man consists in that faith and charity put into vital practice, not in any external dominion exercised by merely human means.

Moreover, in virtue of her mission and nature, she is bound to no particular form of human culture, nor to any political, economic, or social system. Hence the Church by her very universality can be a very close bond between diverse human communities and nations, provided these trust her and truly acknowledge her right to true freedom in fulfilling her mission. For this reason, the Church admonishes her own sons, but also humanity as a whole, to overcome all strife between nations and races in this family spirit of God's children, and in the same way, to give internal strength to human associations which are just. *(World, No.42)*

C. Some Guidelines for True Christian Unity

Catholics, especially, are offered some pointed guidelines with respect to achieving a balanced effort toward unity with their Christian brethren. The first is prudence of action lest, with a false conciliatory attitude, rash zealots may arrive at ecumenical meetings with little to contribute. Specifically, Catholics should know their doctrine accurately, live it sincerely, and present it clearly. Also, genuine self-renewal in the light of the Council's guidelines is certainly the best means for fostering Christian unity with others.

Open communication among all followers of Christ shows forth one of the deepest desires of the Catholic Church in modern times. To this end, newer formulations of traditional and consistent doctrine must be worked out in terms which are intelligible to non-Catholics. While preserving unity in essentials, Catholics are reminded by the conciliar passages that a proper freedom in the various forms of the spiritual life and of discipline belongs by right to the universal Church. The authorized variety of liturgical rites and even the theological elaborations of revealed truths are not to become stifled or stilted. The dynamic growth of the living organism, which is the Church, must be allowed to appeal openly to contemporary man in language and images he can easily understand and embrace.

229. Implications of the Ecumenical Movement for Christians

The "ecumenical movement" means those activities and enterprises which, according to various needs of the Church and opportune occasions, are started and organized for the fostering of unity among Christians. These are: first, every effort to eliminate words, judgments, and actions which do not respond to the condition of separated brethren with truth and fairness and so make mutual relations between them more difficult; then, "dialogue" between competent experts from different Churches and Communities. In their meetings, which are organized in a religious spirit, each explains the teaching of his Communion in greater depth and brings out clearly its distinctive features. Through such dialogue, everyone gains a truer knowledge and more just appreciation of the teaching and religious life of both Communions. In addition, these Communions cooperate more closely in whatever projects a Christian conscience demands for the common good. They also come together for common prayer, where this is permitted. Finally, all are led to examine their own faithfulness to Christ's will for the Church and, wherever necessary, undertake with vigor the task of renewal and reform. *(Ecumenism, No.4)*

230. Catholic Guidelines for Christian Unity

When such actions are carried out by the Catholic faithful with prudence, patience, and the vigilance of their spiritual shepherds, they contribute to the blessings of justice and truth, of concord and collaboration, as well as of the spirit of brotherly love and unity. The result will be that, little by little, as the obstacles to perfect ecclesiastical communion are overcome, all Christians will be gathered, in a common celebration of the Eucharist, into that unity of the one and only Church which Christ bestowed on His Church from the beginning. This unity, we believe, dwells in the Catholic Church as something she can never lose, and we hope that it will continue to increase until the end of time.

However, it is evident that the work of preparing and reconciling those individuals who wish for full Catholic communion is of its nature distinct from ecumenical action. But there is no opposition between the two, since both proceed from the wondrous providence of God.

In ecumenical work, Catholics must assuredly be concerned for their separated brethren, praying for them, keeping them informed about the Church, making the first approaches towards them. But their primary duty is to make an honest and careful appraisal of whatever needs to be renewed and achieved in the Catholic household itself, in order that its life may bear witness more loyally and luminously to the teachings and ordinances which have been handed down from Christ through the apostles. *(Ecumenism, No.4)*

202 EXPLORING VATICAN II

231. Catholic Unity of Belief Amid Variety of Structures

While preserving unity in essentials, let all members of the Church, according to the office entrusted to each, preserve a proper freedom in the various forms of spiritual life and discipline, in the variety of liturgical rites, and even in the theological elaborations of revealed truth. In all things let charity be exercised. If the faithful are true to this course of action, they will be giving ever richer expression to the authentic catholicity of the Church, and, at the same time, to her apostolicity.

On the other hand, Catholics must joyfully acknowledge and esteem the truly Christian endowments from our common heritage which are to be found among our separated brethren. It is right and salutary to recognize the riches of Christ and virtuous works in the lives of others who are bearing witness to Christ, sometimes even to the shedding of their blood. For God is always wonderful in His works and worthy of admiration. *(Ecumenism, No.4)*

232. Removing Divisions Which Violate Christ's Teachings and Disrupt Unity

Nor should we forget that what ever is wrought by the grace of the Holy Spirit in the hearts of our separated brethren can contribute to our own edification. Whatever is truly Christian never conflicts with the genuine interests of the faith; indeed, it can always result in a more ample realization of the very mystery of Christ and the Church.

Nevertheless, the divisions among Christians prevent the Church from effecting the fullness of catholicity proper to her in those of her sons who, though joined to her by baptism, are yet separated from full communion with her. Furthermore, the Church herself finds it more difficult to express in actual life her full catholicity in all its aspects.

This sacred Synod is gratified to note that participation by the Catholic faithful in ecumenical work is growing daily. It commends this work to bishops everywhere in the world for their skillful promotion and prudent guidance. *(Ecumenism, No.4)*

233. The Unity of Christians Aids the Spread of Christianity

Before the whole world, let all Christians profess their faith in God, one and three, in the incarnate Son of God, our Redeemer and

Lord. United in their efforts, and with mutual respect, let them bear witness to our common hope, which does not play us false. Since in our times cooperation in social matters is very widely practiced, all men without exception are summoned to united effort. Those who believe in God have a stronger summons, but the strongest claims are laid on Christians, since they have been sealed with the name of Christ. *(Ecumenism, No.12)*

234. Cooperation among Christian Churches Helps Mankind

Cooperation among all Christians vividly expresses that bond which already unites them, and it sets in clearer relief the features of Christ the Servant. Such cooperation, which has already begun in many countries, should be ever increasingly developed, particularly in regions where a social and technical evolution is taking place. It should contribute to a just appreciation of the dignity of the human person, the promotion of the blessings of peace, the application of gospel principles to social life. and the advancement of the arts and sciences in a Christian spirit. Christians should also work together in the use of every possible means to relieve the afflictions of our times, such as famine and natural disasters, illiteracy and poverty, lack of housing, and the unequal distribution of wealth. Through such cooperation, all believers in Christ are able to learn easily how they can understand each other better and esteem each other more, and how the road to the unity of Christians may be made smooth. *(Ecumenism, No.12)*

2. REQUIREMENTS FOR THE ADVANCEMENT OF CHRISTIAN UNITY

A. Acknowledging Mutual Rights, Agreements, and Differences

The true and beautiful elements in any religion should always be respected by Christians. So too, the differences among the various denominations of Christianity deserve careful consideration and should be accorded appropriate respect. Repeatedly, Catholics are asked to know their faith well and learn to explain it in terms readily understandable by those of different religious, cultural or ethnical backgrounds.

Admittedly, some deep-seated, complex differences have long existed among the various Christian communities. Some of these divergent views involve very serious matters pertaining even to the interpretation of revealed truth and its application to the moral order. Denial of the existence of religious differences would be grossly unrealistic, as well as posing an obstacle to the ultimate solution of these difficulties.

In addition to the mere desire for Christian unity, prayer and concerted effort are required to climb the steep ladder of ecumenism. Step by step, prejudices can be removed, misunderstandings resolved, and open dialogue established in the ascent toward unity. As communication becomes clearer, mutual trust and respect should bring out more sharply the distinctive mark on the Christian seal — charity. Where respect, trust and charity exist, differences can be better understood with greater possibility of their being resolved.

235. The Expression of Catholic Doctrine Should Not Obstruct Dialogue

The manner and order in which Catholic belief is expressed should in no way become an obstacle to dialogue with our brethren. It is, of course, essential that doctrine be clearly presented in its entirety. Nothing is so foreign to the spirit of ecumenism as a false conciliatory approach which harms the purity of Catholic doctrine and obscures its assured genuine meaning.

At the same time, Catholic belief needs to be explained more profoundly and precisely, in ways and in terminology which our separated brethren too can really understand.

Furthermore, Catholic theologians engaged in ecumenical dialogue, while standing fast by the teaching of the Church and searching together with separated brethren into the divine mysteries, should act with love for truth, with charity, and with humility. When comparing doctrines, they should remember that in Catholic teaching there exists an order or "hierarchy" of truths, since they vary in their relationship to the foundation of the Christian faith. Thus the way will be opened for this kind of fraternal rivalry to incite all to a deeper realization and a clearer expression of the unfathomable riches of Christ (cf. Eph. 3:8). *(Ecumenism, No.11)*

236. Unity Among Christians Contains Some Thorny Difficulties

Although the ecumenical movement and the desire for reconciliation with the Catholic Church have not yet grown universally strong, it is our hope that the ecumenical spirit and mutual esteem will gradually increase among all men.

At the same time, however, one should recognize that between these Churches and Communities on the one hand, and the Catholic Church on the other, there are very weighty differences not only of a historical, sociological, psychological, and cultural nature, but especially in the interpretation of revealed truth. That ecumenical dialogue may be more easily undertaken despite these differences, we desire to propose in what follows some considerations which can and ought to serve as a basis and motivation for such dialogue. *(Ecumenism, No.19)*

237. The Search for Mutual Agreement Among Christian Churches

Our thoughts are concerned first of all with those Christians who openly confess Jesus Christ as God and Lord and as the sole Mediator between God and man unto the glory of the one God, Father, Son, and Holy Spirit. We are indeed aware that among them views are held considerably different from the doctrine of the Catholic Church even concerning Christ, God's Word made flesh, and the work of redemption, and thus concerning the mystery and ministry of the Church and the role of Mary in the work of salvation. But we rejoice to see our separated brethren looking to Christ as the source and center of ecclesiastical communion. Inspired by longing for union with Christ, they feel compelled to search for unity ever more ardently, and to bear witness to their faith among all the peoples of the earth. *(Ecumenism, No.20)*

238. Differences on Doctrinal and Moral Questions among Christian Churches

And if in moral matters there are many Christians who do not always understand the gospel in the same way as Catholics, and do not admit the same solutions for the more difficult problems of modern society, nevertheless they share our desire to cling to Christ's word as the source of Christian virtue and to obey the apostolic command: "Whatever you do in word or in work, do all in the name of the Lord Jesus, giving thanks to God the Father through him" (Col. 3:17). Hence, the ecumenical dialogue could start with discussions concerning the application of the gospel to moral questions. *(Ecumenism, No.23)*

239. Striving to Reconcile Differences Among Christians

So, after this brief exposition of the circumstances within which ecumenical activity has to operate and of the principles by which it would be guided, we confidently look to the future. This most sacred Synod urges the faithful to abstain from any superficiality or imprudent zeal, for these can cause harm to true progress towards unity. Their ecumenical activity must not be other than fully and sincerely Catholic, that is, loyal to the truth we have received from the apostles and the Fathers, and in harmony with the faith which the Catholic Church has always professed, and at the same time tending toward that fullness with which our Lord wants His body to be endowed in the course of time.

This most sacred Synod urgently desires that the initiatives of the sons of the Catholic Church joined with those of the separated brethren, go forward without obstructing the ways of divine Providence and without prejudging the future inspiration of the Holy Spirit. Further, this Synod declares its realization that the holy task of reconciling all Christians in the unity of the one and only Church of Christ transcends human energies and abilities. It therefore places its hope entirely in the prayer of Christ for the Church, in the love of the Father for us, and in the power of the Holy Spirit. "And hope does not disappoint, because the charity of God is poured forth in our hearts by the Holy Spirit who has been given to us" (Rom. 5:5). *(Ecumenism, No.24)*

B. Promoting Practices of Ecumenism Among Christians

The practical applications of ecumenism must start within the souls of Christians. Only in deep faith, love and service of God the Father, Son, and Holy Spirit can the foundations of Christian unity stand firm. The practices of ecumenism must have clear motives and solid bases for various actions such as common liturgical celebrations. Unless a sound foundation of faith upholds common worship, it could hardly be considered more than a fellowship gathering, not genuine liturgical worship in oneness of belief. Certainly, fellowship and friendship provide excellent preambles to genuine ecumenism as do social events and collaboration in good works.

On the other hand, the ecumenical movement is far too precious and worthwhile to allow dilution through unthoughtful or hasty happenings such as integrated services which can be devoid of basic meaning when not substantiated by common belief. Certainly there could be no substantial progress toward true ecumenism through watering down of basic and cherished religious beliefs. Such a false conciliatory attitude would be disastrous to Christianity, insulting to the gospel of Christ, and a betrayal of conscience. Ecumenism is too serious and important a movement of the Spirit and of the Church to allow for a sham substitute for the faith.

The Catholic should be certain and proud of his beliefs as he engages in discussion of dogmas, while respecting, in charity, the rights of others to believe otherwise. Most likely those who are strong and knowledgeable in their faith will best advance the great cause of true unity among Christians. Certainly, the goodwilled and prudent efforts toward genuine unity among Christians will earn the blessing of the Good Shepherd who desires oneness and charity within His flock.

240. Within the Universal Church, Particular Churches Hold a Rightful Place

Within the Church particular Churches hold a rightful place. These Churches retain their own traditions without in any way lessening the primacy of the Chair of Peter. This Chair presides over the whole assembly of charity and protects legitimate differences, while at the same time it sees that such differences do not hinder unity but rather contribute toward it. Finally, between all the parts of the Church there remains a bond of close communion with respect to spiritual riches, apostolic workers, and temporal re - sources. For the members of the People of God are called to share these goods, and to each of the Churches the words of the Apostle apply: "According to the gift that each has received, administer it to one another as good stewards of the manifold grace of God" (1 Pet. 4:10).

All men are called to be part of this catholic unity of the People of God, a unity which is harbinger of the universal peace it promotes. And there belong to it or are related to it in various ways, the Catholic faithful as well as all who believe in Christ, and indeed the whole of mankind. For all men are called to salvation by the grace of God. *(Church, No.13)*

241. Widespread Interest in Christian Unity

Concern for restoring unity pertains to the whole Church, faithful and clergy alike. It extends to everyone, according to the potential of each, whether it be exercised in daily Christian living or in theological and historical studies. This very concern already reveals to some extent the bond of brotherhood existing among all Christians, and it leads toward that full and perfect unity which God lovingly desires. *(Ecumenism, No.5)*

242. True Ecumenism Begins with Individual Renewal

There can be no ecumenism worthy of the name without a change of heart. For it is from newness of attitudes (cf. Eph. 4:23), from self-denial and unstinted love, that yearnings for unity take their rise and grow toward maturity. We should therefore pray to the divine Spirit for the grace to be genuinely self-denying, humble, gentle in the service of others, and to have an attitude of brotherly generosity toward them. The Apostle of the Gentiles says: "I, therefore, the prisoner in the Lord, exhort you to walk in a manner worthy of the calling with which you were called, with all humility and meekness, with patience, bearing with one another in love, careful to preserve the unity of the Spirit in the bond of peace" (Eph. 4:1-3). This exhortation applies especially to those who have been raised to sacred orders so that the mission of Christ may be carried on. He came among us "not to be served but to serve" (Mt. 20:28).

St. John has testified: "If we say that we have not sinned, we make him a liar, and his word is not in us" (1 Jn. 1:10). This holds good for sins against unity. Thus, in humble prayer, we beg pardon of God and of our separated brethren, just as we forgive those who trespass against us.

Let all Christ's faithful remember that the more purely they strive to live according to the gospel, the more they are fostering and even practicing Christian unity. For they can achieve depth and ease in strengthening mutual brotherhood to the degree that they enjoy profound communion with the Father, the Word, and the Spirit. *(Ecumenism, No.7)*

243. Common Prayer as an Aid to Achieving Christian Unity

This change of heart and holiness of life, along with public and private prayer for the unity of Christians, should be regarded as the soul of the whole ecumenical movement, and can rightly be called "spiritual ecumenism."

Catholics already have a custom of uniting frequently in that prayer for the unity of the Church with which the Savior Himself, on the eve of His death, appealed so fervently to His Father: "That all may be one" (Jn. 17:21).

In certain special circumstances, such as in prayer services "for unity" and during ecumenical gatherings, it is allowable, indeed desirable, that Catholics should join in prayer with their separated brethren. Such prayers in common are certainly a very effective means of petitioning for the grace of unity, and they are a genuine expression of the ties which even now bind Catholics to their separated brethren. "For where two or three are gathered together for my sake, there am I in the midst of them" (Mt. 18:20). *(Ecumenism, No.8)*

244. Dialogue with Our Separated Brethren Is Built on Understanding

We must come to understand the outlook of our separated brethren. Study is absolutely required for this, and should be pursued with fidelity to truth and in a spirit of good will. When they are properly prepared for this study, Catholics need to acquire a more adequate understanding of the distinctive doctrines of our separated brethren, as well as of their own history, spiritual and liturgical life, their religious psychology and cultural background. Of great value for this purpose are meetings between the two sides, especially for discussion of theological problems, where each can deal with the other on an equal footing. Such meetings require that those who take part in them under authoritative guidance be truly competent. From dialogue of this sort will emerge still more clearly what the true posture of the Catholic Church is. In this way, too, we will better understand the attitude of our separated brethren and more aptly present our own belief. *(Ecumenism, No.9)*

245. Charity among Catholic Clergy and Protestant Leaders

Instruction in sacred theology and other branches of knowledge, especially those of a historical nature, must also be presented from an ecumenical point of view, so that at every point they may more accurately correspond with the facts of the case.

For it is highly important that future bishops and priests should have mastered a theology carefully worked out in this way and not polemically, especially in what concerns the relations of separated brethren with the Catholic Church. For it is upon the formation which priests receive that the necessary instruction and spiritual formation of the faithful and of religious depend so very greatly.

Moreover, Catholics engaged in missionary work, in the same territories as other Christians, ought to know, particularly in these times, the problems and the benefits which affect their apostolate because of the ecumenical movement. *(Ecumenism, No.10)*

3. TOWARD STRONGER UNITY OF EASTERN AND WESTERN CHURCHES IN CHRIST

A. Respecting the Various Eastern and Western Rites in the Church

Unity among the followers of Christ rises above nationality, race, color and cultural backgrounds. Indeed, legitimate diversity of traditions, customs and even varying forms of administration and liturgical rites receive encouragement. Unity of faith amid diversity of customs distinguishes the universal Catholic Church. All legitimate churches or rites within the Catholic fold, regardless of comparative numbers and diversity of customs, deserve equal honor and enjoy equal rights. No East-West or North-South divisions belong in the Catholic community.

Those Christians united with the successor of St. Peter, who serves as the principle of unity in the Catholic Apostolic Church, share the common heritage of the deposit of faith. They also partake of all means for sanctification in Christ Jesus. Ecclesiastical regulations and customs, as well as liturgical variations throughout the world, serve all the more to disclose the universality of the Church founded by Christ for every class and nation of men. United in Christ and directed by the Holy Spirit, a variety of Churches or rites within the one Church, displays a wonderful diversity of means toward a unity of purpose among Christ's people. For instance, supposing in the future that a Pope was elected from a smaller rite of the Roman Catholic Church, this should in no way lessen the prestige of the largest or Latin rite in the universal Church since all rites united with the See of Peter are equal in the faith.

Since the beginning of Christianity there has been legitimate diversity of expression of one and the same faith. Unity of belief does not demand invariable or uniform means for its transmission either in formulation of orthodox doctrine or in manner of liturgical usage, provided the faith itself in its basic application remains consistently one and the same throughout the world. The universal mission of the Church thrives on variety of practice within the unity of genuine doctrinal belief. This is so because the Church of Christ readily adapts herself to every true culture, civilization and tradition.

246. Various Rites within the Catholic Church

That Church, Holy and Catholic, which is the Mystical Body of Christ, is made up of the faithful who are organically united in the Holy Spirit through the same faith, the same sacraments, and the same government and who, combining into various groups held together by a hierarchy, form separate Churches or rites. Between these, there flourishes such an admirable brotherhood that this variety within the Church in no way harms her unity, but rather manifests it. For it is the mind of the Catholic Church that each individual Church or rite retain its traditions whole and entire, while adjusting its way of life to the various needs of time and place. *(Easterns, No.2)*

247. The Sovereign Pontiff, Principle of Unity

Such individual Churches, whether of the East or of the West, although they differ somewhat among themselves in what are called rites (that is, in liturgy, ecclesiastical discipline, and spiritual heritage) are, nevertheless, equally entrusted to the pastoral guidance of the Roman Pontiff, the divinely appointed successor of St. Peter in supreme governance over the universal Church. They are consequently of equal dignity, so that none of them is superior to the others by reason of rite. They enjoy the same rights and are under the same obligations, even with respect to preaching the gospel to the whole world (cf. Mk. 16:15) under the guidance of the Roman Pontiff. *(Easterns, No.3)*

248. Eastern and Western Churches Uniting in Christ

Therefore, attention should everywhere be given to the preservation and growth of each individual Church. For this purpose, parishes and a special hierarchy should be established for each where the spiritual good of the faithful so demands. The Ordinaries of the various individual Churches which have jurisdiction in the same territory should, by taking common counsel in regular meetings, strive to promote unity of action. Through common endeavor let them sustain common tasks, the better to further the good of religion and the more effectively to safeguard clerical discipline.

All clerics and those aspiring to sacred orders should be well instructed in various rites and especially in the principles which are involved in interritual questions. As part of their catechetical education, the laity, too, should be taught about these rites and their rules.

Finally, each and every Catholic, as also the baptized number of every non-Catholic Church or community who enters into the fullness of Catholic communion, should everywhere retain his proper rite, cherish it, and observe it to the best of his ability. This rule does not deny the right whereby persons, communities, or areas may in special cases have recourse to the Apostolic See, which, as the supreme judge of interchurch relations, will directly or through other authorities meet the needs of the occasion in an ecumenical spirit and issue opportune directives, decrees, or rescripts. *(Easterns, No.4)*

249. The Age-old Traditions of the Eastern Churches

History, tradition, and numerous ecclesiastical institutions manifest luminously how much the universal Church is indebted to the Eastern Churches. This sacred Synod, therefore, not only honors this ecclesiastical and spiritual heritage with merited esteem and rightful praise, but also unhesitatingly looks upon it as the heritage of Christ's universal Church. For this reason, it solemnly declares that the Churches of the East, as much as those of the West, fully enjoy the right, and are in duty bound, to rule themselves. Each should do so according to its proper and individual procedures, inasmuch as practices sanctioned by a noble antiquity harmonize better with the customs of the faithful and are seen as more likely to foster the good of souls. *(Easterns, No.5)*

250. Sources of Unity in the Western and Eastern Churches

All Eastern rite members should know and be convinced that

they can and should always preserve their lawful liturgical rites and their established way of life, and that these should not be altered except by way of an appropriate and organic development. Easterners themselves should honor all these things with the greatest fidelity. Besides, they should acquire an ever greater knowledge and a more exact use of them. If they have improperly fallen away from them because of circumstances of time or personage, let them take pains to return to their ancestral ways.

Those who, by reason of their office or an apostolic assignment, are in frequent communication with the Eastern Churches or their faithful should, in proportion to the gravity of their task, be carefully trained to know and respect the rites, discipline, doctrine, history, and characteristics of Easterners. Religious societies and associations of the Latin rite working in Eastern countries or among Eastern faithful are earnestly counseled to multiply the success of their apostolic labors by founding houses or even provinces of Eastern rite, as far as this can be done. *(Easterns, No.6)*

B. Advancing Greater Union
   with Separated Churches

The considered policy of the post-Vatican II Church calls for greater tolerance with regard to the various Orthodox Churches which are not in full accord with all tenets of the Roman Catholic Church. The Council calls for closer union with Eastern Churches which respect but do not now submit fully to the jurisdiction of the Bishop of Rome as the Vicar of Christ and the center of unity.

Significantly, the conciliar documents even allow for interparticipation, within limits, between certain liturgies and sacramental practices of some Orthodox Churches and those of the Roman Church.

The Roman Catholic Church humbly acknowledges its belief that it has been entrusted by Christ, the Lord, with the fullness of His revelation. However, members of so-called dissident Churches, not in complete accord with Rome, participate in the graces of the Holy Spirit and share in the blessings of the entire Church of Christ.

251. Maintaining the Integrity of Catholic Doctrine and Unity

Divine Law forbids any common worship *(communicatio in sacris)* which would damage the unity of the Church, or involve formal acceptance of falsehood or the danger of deviation in the

214 EXPLORING VATICAN II

faith, or scandal, or of indifferentism. At the same time, pastoral experience clearly shows that with respect to our Eastern brethren there should and can be taken into consideration various circumstances affecting individuals, wherein the unity of the Church is not jeopardized nor are intolerable risks involved, but in which salvation itself and the spiritual profit of souls are urgently at issue.

Hence, in view of special circumstances of time, place, and personage, the Catholic Church has often adopted and now adopts a milder policy, offering to all the means of salvation and an example of charity among Christians through participation in the sacraments and in other sacred functions and objects. With these considerations in mind, and "lest because of the harshness of our judgment we prove an obstacle to those seeking salvation," and in order to promote closer union with the Eastern Churches separated from us, this sacred Synod lays down the following policy: *(Easterns, No.26)*

252. Validity of Western and Eastern Consecrations

In view of the principles recalled above, Eastern Christians who are separated in good faith from the Catholic Church, if they ask of their own accord and have the right dispositions, may be granted the sacraments of penance, the Eucharist, and the anointing of the sick. Furthermore, Catholics may ask for these same sacraments from those non-Catholic ministers whose Churches possess valid sacraments, as often as necessity or a genuine spiritual benefit recommends such a course of action, and when access to a Catholic priest is physically or morally impossible. *(Easterns, No.27)*

253. Toward Unity in Worship among Eastern and Western Churches

Again, in view of these very same principles, Catholics may for a just cause join with their separated Eastern brethren in sacred functions, things, and places. *(Easterns, No.28)*

254. The Hierarchy Must Guide Practices of Ecumenism

This more lenient policy with regard to common worship involving Catholics and their brethren of the separated Eastern Churches is entrusted to the care and execution of the local Ordinaries so that, by taking counsel among themselves and, if circumstances warrant, after consultation also with the Ordinaries of the separated Churches, they may govern relations between Christians by timely and effective rules and regulations. *(Easterns, No.28)*

Much reflection and care will be required before the full flowering of the foregoing conciliar passages can be nurtured to blossom in the hearts of adherents to the various Churches or forms of Christianity. Before the ideal of unity can be realized, self-effort is required to weed out hidden prejudices and preconceptions which may lie beneath the surface and subtly stunt the growth of unity. The very uprooting of infectious tendencies may require repentance and renewal which seem to be the forerunners of unity among the believers and lovers of Christ and His dynamic Church-community throughout the world.

We must not only desire fervently but also work mightily for this ideal to become an actuality. In this age of over-reliance upon plans and practical procedures and upon the value of the visible and the tangible, let all Christians not fail to call upon the power of prayer to propel unity among us and among all mankind.

Chapter X

CHRIST'S PASCHAL MYSTERY TODAY

Alive in the Liturgy

The Paschal Mystery of our Lord's death and resurrection communicates spiritual life to us through His continual presence, mystical but real, in the liturgical rites of the Church. Over the centuries the sanctifying actions of Christ for His people have been variously named. The term "liturgy" includes all the official public acts of prayer and worship offered by Christ's community in His name. Liturgy embraces all the corporate acts of praise, adoration, petition and supplication accomplished by the Church body. Liturgy also differentiates the grace-bringing actions of the Church's public spiritual works from the prayers and acts of piety done in private.

Hence, when we speak of liturgical celebrations, we refer in one breath to the Eucharistic Sacrifice of the Mass, the special graces of the seven sacraments, the various sacramentals, and all official prayers and sacred rites of the Church. Likewise, the proclaiming of the holy Scriptures is also called the liturgy of the word of God.

Since Christ Himself becomes present and effective in our souls and in our midst through these holy rites, they are eminently sacred. It is precisely as a member of the Catholic Church-community participating in these grace-bringing rites that the individual advances in the Christian life, of which the liturgy is the very heart. Due to Christ's action, the liturgy remains the richest source of sanctification and a pledge of eternal salvation. In these liturgical actions we find the most authentic channels for delivering to men the blessings of Jesus Christ in the lives of His followers.

The spiritual life of Catholics is essentially crystalized in their participation in the liturgical vitality of the Church (Section 1). It is especially in the Mass and the sacraments that the visible is brought to embrace the invisible and life becomes more spiritually enriched since Christ there joins Himself more fully with His people (Section 2). Human beings, responding in love to the action of their Lord, require the enrichment of their liturgical life through appropriate ceremonies which enhance their participation in the liturgy of the Christian community (Section 3).

Our full participation in the liturgical celebrations of the Church constitutes the chief means of our living in the paschal mystery of our risen Savior today. Since Christ is present in the liturgical life of His Church-community at worship, we can do nothing better than to be united with our Lord in sacred liturgical actions, and, thereby, become more closely united with one another. From this unity in Christ Jesus, the Christian community draws its power to be the beacon enlightening the world through Him who is the world's true Light. Like rays from the sun, the power of Christ's death on the cross and His resurrection from the tomb radiate throughout the world.

1. ESSENTIALS FOR EFFECTIVE PARTICIPATION IN LITURGICAL ACTIONS

A. Prerequisites for Deriving Sanctification from Liturgical Participation

Before a person can meaningfully participate in the liturgy he must, assuredly, have religious belief in the liturgical actions being performed. The adequate worship of the Lord consists principally in the giving of one's self in response to God's love for us. The grace and goodness of Christ and the predispositions with which we approach liturgical functions determine their efficacy in our lives.

At the outset it must be recalled that the conciliar documents strongly urge the use of traditional practices for nurturing personal piety. Private prayer and individual virtue must always remain in the Christian spiritual tradition since they are divine injunctions. Consequently, when we consider the important community-worship functions of the liturgy we should not overlook the necessity of private devotional practices and the acquisition of personal virtues.

Throughout the history of the Church various devotional practices emerged, which benefitted the faithful for a period, and then fell into disuse as newer forms of devotion took precedence. Among Catholics in the Western world, visits to the Blessed Sacrament, making spiritual retreats, stations of the cross, novenas, and the rosary have highlighted religious practices of personal piety. In the East, our fellow-Christians chant litanies quite often, they incense their icons or sacred pictures, and they frequently offer at a shrine some drawing, perhaps of a home or of a human heart, as vivid portrayals of their petition of need or their gratitude for graces received. Whatever practices of piety are approved for individual spiritual advancement, they should bear a relationship to the sacred liturgical rites of the universal Church.

Personal sanctity builds up the spiritual vitality of the whole Christian community. In addition to the necessity of private prayer, the place of self-denial must ever be acknowledged as essential for leading a true Christian life. Thus, the effectiveness of liturgical action in a Christian community increases with the personal sanctity of its members.

255. People Need Lively Faith to Participate Fruitfully in the Liturgy

Before men can come to the liturgy they must be called to faith and to conversion: "How then are they to call upon him in whom they have not believed? But how are they to believe him whom they have not heard? And how are they to hear, if no one preaches? And how are men to preach unless they be sent?" (Rom. 10:14-15).

Therefore the Church announces the good tidings of salvation to those who do not believe, so that all men may know the true God and Jesus Christ whom He has sent, and may repent and mend their ways (cf. Jn. 17:3; Lk. 24:27; Acts 2:38). To believers also the Church must ever preach faith and repentance. She must prepare them for the sacraments, teach them to observe all that Christ has commanded (cf. Mt. 28:20), and win them to all the works of charity, piety, and the apostolate. For all these activities make it clear that Christ's faithful, though not of this world, are the light of the world and give glory to the father in the sight of men. (Liturgy, No.9)

256. Personal Prayer and Self-denial Help Us to Profit More from Liturgical Actions

The spiritual life, however, is not confined to participation in the liturgy. The Christian is assuredly called to pray with his brethren, but he must also enter into his chamber to pray to the Father in secret (cf. Mt. 6:6); indeed, according to the teaching of the Apostle Paul, he should pray without ceasing (cf. 1 Th. 5:17). We learn from the same Apostle that we must always carry about in our body the dying of Jesus, so that the life of Jesus too may be made manifest in our bodily frame (cf. 2 Cor. 4:10-11). This is why we ask the Lord in the sacrifice of the Mass that, "receiving the offering of the spiritual victim," He may fashion us for Himself "as an eternal gift." *(Liturgy, No.12)*

B. Full and Active Participation in Liturgical Celebrations

In no phase of the practice of their faith are Catholics more profoundly moved than in the liturgical actions of the Mass, the sacraments and other rites of the Church. Any changes in ceremonies and rites within the liturgy have vast ramifications throughout the liturgical and devotional life of the faithful. However, since active participation is the prime requisite for fruitful liturgical actions, the present or future adaptations of the liturgy have this sanctifying aim in view. Full, active, and knowledgeable participation starts with interior response to Christ's presence in liturgical celebrations. There should be times for song as well as for silence; vocal responses fulfill their function and reverent observance has its place in divine worship.

"Union" summarizes the purpose of the sacred liturgy; union with Christ and thereupon with fellow worshippers. All liturgical celebrations, although they should develop amicable human relationships, transcend the mere increasing of fellowship; they unite Christians first with Christ, then in Him with one-another, and, hopefully, with all mankind.

In addition to being the core of Christian unanimity in faith and charity, the liturgy is an excellent source of religious instruction for the faithful. In the ceremonies of Mass and the sacraments, the holy Scriptures are proclaimed, instruction is imparted, faith is strengthened, and love is increased. Active participation in the sacred religious rites of the Church is the best means for living in the Christian spirit of our risen Savior. It is also a foretaste of sharing with loved ones our future glorification in Christ.

257. Wholehearted Participation of the Faithful Is the Desired Goal in the Liturgy

Mother Church earnestly desires that all the faithful be led to that full, conscious, and active participation in liturgical celebrations which is demanded by the very nature of the liturgy. Such participation by the Christian people as "a chosen race, a royal priesthood, a holy nation, a purchased people" (1 Pet. 2:9; cf. 2:4-5), is their right and duty by reason of their baptism.

In the restoration and promotion of the sacred liturgy, this full and active participation by all the people is the aim to be considered before all else; for it is the primary and indispensable source from which the faithful are to derive the true Christian spirit. *(Liturgy, No.14)*

258. Liturgical Services Are Actions of the Church Community

Liturgical services are not private functions, but are celebrations of the Church, which is the "sacrament of unity," namely, a holy people united and organized under their bishops.

Therefore liturgical services pertain to the whole body of the Church; they manifest it and have effects upon it; but they concern individual members of the Church in different ways, according to the diversity of holy orders, functions, and degrees of participation. *(Liturgy, No.26)*

259. The Faithful Should Participate Knowingly, Actively, Fruitfully

But in order that the sacred liturgy may produce its full effect, it is necessary that the faithful come to it with proper dispositions, that their thoughts match their words, and that they cooperate with divine grace lest they receive it in vain (cf. 2 Cor. 6:1). Pastors of souls must therefore realize that, when the liturgy is celebrated, more is required than the mere observance of the laws governing valid and licit celebration. It is their duty also to ensure that the faithful take part knowingly, actively, and fruitfully. *(Liturgy, No.11)*

260. Fulfilling One's Function in Liturgical Celebrations

By way of promoting active participation, the people should be encouraged to take part by means of acclamations, responses, psalmody, antiphons, and songs, as well as by actions, gestures, and bodily attitudes. And at the proper times all should observe a reverent silence. *(Liturgy, No.30)*

261. Liturgy Primarily Embraces Worship of God and Includes Religious Instruction

Although the sacred liturgy is above all things the worship of the divine Majesty, it likewise contains abundant instruction for the faithful. For in the liturgy God speaks to His people and Christ is still proclaiming His gospel. And the people reply to God both by song and by prayer.

Moreover, the prayers addressed God by the priest who presides over the assembly in the person of Christ are said in the name of the entire holy people as well as of all present. And the visible signs used by the liturgy to signify invisible divine things have been chosen by Christ or the Church. Thus, not only when things are read "which have been written for our instruction" (Rom.15:4), but also when the Church prays or sings or acts, the faith of those taking part is nourished and their minds are raised to God, so that they may offer Him the worship which reason required and more copiously receive His grace. *(Liturgy, No.33)*

C. The Up-Dating of Liturgical Rites to Encourage Fuller Participation

While the sanctifying effects conveyed through the liturgy remain the same, changes in ceremonies become advisable from time to time in order to keep the Church's liturgical rites meaningful in terms of current cultures and needs of people. Consequently, when the wisdom of the Church, in the exercise of competent authority, directs changes and readjustments of sacred rites, the faithful should welcome them as conducive for fostering greater sanctity.

All over the world, until the end of time, the spiritual power of the sacred liturgy will continue to strengthen those who participate in these sanctifying rites. The essential and unchangeable elements within the Church's liturgy will, obviously, remain the same until the heavenly liturgy begins in eternity. The Holy Eucharistic sacrifice and the sacraments can never lose their intrinsic value or power. But rubrical adaptions will, as they have throughout Church history, continue to be made whenever ceremonies need revision for producing more mean-

ingful participation in the liturgical gatherings of Christians. The up-
dating of liturgical rites must take into consideration the various cultural backgrounds, customs, languages, and manners of thinking of
people everywhere. The revisions of liturgical rites, therefore, must
maintain both stability in essentials and variety in the ways in which
Christ's presence can be realized more fully in the liturgical life of the
various Catholic communities throughout the world of today.

262. Holy Rites Should Be More Understood by Those Attending Them

With the passage of time, however, there have crept into the
rites of the sacraments and sacramentals certain features which have
rendered their nature and purpose less clear to the people of today;
and hence to that extent the need arises to adjust certain aspects of
these rites to the requirements of our times. *(Liturgy, No.62)*

263. The Unchangeable Elements Remain When Rubrical Changes Are Made

In order that the Christian people may more securely derive
an abundance of graces from the sacred liturgy, holy Mother Church
desires to undertake with great care a general restoration of the
liturgy itself. For the liturgy is made up of unchangeable elements
divinely instituted, and elements subject to change. The latter not
only may but ought to be changed with the passing of time if
features have by chance crept in which are less harmonious with the
intimate nature of the liturgy, or if existing elements have grown
less functional.

In this restoration, both texts and rites should be drawn up so
that they express more clearly the holy things which they signify.
Christian people, as far as possible, should be able to understand
them with ease and to take part in them fully, actively, and as befits
a community. *(Liturgy, No.21)*

264. Simplicity and Clarity of Liturgical Rites

The rites should be distinguished by a noble simplicity; they
should be short, clear, and unencumbered by useless repetitions;
they should be within the people's powers of comprehension, and
normally should not require much explanation. *(Liturgy, No.34)*

265. Variety in Liturgical Rites as Adapted to the Different Races and Cultures

Even in the liturgy, the Church has no wish to impose a rigid uniformity in matters which do not involve the faith or the good of the whole community. Rather she respects and fosters the spiritual adornments and gifts of the various races and peoples. Anything in their way of life that is not indissolubly bound up with superstition and error she studies with sympathy and, if possible, preserves intact. Sometimes in fact she admits such things into the liturgy itself, as long as they harmonize with its true and authentic spirit.

Provided that the substantial unity of the Roman rite is maintained, the revision of liturgical books should allow for legitimate variations and adaptations to different groups, regions, and peoples, especially in mission lands. Where opportune, the same rule applies to the structuring of rites and the devising of rubrics. *(Liturgy, No.37-38)*

266. Zeal for the Promotion of Liturgy as a Movement of the Holy Spirit

Zeal for the promotion and restoration of the liturgy is rightly held to be a sign of the providential dispositions of God in our time, as a movement of the Holy Spirit in His Church. It is today a distinguishing mark of the Church's life, indeed of the whole tenor of contemporary religious thought and action. *(Liturgy, No.43)*

2. THE BENEFITS AND EFFICACY OF LITURGICAL CELEBRATIONS

A. Christ's Presence Makes Liturgical Celebrations Fruitful

The underlying fact which vitalizes liturgical exercises is Christ's presence in them and His dispensation of grace to us through them. The effects of the paschal mystery of Christ's passion, resurrection, and ascension and of His sending of the Holy Spirit are renewed whenever His people assemble for participation in liturgical celebrations.

There is one priesthood of Christ and all participants in the liturgy, clergy and laity alike, share in our Lord's priestly presence among

His people. The risen Savior dwells and acts in our midst particularly when His people worship together and partake of the sacramental life of the Church.

267. The Holy Sacrifice and The Sacraments Are the Chief Means of Sanctification

Just as Christ was sent by the Father, so also He sent the apostles, filled with the Holy Spirit. This He did so that, by preaching the gospel to every creature (cf. Mk. 16:15), they might proclaim that the Son of God, by His death and resurrection, had freed us from the power of Satan (cf. Acts 26:18) and from death, and brought us into the kingdom of His Father. His purpose was also that they might exercise the work of salvation which they were proclaiming, by means of sacrifice and sacraments, around which the entire liturgical life revolves. *(Liturgy, No.6)*

268. The Effectiveness of Christ's Presence in All liturgical Celebrations

To accomplish so great a work, Christ is always present in His Church, especially in her liturgical celebrations, He is present in the sacrifice of the Mass, not only in the person of His minister, "the same one now offering, through the ministry of priests, who formerly offered himself on the cross," but especially under the Eucharistic species. By His power He is present in the sacraments, so that when a man baptizes it is really Christ Himself who baptizes. He is present in His word, since it is He Himself who speaks when the holy Scriptures are read in the church. He is present, finally, when the Church prays and sings, for He promised: "Where two or three are gathered together for my sake, there am I in the midst of them" (Mt. 18:20).

Christ indeed always associates the Church with Himself in the truly great work of giving perfect praise to God and making men holy. The Church is His dearly beloved Bride who calls to her Lord, and through Him offers worship to the Eternal Father.

Rightly, then, the liturgy is considered as an exercise of the priestly office of Jesus Christ. In the liturgy the sanctification of man is manifested by signs perceptible to the senses, and is effected in a way which is proper to each of these signs; in the liturgy full public worship is performed by the Mystical Body of Jesus Christ, that is, by the Head and His members.

From this it follows that every liturgical celebration, because it is an action of Christ the priest and of His Body the Church, is a sacred action surpassing all others. No other action of the Church can match its claim to efficacy, nor equal the degree of it. *(Liturgy, No. 7)*

269. Liturgical Vitality Is the Highest Activity of the Christian Community

The liturgy is the summit toward which the activity of the Church is directed; at the same time it is the fountain from which all her power flows. For the goal of apostolic works is that all who are made sons of God by faith and baptism should come together to praise God in the midst of His Church, to take part in her sacrifice, and to eat the Lord's supper.

The liturgy in its turn inspires the faithful to become "of one heart in love" when they have tasted to their full of the paschal mysteries; it prays that "they may grasp by deed what they hold by creed." The renewal in the Eucharist of the covenant between the Lord and man draws the faithful into the compelling love of Christ and sets them afire. From the liturgy, therefore, and especially from the Eucharist, as from a fountain, grace is channeled into us; and the sanctification of men in Christ and the glorification of God, to which all other activities of the Church are directed as toward their goal, are most powerfully achieved. *(Liturgy, No. 10)*

270. The Liturgy Implements Christ's Work of Redemption

For it is through the liturgy, especially the divine Eucharistic Sacrifice, that "the work of our redemption is exercised." The liturgy is thus the outstanding means by which the faithful can express in their lives, and manifest to others, the mystery of Christ and the real nature of the true Church. It is of the essence of the Church that she be both human and divine, visible and yet invisibly endowed, eager to act and yet devoted to contemplation, present in this world and yet not at home in it. She is all these things in such a way that in her the human is directed and subordinated to the divine, the visible likewise to the invisible, action to contemplation, and this present world to that city yet to come, which we seek (cf. Heb. 13:14). Day by day the liturgy builds up those within the Church into the Lord's holy temple, into a spiritual dwelling for God (cf. Eph. 2:21-22) — an enterprise which will continue until

Christ's full stature is achieved (cf. Eph. 4:13). At the same time the liturgy marvelously fortifies the faithful in their capacity to preach Christ. To outsiders the liturgy thereby reveals the Church as a sign raised above the nations (cf. Is. 11:12). Under this sign the scattered sons of God are being gathered into one (cf. Jn. 11:52) until there is one fold and one shepherd (cf. Jn. 10:16). *(Liturgy, No.2)*

B. The Supreme Value of the Liturgy of the Most Holy Eucharist

Christ's institution of the Holy Eucharist united to His death on the cross have not ceased to be effective as if they were historically completed actions. They remain living events which profoundly influence the lives of His people today. Once we become incorporated into the life of Christ through baptism, or restored to grace through penance, it is the reception of the Holy Eucharist which most fully unites us with Him and with one another. The saving power of our Lord's life, teachings, and paschal mystery converge in the most Holy Eucharist.

The greatest sign of Catholic vitality appears in the active participation of the people in the liturgy of the Eucharistic sacrifice and the receiving of Holy Communion. All apostolic activity of the Catholic community ultimately derives from union with Christ, whose presence is most intimately realized in the Holy Eucharist. Here is the source of the laity's as well as the clergy's inner vitality for outer good works. Holy Communion brings strength to the needy, health of soul to the weak, and out-going charity to all. This sacrament is a pledge of heaven's attainment, the sign of living faith, and the bond uniting Christ's people in His Body for their individual benefit and that of His universal Church.

271. Christ's Sacrifice and Sacrament of Love and Unity

At the Last Supper, on the night when He was betrayed, our Savior instituted the Eucharistic Sacrifice of His Body and Blood. He did this in order to perpetuate the sacrifice of the Cross throughout the centuries until He should come again, and so to entrust to His beloved spouse, the Church, a memorial of His death and resurrection: a sacrament of love, a sign of unity, a bond of charity, a paschal banquet in which Christ is consumed, the mind is filled with grace, and a pledge of future glory is given to us. *(Liturgy, No.47)*

272. The Eucharistic Sacrifice Continues Christ's Work of Redemption

This inauguration and this growth are both symbolized by the blood and water which flowed from the open side of the crucified Jesus (cf. Jn. 19:34), and are foretold in the Lord's words concerning His death on the cross: "And I, if I be lifted up from the earth, will draw all men to myself" (Jn. 12:32, Greek text). As often as the sacrifice of the cross in which "Christ, our passover, has been sacrificed" (1 Cor. 5:7) is celebrated on an altar, the work of our redemption is carried on. At the same time, in the sacrament of the Eucharistic bread the unity of all believers who form one body in Christ (cf. 1 Cor. 10:17) is both expressed and brought about. All men are called to this union with Christ, who is the light of the world, from whom we go forth, through whom we live, and toward whom our journey leads us. *(Church, No.3)*

273. Regarding Full Participation in the Liturgy of the Eucharistic Sacrifice

The Church, therefore, earnestly desires that Christ's faithful, when present at this mystery of faith, should not be there as strangers or silent spectators. On the contrary, through a proper appreciation of the rites and prayers they should participate knowingly, devoutly, and actively. They should be instructed by God's word and be refreshed at the table of the Lord's body; they should give thanks to God; by offering the Immaculate Victim, not only through the hands of the priest, but also with him, they should learn to offer themselves too. Through Christ the Mediator, they should be drawn day by day into ever closer union with God and with each other, so that finally God may be all in all. *(Liturgy, No.48)*

274. The Spirit Behind Attendance at Sunday Mass

By an apostolic tradition which took its origin from the very day of Christ's resurrection, the Church celebrates the paschal mystery every eighth day; with good reason this, then, bears the name of the Lord's day or the day of the Lord. For on this day Christ's faithful should come together into one place so that, by hearing the word of God and taking part in the Eucharist, they may call to mind the passion, the resurrection, and the glorification of the Lord Jesus, and may thank God who "has begotten us again, through the resurrection of Jesus Christ from the dead, unto a living hope" (1 Pet. 1:3). Hence the Lord's day is the original feast day, and it should be proposed to the piety of the faithful and taught to them in such a way that it may become in fact a day of joy and of freedom from work. Other celebrations, unless they be truly of overriding importance, must not have precedence over this day, which is the foundation and nucleus of the whole liturgical year. *(Liturgy, No.106)*

275. Participation in the Eucharistic Sacrifice Should Prompt Works of Charity

In her very early days, the holy Church added the "agape" to the Eucharistic Supper and thus showed herself to be wholly united around Christ by the bond of charity. So, too, in every era she is recognized by this sign of love, and while she rejoices in the undertakings of others, she claims works of charity as her own inalienable duty and right. For this reason, pity for the needy and the sick, and works of charity and mutual aid intended to relieve human needs of every kind are held in special honor by the Church. *(Laity, No.8)*

C. Utilizing the Power Within the Sacraments for Daily Life

The paschal mystery of Christ continues its saving work today, chiefly through the Eucharistic Sacrifice of the Mass and the reception of the seven sacraments. Through the Church's liturgical rites Christ continues the salvific action of His life, death and resurrection. In the great sacramental system He has left for our sanctification, Christ provides for our spiritual welfare from the cradle to the grave. Through these sacraments He intensifies in us at every stage of our lives the charity that unites with the divine while uplifting the human. As our Savior, Christ is more interested in our rise from sin than in our antecedent fall from grace. To help us become holy, Christ renews His sacred presence among us particularly through means of the liturgical events of Mass and the sacraments.

In themselves, the sacraments of the Church cannot fail to produce the benefits Christ intended. However, the faithful must fulfill the necessary conditions for the sacraments to be fruitful, namely, wholehearted response to the action, grace and love which Christ offers through the liturgy. The sanctification that comes from the liturgy is not a luxury; it is the way to eternal life. The sacraments are not intended for angels but for weak, needy men; they provide the sustenance of people hungry for eternal life with their God.

The strength, instruction, and inspiration to be derived from liturgical participation in the sacraments is as relevant to the conditions of modern living as they ever were in history. Christ's saving work was meant to benefit people everywhere until the end of time, regardless of race, political system, cultural attainment or personal circumstances. The sacraments contain the principal source of divine grace to combat the defects and failings of mortal man's weaknesses. From His bounty, God not only sustains us in being, but gives additional support to us when needed according to His wisdom and love, and our requirements. Our Savior has established the sacraments to fulfill man's destiny, uplift his life, and unite all of His people together in their Lord.

276. The Importance of Recourse to the Sacraments

The purpose of the sacraments is to sanctify men, to build up the body of Christ, and finally, to give worship to God. Because they are signs they also instruct. They not only presuppose faith, but by words and objects they also nourish, strengthen, and express it; that is why they are called "sacraments of faith." They do indeed impart grace, but, in addition, the very act of celebrating them disposes the faithful most effectively to receive this grace in a fruitful manner, to worship God duly, and to practice charity.

It is therefore of capital importance that the faithful easily understand the sacramental signs, and with great eagerness have frequent recourse to those sacraments which were instituted to nourish the Christian life. *(Liturgy, No.59)*

277. Christ's Paschal Mystery Uplifts Daily Living

Thus, for well-disposed members of the faithful, the liturgy of the sacraments and sacramentals sanctifies almost every event in their lives; they are given access to the stream of divine grace which flows from the paschal mystery of the passion, death, and resurrection of Christ, the fountain from which all sacraments and sacramentals draw their power. There is hardly any proper use of material things which cannot thus be directed toward the sanctification of men and the praise of God. *(Liturgy, No.61)*

278. Sacraments of Initiation, Baptism and Confirmation

It is through the sacraments and the exercise of the virtues that the sacred nature and organic structure of the priestly community is brought into operation. Incorporated into the Church through baptism, the faithful are consecrated by the baptismal character to the exercise of the cult of the Christian religion. Reborn as sons of God, they must confess before men the faith which they have received from God through the Church. Bound more intimately to the Church by the sacrament of confirmation, they are endowed by the Holy Spirit with special strength. Hence they are more strictly obliged to spread and defend the faith both by word and by deed as true witnesses of Christ. *(Church, No.11)*

279. Strength and Union from Holy Communion

Taking part in the Eucharistic Sacrifice, which is the fount and apex of the whole Christian life, they offer the divine Victim to God, and offer themselves along with It. Thus, both by the act of oblation and through holy Communion, all perform their proper part in this liturgical service, not, indeed, all in the same way but each in that way which is appropriate to himself. Strengthened anew at the holy table by the Body of Christ, they manifest in a practical way that unity of God's People which is suitably signified and wondrously brought about by this most awesome sacrament. *(Church, No.11)*

280. The Sacraments of Penance, Anointing of the Sick and Holy Orders

Those who approach the sacrament of penance obtain pardon from the mercy of God for offenses committed against Him. They are at the same time reconciled with the Church, which they have wounded by their sins, and which by charity, example, and prayer seeks their conversion. By the sacred anointing of the sick and the prayer of her priests, the whole Church commends those who are ill to the suffering and glorified Lord, asking that He may lighten their suffering and save them (cf. Jas. 5:14-16). She exhorts them, moreover, to contribute to the welfare of the whole People of God by associating themselves freely with the passion and death of Christ (cf. Rom. 8:17; Col. 1:24; 2 Tim. 2:11-12; 1 Pet. 4:13). Those of the faithful who are consecrated by holy orders are appointed to feed the Church in Christ's name with the Word and the grace of God. *(Church, No.11)*

281. Marriage, the Sacrament of Christian Family Life

Finally, Christian spouses, in virtue of the sacrament of matrimony, signify and partake of the mystery of that unity and fruitful love which exists between Christ and His Church (cf. Eph. 5:32). The spouses thereby help each other to attain to holiness in their married life and by the rearing and education of their children. And so, in their state and way of life, they have their own special gift among the People of God (cf. 1 Cor. 7:7).

For from the wedlock of Christians there comes the family, in which new citizens of human society are born. By the grace of the Holy Spirit received in baptism these are made children of God, thus perpetuating the People of God through the centuries. The family is, so to speak, the domestic Church, In it parents should, by their word and example, be the first preachers of the faith to their children. They should encourage them in the vocation which is proper to each of them fostering with special care any religious vocation.

Fortified by so many and such powerful means of salvation, all the faithful, whatever their condition or state, are called by the Lord, each in his own way, to that perfect holiness whereby the Father Himself is perfect. *(Church, No.11)*

282. Using the Sacramentals to Best Advantage

Holy Mother Church has, moreover, instituted sacramentals. These are sacred signs which bear a resemblance to the sacraments: they signify effects, particularly of a spiritual kind, which are obtained through the Church's intercession. By them men are disposed to receive the chief effect of the sacraments, and various occasions in life are rendered holy. *(Liturgy, No.60)*

3. ASPECTS WHICH ENHANCE THE CELEBRATION OF THE LITURGY

A. Enriching the Liturgy by Prayer, Music, Art and Ornamentation

Whatever is truly beautiful and uplifting to the human spirit is likewise suitable for liturgical service and worthy of the temple of God. The Church approves of all forms of true art and admits them into divine worship when they show appropriate qualities for man's inspiration when offering praise to God.

Reverence has a common denominator, but the expressions of reverential art-forms may vary with the complexities of many cultural backgrounds. Possibly in one country a pipe-organ may best serve the cause of liturgical music, while in other areas guitars or even tom-toms may express a deeper liturgical meaning to the people. In the Middle and Far East incense may signify what Latin countries portray by the use of candles. Genuflecting in Western cultures displaces the Oriental bow, yet both courtesies manifest the interior reverence which exterior actions are intended to convey.

What is most important is that gestures, ceremonies, music, art and ornamentation should assist the people to grasp the full significance of the particular liturgical action being celebrated. The architecture, art-forms, furnishings and music employed must all convey liturgical significance to contemporary participants and must be consonant with the dignity of the function which gives honor to the divine Majesty.

283. Praising the Lord and Praying for the World in the Divine Office

Christ Jesus, high priest of the new and eternal covenant, taking human nature, introduced into this earthly exile that hymn which is sung throughout all ages in the halls of heaven. He joins the entire community of mankind to Himself, associating it with His own singing of this canticle of divine praise.

For He continues His priestly work through the agency of His Church, which is ceaselessly engaged in praising the Lord and interceding for the salvation of the whole world. This she does not only by celebrating the Eucharist, but also in other ways, especially by praying the divine Office. *(Liturgy, No.83)*

284. Church Music Enriches Liturgical Action

The musical tradition of the universal Church is a treasure of immeasurable value, greater even than that of any other art. The main reason for this pre-eminence is that, as sacred melody united to words, it forms a necessary or integral part of the solemn liturgy.

Holy Scripture, indeed, has bestowed praise upon sacred song (cf. Eph. 5:19; Col. 3:16), and the same may be said of the Fathers of the Church and of the Roman pontiffs who in recent times, led by St. Pius X, have explained more precisely the ministerial function rendered by sacred music in the service of the Lord.

Therefore sacred music increases in holiness to the degree that it is intimately linked with liturgical action, winningly expresses prayerfulness, promotes solidarity, and enriches sacred rites with heightened solemnity. The Church indeed approves of all forms of true art, and admits them into divine worship when they show appropriate qualities. *(Liturgy, No.112)*

285. Church Art and Ornamentation Elevates Liturgical Services

Very rightly the fine arts are considered to rank among the noblest expressions of human genius. This judgment applies especially to religious art and to its highest achievement, which is sacred art. By their very nature both of the latter are related to God's boundless beauty, for this is the reality which these human efforts are trying to express in some way. To the extent that these works aim exclusively at turning men's thoughts to God persuasively and devoutly, they are dedicated to God and to the cause of His greater honor and glory.

Holy Mother Church has therefore always been the friend of the fine arts and has continuously sought their noble ministry, with the special aim that all things set apart for use in divine worship should be truly worthy, becoming, and beautiful, signs and symbols of heavenly realities. For this purpose, too, she has trained artists. In fact, the Church has, with good reason, always reserved to herself the right to pass judgment upon the arts, deciding which of the works of artists are in accordance with faith, piety, and cherished traditional laws, and thereby suited to sacred purposes.

The Church has been particularly careful to see that sacred furnishings should worthily and beautifully serve the dignity of worship, and has welcomed those changes in materials, style, or ornamentation which the progress of the technical arts has brought with the passage of time. *(Liturgy, No.122)*

B. The Celebration and Regulation of the Liturgy by Those Authorized

Just as Christ left to His Apostles and their successors the interpretation of His teachings, so also He ratifies in heaven what they regulate on earth regarding the liturgical practices of the faith. To the bishops belongs the primary responsibility to celebrate and oversee all sacred liturgical exercises. Respectful compliance with episcopal regulations assures orthodoxy and unanimity in the sacred liturgy since, with approval of the Holy See, the variety of forms will bestow full blessings as long as the unity of divine worship is universally maintained.

Whatever revisions of liturgical rites may be forthcoming from legitimate authorities, such adaptations are intended principally to help portray the simple grandeur of divine worship for man's spirit. The ceremonial beauty of liturgical actions helps to enhance both the dignity of God's praise and the intelligibility of these holy rites for the People of God in current times.

286. The Bishops' Responsibility to Regulate Liturgical Practices and Innovations

Every legitimate celebration of the Eucharist is regulated by the bishop, to whom is committed the office of offering the worship of Christian religion to the divine Majesty and of administering it in accordance with the Lord's commandments and with the Church's laws, as further defined by his particular judgment for his diocese. (Church, No.26)

287. Regarding Common Worship among Various Christian Churches

As for common worship, however, it may not be regarded as a means to be used indiscriminately for the restoration of unity among Christians. Such worship depends chiefly on two principles: it should signify the unity of the Church; it should provide a sharing in the means of grace. The fact that it should signify unity generally rules out common worship. Yet the gaining of a needed grace sometimes commends it.

The practical course to be adopted, after due regard has been given to all the circumstances of time, place and personage, is left to the prudent decision of the local episcopal authority, unless the Bishops' Conference according to its own statutes, or the Holy See, has determined otherwise. (Ecumenism, No.8)

288. The Celebration and Regulation of Liturgical Functions by Bishops

By thus praying and laboring for the people, bishops channel the fullness of Christ's holiness in many ways and abundantly. By the ministry of the word they communicate God's power to those who believe unto salvation (cf. Rom. 1:16). Through the sacraments, the regular and fruitful distribution of which they direct by their authority, they sanctify the faithful. They govern the conferring of baptism, by which a sharing in the kingly priesthood of Christ is granted. They are the original ministers of confirmation, dispensers of sacred orders, and the moderators of penitential discipline. They earnestly exhort and instruct their people to carry out with faith and reverence their part in the liturgy and especially in the holy Sacrifice of the Mass. Finally, by the example of their manner of life they must be an influence for good on those over whom they preside, by refraining from all evil and, as far as they are able with God's help, turning evil to good. Thus, together with the flock committed to their care, they can arrive at eternal life. *(Church, No.26)*

The effects of Christ's death and resurrection, His paschal mystery, come to us chiefly through our participation in the sacred liturgical actions of the Eucharistic Sacrifice and the life-giving sacraments. Here we encounter the living Christ, for He is present whenever His people participate in the sacramental and sacrificial rites which He established to feed His flock.

Our wholehearted participation in the liturgical actions of the Mass and the sacraments brings us Christ's legacy for living the Christian life most fully. The liturgy is also the principal source which generates the strength to perform worthwhile and self-sacrificing apostolic works. Our private prayer and devotions, most valuable for fostering the spiritual life, further dispose us to be united with Christ and one another in the sacred liturgical actions of the Church-community at worship. There is no action on earth more truly sublime than Christ's care for His people through His sacred presence in liturgical actions. For it is here that man and matter become infused with God and goodness — in the union of love so significant of the very Incarnation of our Savior and His saving actions.

Summary of Part Three – UNITY

Part Three undertook to help us reflect on the relevance of Christian unity and participation in the sacred liturgy as particularly necessary in our age. The action of unity with our fellow-man must proceed from the inner movement of mind and heart toward other people, as Christ pleaded during His week of passion-suffering (Chapter IX). Drawing strength chiefly from active participation in the sacred liturgical celebrations, the contemporary Christian partakes of Christ's Paschal Mystery as alive and effective in today's world (Chapter X).

The following conciliar passage may serve to crystalize the spirit of Part Three on unity, and reflect the inestimable need of the sacred liturgy for acquiring union with God and, in Him, with all men.

289. May Unity Bring Stronger Relevance of Ecumenism and the Liturgy in Our Age

By virtue of her mission to shed on the whole world the radiance of the gospel message, and to unify under one Spirit all men of whatever nation, race, or culture, the Church stands forth as a sign of that brotherliness which allows honest dialogue and invigorates it.

Such a mission requires in the first place that we foster within the Church herself mutual esteem, reverence, and harmony, through the full recognition of lawful diversity. Thus all those who compose the one People of God, both pastors and the general faithful, can engage in dialogue with everabounding fruitfulness. For the bonds which unite the faithful are mightier than anything which divides them. Hence, let there be unity in what is necessary, freedom in what is unsettled, and charity in any case.

Our hearts embrace also those brothers and communities not yet living with us in full communion. To them we are linked nonetheless by our profession of the Father and the Son and the Holy Spirit, and by the bond of charity. We are mindful that the unity of Christians is today awaited and desired by many, too, who do not believe in Christ. For the further it advances toward truth and love under the powerful impulse of the Holy Spirit, the more this unity will be a harbinger of unity and peace for the world at large. *(World, No.92)*

Once Christians have attained the flowering of charity unto unity with others in love of Christ, they become witnesses to Christianity in the community-life of the world. Part Four, then, will consider the involvement of Christians in uplifting human conditions through the work of the Holy Spirit toward establishing a better world together in God's love.

Part 4
Witness

PART FOUR – WITNESS

THE INVOLVEMENT OF CHRISTIANS IN
UPLIFTING COMMUNITIES OF THE WORLD

When Christians have been imbued with the spirit of renewal and have become committed to Christ in unity with one another, then the indwelling of the Holy Spirit shows forth in the Church-community's vitality in the world. To be a "witness" to Christ means first of all to be a good-living Christian oneself, having the spirit of Christ and thinking with His Church. The involvement of Christians in uplifting the communities of the world begins within the soul of each follower of Christ who exerts some good influence in the various circles in which he lives and works. These communities include the family, the neighborhood, one's business associates, and the organizations to which he belongs. In addition, Christian influence must be exerted in the social and economic spheres and on the national and international levels when possible. Furthermore, the witnessing Christian strives to invite others, who can look on life as he does, into the community of the Church of Christ. Hence, "to strengthen those aspects of the Church which can help to summon all of mankind into her embrace", is the fourth expressed goal of the Vatican II Christian community.

The true witness of Christ manifests Christianity in all circumstances of his life because he is convinced that he can help to improve the here-and-now human condition as a noble work in itself as well as a means for uplifting man's spiritual nature in the furthering of Christ's kingdom on earth. An essential element of this Christian witness is to become involved in the current problems of the communities which are available. Fortified by the Holy Spirit, the convinced Christian strives to propagate Christ's truths in the role of valuable service to his fellow man.

Christians must live in the various communities of the world and become involved in them, yet with a spirit of freedom. St. Paul, the inspired commentator on the practical applications of Christ's gospel message, claims that freedom is the keynote of the witness to Christ. This means freedom from sinfulness, selfishness, or servitude. No worldly power is to be allowed to hamper the spirit of freedom in the Christian's service of Christ, for this is essential to the forward-movement of Christianity. Freedom of soul is the spirit of the gospel for those who live for the risen Christ in His Church-community. The Council re-affirms the right and duty of Christians to live with this enthusiastic freedom as brothers and sisters of Christ.

Those who are united in Christ form the various communities of Christians throughout the world. The unity between all these smaller groups comprises the universal Church-community. The uniting bond resides in the Vicar of Christ for the purpose of strengthening the unity of the community of Christ. In this guiding unity there is freedom of spirit to foster the forward-moving influence of the Church throughout the world.

Hence, we next consider how to apply the gospel message to several fundamental aspects of Christian living in our times. The work of the Holy Spirit and our witnessing to Christ in religious freedom will be considered, as well as our relationship toward non-Christian religions. We will also ponder Christian principles on marriage, the family and the education of children and youth, in addition to considering various matters pertaining to the socio-economic order. Government, Church-state relations, war and peace, and several other points are presented for reflection in the light of the Council's guidelines on the seething issues of concern to all mankind.

At times in the past there seems to have been a tendency to regard the mission of the Church as exclusively spiritual. This, rightly understood, is true. Yet, the mission of God's people in the temporal order is not to be overlooked; rather it is to be fostered. Christ looks to establish His kingdom on earth, since eternity's rewards come from time's good use. The joys of heaven are a consequence of the successful outcome of life's struggles on earth. This world and man's life in it must be used for his benefit according to Christ's teachings, for He knows what is best for man's life and salvation. God is glorified when man moves toward the perfecting of his human life as a reflection of the divine.

The Christian's influence in community enterprises will be effective when the individual follower of Christ becomes a witness to Him and His ways through openness to the operations of the Holy Spirit (Chapter XI). The Christian has a temporal mission to help establish a better world, and by that very fact to build a more Christ-like society, in all areas, on all levels, everywhere that is available to him in the domestic, socio-economic, national and international communities of the world (Chapter XII). The involvement of Christians in uplifting the various societies and communities of the world according to the spirit of the gospels, and their legitimate application to practical situations, will give evidence of the witness expected by Christ from his people in their life-time in His world.

Chapter XI

TODAY'S PENTECOST OF THE SPIRIT

At Work in God's People

After Christ rose from the dead, He commissioned His disciples to go out and bear witness to Him and His teachings in the communities of the world. On Pentecost, the Spirit of Truth descended more fully on Christ's apostles, the first Christians. This same Holy Spirit is just as operative in our times, the Vatican II era. Indeed, some have called our age the new Pentecost, referring to the expected renewal among Christians which should profoundly influence the communities of the modern world in the direction of a more genuine Christianity.

The current movements in the world are leading mankind into a new stage of development. Certainly, the contemporary follower of Christ should attempt to Christianize this new, emerging society. Future historians may call our times the renewed age of the Holy Spirit. This is not to say that indiscriminate claims of the Spirit's working would advance Christ's cause in the world. However, there seems to be a growing and beneficial tendency to listen more attentively to the Spirit of God and to weigh more accurately the effects of various current movements in the Church. This will help us to better discern where the guiding action of the Holy Spirit is at work.

The fuller awareness of the Holy Spirit's actions in the Christian community and His special graces within individuals show themselves in various aspects of Christian life. Some of these are discernable in the growing sense of personal responsibility for the Church and her mission in the world, and in the emerging position of the laity in social, charitable, political and ecclesial matters. There is, likewise, a widespread sense of freedom and more openness in several aspects of modern living, including attitudes within the Church.

In the present chapter we consider the dynamic activity and

mission of the Holy Spirit in the world (Section 1). It is by our giving witness to Christianity that we evidence the workings of this Advocate within us as individuals and as members of the universal Christian community (Section 2). The work of the Paraclete prospers in an atmosphere where religious freedom exists (Section 3). In addition, though the Spirit of Truth works most definitely in the Catholic Church, He also assists sincere people of other religions with whom Christians are to cooperate in dialogue and good works.

Just as Christ's divinity operated through His human nature, so also the divine Holy Spirit operates through the human persons who welcome His activity in them. It is our privilege and commission from Christ so to prepare ourselves in sanctity that He may freely use us as instruments of His saving and strengthening influence in the world of today.

1. THE MISSION OF THE HOLY SPIRIT IN THE WORLD

A. Christ Sends the Holy Spirit to Complete His Work

Christ's work for man's salvation will continue until His second coming at the fulfillment of time. Until then, He accomplishes man's sanctification and salvation through the Holy Spirit whom Christ sends to activate people with divine strength which unites with God and inspires acts of righteousness, charity and zeal.

The Christian's function is so to prepare himself that the obstacles to steady faith, to staunch morality, and to steadfast dedication are removed in order that the working of the Spirit may continue to operate freely and effectively in the world through us. The sacraments of initiation, baptism and confirmation, enliven Christ's people to cooperate with Him in the fulfillment of His mission from the Father through the operation of the Holy Spirit in the Church.

290. Spreading Christ's Gospel throughout the World

By His death and His resurrection the Lord completed once for all in Himself the mysteries of our salvation and of the renewal of all things. He had received all power in heaven and on earth (cf. Mt. 28:18). Now, before He was taken up into heaven (cf. Acts 1:11), He founded His Church as the sacrament of salvation, and sent His apostles into all the world just as He Himself had been sent by His Father (cf. Jn. 20:21). He gave them this command: "Go, therefore, and make disciples of all nations, baptizing them in the name of the Father, and of the Son, and of the Holy Spirit, teaching them to observe all that I have commanded you" (Mt. 28:19 f.). "Go into the whole world; preach the gospel to every creature. He who believes and is baptized shall be saved, but he who does not believe shall be condemned" (Mk. 16:15 f.). *(Missions, No.5)*

291. The Holy Spirit Continues Christ's Mission in the World

When the work which the Father had given the Son to do on earth (cf. Jn. 17:4) was accomplished, the Holy Spirit was sent on the day of Pentecost in order that He might forever sanctify the Church, and thus all believers would have access to the Father through Christ in the one Spirit (cf. Eph. 2:18). He is the Spirit of life, a fountain of water springing up to life eternal (cf. Jn. 4:14; 7:38-39). Through Him the Father gives life to men who are dead from sin, till at last He revives in Christ even their mortal bodies (cf. Rom. 8:10-11).

The Spirit dwells in the Church and in the hearts of the faithful as in a temple (cf. 1 Cor. 3:16; 6:19). In them He prays and bears witness to the fact that they are adopted sons (cf. Gal. 4:6; Rom. 8:15-16 and 26). The Spirit guides the Church into the fullness of truth (cf. Jn. 16:13) and gives her a unity of fellowship and service. He furnishes and directs her with various gifts, both hierarchical and charismatic, and adorns her with the fruits of His grace (cf. Eph. 4:11-12; 1 Cor. 12:4; Gal. 5:22). By the power of the gospel He makes the Church grow, perpetually renews her, and leads her to perfect union with her Spouse. The Spirit and the Bride both say to the Lord Jesus, "Come!" (cf. Apoc. 22:17).

Thus, the Church shines forth as "a people made one with the unity of the Father, the Son, and the Holy Spirit." *(Church, No.4)*

292. Through the Holy Spirit the Church Extends to All Times and Places

While she transcends all limits of time and of race, the Church is destined to extend to all regions of the earth and so to enter into the history of mankind. Moving forward through trial and tribulation, the Church is strengthened by the power of God's grace promised to her by the Lord, so that in the weakness of the flesh she may not waver from perfect fidelity, but remain a bride worthy of her Lord; that moved by the Holy Spirit she may never cease to renew herself, until through the cross she arrives at the light which knows no setting. *(Church, No.9)*

B. The Holy Spirit Works Through Our Witness of Christianity

The fullness of God's help to man derives from His divine Son, sent to save His people from sin and degradation. Christ's gospel message is not confined to mere words in a book; it proclaims God's way of life for man. When His word and His Church are embraced with mind, heart, and soul, they transform life. The "good news" means Christ's dynamic power, imparted by the Holy Spirit, bringing His grace for our enlightenment and zeal in a world so badly in need of Christian action.

In large measure, man is assisted to respond to God's love through other people who reflect godliness in their lives and actions. Just as a transmitting satellite can instantly bring the same picture to millions of television screens, so also, through the Holy Spirit, God's people can reflect the same Christ to countless others. Christians can be witnesses and projections of His image and His word throughout the world.

293. As Christ Sent His Apostles, He Sends Us Today

Just as the Son was sent by the Father, so He too sent the apostles (cf. Jn. 20:21), saying: "Go, therefore, and make disciples of all nations, baptizing them in the name of the Father and of the Son and of the Holy Spirit, teaching them to observe all that I have commanded you; and behold, I am with you all days even unto the consummation of the world" (Mt. 28:18-20).

The Church has received from the apostles as a task to be discharged even to the ends of the earth this solemn mandate of Christ to proclaim the saving truth (cf. Acts 1:8). Hence she makes the words of the Apostle her own: "Woe to me, if I do not preach the gospel" (1 Cor. 9:16), and continues unceasingly to send heralds of the gospel until such time as the infant churches are fully established and can themselves carry on the work of evangelizing. For the Church is compelled by the Holy Spirit to do her part towards the full realization of the will of God, who has established Christ as the source of salvation for the whole world. By the proclamation of the gospel, she prepares her hearers to receive and profess the faith disposes them for baptism, snatches them from the slavery of error, and incorporates them into Christ so that through charity they may grow up into full maturity in Christ. *(Church, No.17)*

294. The Church Is Christ's Universal Sacrament of Salvation

The Church has been divinely sent to all nations that she might be "the universal sacrament of salvation." Acting out of the innermost requirements of her own catholicity and in obedience to her Founder's mandate (cf. Mk. 16:16), she strives to proclaim the gospel to all men. For the Church was founded upon the apostles, who, following in the footsteps of Christ, "preached the message of truth and begot Churches." Upon their successors devolves the duty of perpetuating this work through the years. Thus "the word of God may run and be glorified" (2 Th. 3:1) and God's kingdom can be everywhere proclaimed and established.

The present historical situation is leading humanity into a new stage. As the salt of the earth and light of the world (cf. Mt. 5:13-14), the Church is summoned with special urgency to save and renew every creature. In this way all things can be restored in Christ, and in Him mankind can compose one family and one people. *(Missions, No.1)*

295. The Holy Spirit of Christ Actively Helps Us

To accomplish this goal, Christ sent the Holy Spirit from the Father. The Spirit was to carry out His saving work inwardly and to impel the Church toward her proper expansion. Doubtless, the Holy Spirit was already at work in the world before Christ was glorified. Yet on the day of Pentecost, He came down upon the disciples to remain with them forever (cf. Jn. 14:16). On that day the Church was publicly revealed to the multitude, the gospel began to spread among the nations by means of preaching, and finally there occurred a foreshadowing of that union of all peoples in a universal faith.

That union was to be achieved by the Church of the New Covenant, a church which speaks all tongues, which lovingly understands and accepts all tongues, and thus overcomes the divisiveness of Babel. For it was from Pentecost that the "Acts of the Apostles" took their origin. In a similar way Christ was conceived when the Holy Spirit came upon the Virgin Mary. Thus too Christ was impelled to the work of His ministry when the same Holy Spirit descended upon Him at prayer.

Now, before freely giving His life for the world, the Lord Jesus so arranged the ministry of the apostles and so promised to send the Holy Spirit, that both they and the Spirit were to be associated in effecting the work of salvation always and everywhere. Throughout all ages, the Holy Spirit gives the entire Church "unity in fellowship and in service; He furnishes her with various gifts, both hierarchical and charismatic." He vivifies ecclesiastical institutions as a kind of soul and instills into the hearts of the faithful the same mission spirit which motivated Christ Himself. Sometimes He visibly anticipates the apostles' action, just as He unceasingly accompanies and directs it in different ways. *(Missions, No.4)*

2. WE GIVE WITNESS TO THE LIVING PENTECOST BY OUR APOSTOLIC WORKS

A. Spreading the Faith at Home and in the Missions

Although important events of secular history undoubtedly have a bearing on contemporary situations, they are essentially actions which took place in the past and are now completed. To the contrary, through the living presence of God in His world, the important events of salvation history maintain a constant and effective vitality from age to age. Such it is with the Pentecost of the Spirit which is active today. The Holy Spirit not only descended on the apostles as an historical event, but His activity continues to be operative, working for the salvation and apostolic activity of God's people in our times.

The gift of faith is a treasure to be cherished, but it likewise contains an inner dynamism for diffusion of itself to ever increasing numbers of people. The Church is not merely another one of many societies or movements in the world competing for membership. It far supercedes the aims of all other causes. The Holy Spirit inspires people to affiliation in the supernatural society of the Mystical Body of Christ to which all mankind is invited.

The full religious formation of Catholics from the tender years of first Holy Communion through subsequent stages of their spiritual maturity requires more than the "I-thou" relationship with Christ. Union with our Lord should include a growing interest in spreading His religion among others out of gratitude for this gift, and for the benefits it brings to the lives of others. Briefly, the nature of Christian witness is epitomized in the mission zeal for the spread of the faith.

While the number of Christians is important, it is not as significant as the vitality they possess and the quality of Christianity to which they bear witness in action. The salvific mission of the Church throughout the modern world, made possible by the exertion of Christian vitality as impelled by cooperation with the Holy Spirit, fosters the progress of Christ's cause at home and in the foreign missions. Hundreds of millions of searching people are still uncommitted to Christ's cause or unconcerned with His gospel, intended for man's happiness and salvation. To these, mostly, the Holy Spirit would have us be witnesses of vital Christianity in our time.

296. The Laity's Vocation to Spread the Faith

Wishing to intensify the apostolic activity of the People of God, this most holy Synod earnestly addresses itself to the laity, whose proper and indispensable role in the mission of the Church it has already called to mind in other documents. The layman's apostolate derives from his Christian vocation, and the Church can never be without it. Sacred Scripture clearly shows how spontaneous and fruitful such activity was at the very beginning of the Church (cf. Acts 11:19-21; 18:26; Rom. 16:1-16; Phil. 4:3).

Our own times require of the laity no less zeal. In fact, modern conditions demand that their apostolate be thoroughly broadened and intensified. The constant expansion of population, scientific and technical progress, and the tightening of bonds between men have not only immensely widened the field of the lay apostolate, a field which is for the most part accessible only to them. These developments have themselves raised new problems which cry out for the skillful concern and attention of the laity. This apostolate becomes more imperative in view of the fact that many areas of human life have become very largely autonomous. This is as it should be, but it sometimes involves a certain withdrawal from ethical and religious influences and a serious danger to Christian life. Besides, in many places where priests are very few or, in some instances, are deprived of due freedom in their ministry, the Church could scarcely be present and functioning without the activity of the laity.

An indication of this manifold and pressing need is the unmistakable work of the Holy Spirit in making the laity today even more conscious of their own responsibility and inspiring them everywhere to serve Christ and the Church. *(Laity, No.1)*

297. The Kingdom of Christ Spreads through a Vital Mission Spirit

This missionary activity finds its reason in the will of God, "who wishes all men to be saved and to come to the knowledge of the truth. For there is one God, and one Mediator between God and men, himself man, Christ Jesus, who gave himself a ransom for all" (1 Tim. 2:4-5), "neither is there salvation in any other" (Acts 4:12).

Therefore, all must be converted to Him as He is made known by the Church's preaching. All must be incorporated into Him by baptism, and into the Church which is His body. For Christ Himself "in explicit terms . . . affirmed the necessity of faith and baptism (cf. Mk. 16:16; Jn. 3:5) and thereby affirmed also the necessity of the Church, for through baptism as through a door men enter the Church. Whosoever, therefore, knowing that the Catholic Church was made necessary by God through Jesus Christ, would refuse to enter her or to remain in her could not be saved."

Therefore, though God in ways known to Himself can lead those inculpably ignorant of the gospel to that faith without which it is impossible to please Him (Heb. 11:6), yet a necessity lies upon the Church (cf. 1 Cor. 9:16), and at the same time a sacred duty, to preach the gospel. Hence missionary activity today as always retains its power and necessity.

By means of this activity, the Mystical Body of Christ unceasingly gathers and directs its forces toward its own growth (cf. Eph. 4:11-16). The members of the Church are impelled to carry on such missionary activity by reason of the love with which they love God and by which they desire to share with all men in the spiritual goods of both this life and the life to come.

Finally, by means of this missionary activity, God is fully glorified, provided that men consciously and fully accept His work of salvation, which He has accomplished in Christ. Through this activity that plan of God is thus fulfilled to which Christ was obediently and lovingly devoted for the glory of the Father who sent Him. According to this plan, the whole human race is to form one People of God, coalesce into the one body of Christ, and be built up into one temple of the Holy Spirit. Since it concerns brotherly concord, this design surely corresponds with the inmost wishes of all men.

And so the plan of the Creator, who formed man to His own image and likeness, will be realized at last when all who share one human nature, regenerated in Christ through the Holy Spirit and beholding together the glory of God, will be able to say "Our Father." *(Missions, No. 7)*

298. Missionary Activity Manifests Christ and Uplifts Mankind

Missionary activity is closely bound up too with human nature itself and its aspirations. By manifesting Christ, the Church reveals to men the real truth about their condition and their total vocation. For Christ is the source and model of that renewed humanity, penetrated with brotherly love, sincerity, and a peaceful spirit, to which all aspire. Christ and the Church, which bears witness to Him by preaching the gospel, transcend every particularity of race or nation and therefore cannot be considered foreign anywhere or to anybody. Christ Himself is the Truth and the Way. The preaching of the gospel opens them up to all when it proclaims to all these words of the same Christ: "Repent, and believe in the gospel" (Mk. 1:15).

Now, since he who does not believe is already judged (cf. Jn. 3:18), the words of Christ are at one and the same time words of judgment and of grace, of death and of life. For it is only by putting to death what is old that we are able to come to a newness of life. This fact applies first of all to persons, but it holds also for the various goods of this world, which bear the mark both of man's sin and of God's blessing; for "all have sinned and have need of the glory of God" (Rom. 3:23). By himself and by his own power, no one is freed from sin or raised above himself, or completely rid of his sickness or his solitude or his servitude. On the contrary, all stand in need of Christ, their Model, their Mentor, their Liberator, their Savior, their Source of life.

The gospel has truly been a leaven of liberty and progress in human history, even in its temporal sphere, and always proves itself a leaven of brotherhood, of unity, and of peace. Therefore, not without cause is Christ hailed by the faithful as "the expected of the nations, and their Savior." *(Missions, No. 8)*

299. The Mission Spirit Is the Spirit of Christ and His People

And so the time for missionary activity extends between the first coming of the Lord and the second. Then from the four winds the Church will be gathered like a harvest into the kingdom of God. For the gospel must be preached to all nations before the Lord returns (cf. Mk. 13:10).

Missionary activity is nothing else and nothing less than a manifestation of epiphany of God's will, and the fulfillment of that will in the world and in world history. In the course of this history God plainly works out the history of salvation by means of mission. By the preaching of the word and by the celebration of the sacraments, whose center and summit is the most holy Eucharist, missionary activity brings about the presence of Christ, the Author of salvation.

But whatever truth and grace are to be found among the nations, as a sort of secret presence of God, this activity frees from all taint of evil and restores to Christ its maker, who overthrows the devil's domain and wards off the manifold malice of vice. And so, whatever good is found to be sown in the hearts and minds of men, or in the rites and cultures peculiar to various peoples, is not lost. More than that, it is healed, ennobled, and perfected for the glory of God, the shame of the demon, and the bliss of men.

Thus, missionary activity tends toward the fulfillment which will come at the end of time. For by it the People of God advances toward that degree of growth and that time of completion which the Father has fixed in His power (cf. Acts 1:7). To this people it was said in prophecy: "Enlarge the space for your tent, spread out your tent cloths unsparingly" (Is. 54:2). By missionary activity, the mystical body grows to the mature measure of the fullness of Christ (cf. Eph. 4:13). The spiritual temple, where God is adored in spirit and in truth (cf. Jn. 4:23), grows and is built up upon the foundation of the apostles and prophets with Christ Jesus Himself remaining the chief cornerstone (Eph. 2:20). *(Missions, No.9)*

300. The Laity's Special Role in Modern Times

There are innumerable opportunities open to the laity for the exercise of their apostolate of making the gospel known and men holy. The very testimony of their Christian life, and good works done in a supernatural spirit, have the power to draw men to belief and to God; for the Lord says, "Even so let your light shine before men, in order that they may see your good works and give glory to your Father in heaven" (Mt. 5:16).

However, an apostolate of this kind does not consist only in the witness of one's way of life; a true apostle looks for opportunities to announce Christ by words addressed either to non-believers with a view to instructing and strengthening them, and motivating them toward a more fervent life. "For the love of Christ impels us" (2 Cor. 5:14), and the words of the Apostle should echo in every Christian heart: "For woe to me if I do not preach the gospel" (1 Cor. 9:16).

Since, in this age of ours, new problems are arising and extremely serious errors are gaining currency which tend to undermine the foundations of religion, the moral order, and human society itself, this sacred Synod earnestly exhorts laymen, each according to his natural gifts and learning, to be more diligent in doing their part according to the mind of the Church, to explain and defend Christian principles, and to apply them rightly to the problems of our era. *(Laity, No.6)*

B. Using Modern Means to Foster the Church's Mission

Since he is made in the image of God, man has within himself something of the creative instinct. Man proves himself truly alive with the breath of God when he keeps striving to resolve the inevitable conflict between mind and matter, flesh and spirit, time and eternity. Man looks outward and yearns to communicate and unite with material creation and his fellow humans. Man looks inward and tries to express to himself and to others the inner ideas and feelings of his being. Thus, he longs to communicate – to love and to be loved, to give and to receive, to understand and to be understood. He strives to express in various forms his inner self while absorbing the self-expression of others. In the widest sense, life is a fine art because it is both creative by its self-expression to others and redemptive by its self-communication for others.

The current times are marked by tensions and conflicts which will plague mankind for years to come. During periods of tension, the facility to express oneself so as to be understood by others, no less than the ability to understand others, tend to break down. In intercommunication, the message becomes clear only when the medium through which it is expressed is meaningful both to those who wish to communicate an idea and to those for whom the message is intended. The complex subject of social communication of ideas and feelings between people may be compressed into the twofold fields of verbal expression and of visual portrayal. Both are essential for communicating the Church's message.

In importance for this or any age, nothing surpasses the Gospel message of Christ. This good-news-message of attainable salvation has not lost its pertinence to mankind's destiny today. Consequently, the message of Christ's Church deserves to be proclaimed through the most meaningful means of verbal and visual communications available to modern man.

The conciliar passages give the green light for exploring the vast potential in the modern means of communication, both for their own contribution to mankind and for the advancement of Christ's cause among men. All suitable forms of verbal and visual aids should be employed when they can foster the Church's mission on earth. All advanced media of social communication, such as the art-forms, music, drama, the press, radio, television, films, tapes, records, and future means should be used when they can successfully convey to contemporary man the message of Christ and His Church.

301. Utilizing Modern Communications Media to Spread the Faith

By divine favor, especially in modern times, human genius has produced from natural material astonishing inventions in the field of technology. Some of these have extraordinary bearing on the human spirit, since they open up new and highly effective avenues of communication for all kinds of information, ideas, and directives.

As a Mother, the Church welcomes and watches such inventions with special concern. Chief among them are those which by their very nature can reach and influence not only individual men, but the masses themselves, even the whole of society. Such would be the press, the cinema, radio, television, and similar media, which can be properly classified as instruments of social communication. *(Communications, No.1)*

302. Preaching the Word through Advanced Techniques Available

The Catholic Church has been commissioned by the Lord Christ to bring salvation to every man, and is consequently bound to proclaim the gospel. Hence she judges it part of her duty to preach the news of redemption with the aid of the instruments of social communication, and to instruct mankind as well in their worthy use.

Therefore the Church claims as a birthright the use and possession of all instruments of this kind which are necessary or useful for the formation of Christians and for every activity undertaken on behalf of man's salvation.

On religious shepherds devolves the task of so training and directing the faithful that by the help of these instruments, too, they may pursue their own salvation and fulfillment, and that of the entire human family.

For the rest, it is the layman's particular obligation to animate these instruments with a humane and Christian spirit. Thus will they abundantly satisfy the high hopes of mankind and the will of God Himself. *(Communications, No.3)*

303. Evaluating the Best Means for Reaching Modern Man

With common heart and mind, let all the sons of the Church strive immediately and most energetically to use the instruments of social communication effectively in the many fields of the apostolate, as the circumstances and the times require. These efforts should head off hurtful enterprises, especially in those places where moral and religious needs dictate a more active zeal.

Religious shepherds should speedily fulfill their duties in this field, closely connected as it is with their normal preaching responsibilities. Laymen who have a role in using these instruments should be busy giving witness to Christ, especially by performing their duties skillfully and with apostolic ardor. In their own way, let them also lend direct aid to the pastoral action of the Church through their technical, economic, cultural, and artistic abilities. *(Communications, No.13)*

3. THE WORK OF THE HOLY SPIRIT PROSPERS IN AN ATMOSPHERE OF RELIGIOUS FREEDOM

A. Religious Freedom is Man's Right and It Can Enhance Religious Practice

The exercise of religion consists in those internal and free acts whereby man, responding to God's impulses of grace and love, sets the course of his life toward his Lord. No merely human power can either command or prohibit acts of this kind, since man's response to God is his right. Consonant with the innate dignity of man as implanted by his Creator, all men as free beings are naturally entitled to the exercise of freedom in their religious acts in accordance with laws of nature as established by the Author of life.

This religious freedom of man must be genuine; it should not be motivated by either reluctant approval or tentative concession, looking toward a future ensnarement. True freedom is a fundamental right and it furnishes a condition conducive for man's internal acceptance and external practice of religion. Furthermore, religious liberty includes freedom from psychological as well as external coercion. The Catholic Church has repeatedly proclaimed that human dignity and freedom belong to man by God-given right. Not by the sword will men's allegiance to God be won; only by the two-edged piercing power of truth and love will men's hearts be opened to accept God's invitation freely.

The document on religious freedom contains overtones and undertones which should strike a responsive chord in homes, schools, parishes, religious houses, seminaries, dioceses, etc. Catholic and otherwise. However, human nature has a tendency to favor itself. Freedom can be misinterpreted to mean license and conscience can sometimes be warped to express self-love. As with other documents of Vatican II, this one, too, will require balanced consideration, lest religious freedom's purpose of assisting people toward God should become distorted to signify merely nebulous beliefs, a limpid moral order, and personal liberty to believe and do almost anything while claiming full allegiance to the Catholic faith — all in the guise of religious freedom.

Nevertheless, the climate in which the Holy Spirit can best prosper His work is one in which people are genuinely free to follow their religious convictions. A person's conscience is his inner sanctuary before the throne of God. Just as love blossoms best in an atmosphere of mutual trust and confidence so do religious acts develop to the fullest when they are freely given. Genuine freedom and true love are intimately united. Since God is the main source of both, man is morally obliged to respect both. God alone will pass the ultimate sanction on the worth of a man's life. He will evaluate a person's response to His revelation, His grace, His Church, and His love.

304. The Free Exercise of Religion in Society

A sense of the dignity of the human person has been impressing itself more and more deeply on the consciousness of contemporary man. And the demand is increasingly made that men should act on their own judgment, enjoying and making use of a responsible freedom, not driven by coercion but motivated by a sense of duty. The demand is also made that constitutional limits should be set to the powers of government, in order that there may be no encroachment on the rightful freedom of the person and of associations.

This demand for freedom in human society chiefly regards the quest for the values proper to the human spirit. It regards, in the first place, the free exercise of religion in society. *(Freedom, No.1)*

305. Human Dignity Requires Religious Freedom

This Vatican Synod declares that the human person has a right to religious freedom. This freedom means that all men are to be immune from coercion on the part of individuals or of social groups and of any human power, in such wise that in matters religious no one is to be forced to act in a manner contrary to his own beliefs. Nor is anyone to be restrained from acting in accordance with his own beliefs, whether privately or publicly, whether alone or in association with others, within due limits.

The Synod further declares that the right to religious freedom has its foundation in the very dignity of the human person, as this dignity is known through the revealed Word of God and by reason itself. This right of the human person to religious freedom is to be recognized in the constitutional law whereby society is governed. Thus it is to become a civil right. *(Freedom, No.2)*

306. Though Morally Bound to Seek Truth, People May Not Be Forced

It is in accordance with their dignity as persons—that is, beings endowed with reason and free will and therefore privileged to bear personal responsibility—that all men should be at once impelled by nature and also bound by a moral obligation to seek the truth, especially religious truth. They are also bound to adhere to the truth, once it is known, and to order their whole lives in accord with the demands of truth.

However, men cannot discharge these obligations in a manner in keeping with their own nature unless they enjoy immunity from external coercion as well as psychological freedom. Therefore, the right to religious freedom has its foundation, not in the subjective disposition of the person, but in his very nature. In consequence, the right to this immunity continues to exist even in those who do not live up to their obligation of seeking the truth and adhering to it. Nor is the exercise of this right to be impeded, provided that the just requirements of public order are observed. *(Freedom, No.2)*

307. Educating Youth and Others to Personal Responsibility

Therefore, this Vatican Synod urges everyone, especially those who are charged with the task of educating others, to do their utmost to form men who will respect the moral order and be obedient to lawful authority. Let them form men too who will be lovers of true freedom—men, in other words, who will come to decisions on their own judgment and in the light of truth, govern their activities with a sense of responsibility, and strive after what is true and right, willing always to join with others in cooperative effort.

Religious freedom, therefore, ought to have this further purpose and aim, namely, that men may come to act with greater responsibility in fulfilling their duties in community life. *(Freedom, No.8)*

308. Divine Law Attracts When People Are Free from Coercion

Further light is shed on the subject if one considers that the highest norm of human life is the divine law—eternal, objective, and universal—whereby God orders, directs, and governs the entire universe and all the ways of the human community, by a plan conceived in wisdom and love. Man has been made by God to participate in this law, with the result that, under the gentle disposition of divine Providence, he can come to perceive ever increasingly the unchanging truth. Hence every man has the duty, and therefore the right, to seek the truth in matters religious, in order that he may with prudence form for himself right and true judgments of conscience, with the use of all suitable means.

Truth, however, is to be sought after in a manner proper to the dignity of the human person and his social nature. The inquiry is to be free, carried on with the aid of teaching or instruction, communication, and dialogue. In the course of these, men explain to one another the truth they have discovered, or think they have discovered, in order thus to assist one another in the quest for truth. Moreover, as the truth is discovered, it is by a personal assent that men are to adhere to it.

On his part, man perceives and acknowledges the imperatives of the divine law through the mediation of conscience. In all his activity a man is bound to follow his conscience faithfully, in order that he may come to God, for whom he was created. It follows that he is not to be forced to act in a manner contrary to his conscience. Nor, on the other hand, is he to be restrained from acting in accordance with his conscience, especially in matters religious.

For, of its very nature, the exercise of religion consists before all else in those internal, voluntary, and free acts whereby man sets the course of his life directly toward God. No merely human power can either command or prohibit acts of this kind. *(Freedom, No.3)*

309. Governments Should Provide the Climate of Freedom for Religion

However, the social nature of man itself requires that he should give external expression to his internal acts of religion; that he should participate with others in matters religious; that he should profess his religion in community. Injury, therefore, is done to the human person and to the very order established by God for human life, if the free exercise of religion is denied in society when the just requirements of public order do not so require.

There is a further consideration. The religious acts whereby men, in private and in public and out of a sense of personal conviction, direct their lives to God transcend by their very nature the order of terrestrial and temporal affairs. Government, therefore, ought indeed to take account of the religious life of the people and show it favor, since the function of government is to make provision for the common welfare. However, it would clearly transgress the limits set to its power were it to presume to direct or inhibit acts that are religious. *(Freedom, No.3)*

310. No One Is to Be Forced to Embrace the Catholic Religion

It is one of the major tenets of Catholic doctrine that man's response to God in faith must be free. Therefore no one is to be forced to embrace the Christian faith against his own will. This doctrine is contained in the Word of God and it was constantly proclaimed by the Fathers of the Church. The act of faith is of its very nature a free act. Man, redeemed by Christ the Savior and through Christ Jesus called to be God's adopted son, cannot give his adherence to God revealing Himself unless the Father draw him to offer to God the reasonable and free submission of faith.

It is therefore completely in accord with the nature of faith that in matters religious every manner of coercion on the part of men should be excluded. In consequence, the principle of religious freedom makes no small contribution to the creation of an environment in which men can without hindrance be invited to Christian faith, and embrace it of their own free will, and profess it effectively in their whole manner of life. *(Freedom, No.10)*

311. Christ Invited and Won People to Believe in Him

God calls men to serve Him in spirit and in truth. Hence they are bound in conscience but they stand under no compulsion. God has regard for the dignity of the human person whom He Himself created; man is to be guided by his own judgment and he is to enjoy freedom.

This truth appears at its height in Christ Jesus, in whom God perfectly manifested Himself and His ways with men. Christ is our Master and our Lord. He is also meek and humble of heart. And in attracting and inviting His disciples He acted patiently. He wrought miracles to shed light on His teaching and to establish its truth. But His intention was to rouse faith in His hearers and to confirm them in faith, not to exert coercion upon them. *(Freedom, No.11)*

312. Conscience Must Be Free to Respond to God's Grace Unforced

He did indeed denounce the unbelief of some who listened to Him; but He left vengeance to God in expectation of the day of judgment. When He sent His apostles into the world, He said to them: "He who believes and is baptized shall be saved, but he who does not believe shall be condemned" (Mk. 16:16); but He Himself, noting that cockle had been sown amid the wheat, gave orders that both should be allowed to grow until the harvest time, which will come at the end of the world.

He refused to be a political Messiah, ruling by force; He preferred to call Himself the Son of Man, who came "to serve and to give his life as a ransom for many" (Mk. 10:45) He showed Himself the perfect Servant of God; "a bruised reed he will not break, and a smoking wick he will not quench" (Mt. 12:20).

He acknowledged the power of government and its rights, when He commanded that tribute be given to Caesar. But He gave clear warning that the higher rights of God are to be kept inviolate: "Render, therefore, to Caesar the things that are Caesar's, and to God the things that are God's (Mt. 22:21). *(Freedom, No.11)*

B. The Christians' Relationship
   ### With Non-Christian Religions

Christians should respect the religious beliefs and practices of people who in sincerity profess religions other than Christianity. The conciliar documents remove the ground from under any theory or practice which would lead to a distinction between people regarding their basic human dignity and the rights which flow from it. As a consequence, the Catholic Church rejects as foreign to the mind of Christ, discrimination against people or harassment of them because of their race, color, condition of life, or religion.

Christians are exhorted to engage in dialogue toward mutual understanding and collaboration for fostering good works with followers of other religions. While being witnesses of the Christian faith and way of life, the followers of Christ should acknowledge and preserve the spiritual and moral values of non-Christian religions as well as the rich heritage of their social, artistic, and cultural contributions to the world's civilizations.

In some Christian European towns, the church bells that announce liturgical services bear the names of saints; in the middle-East, towers abound from which a man's voice can be heard for miles around, calling non-Christian people to prayer. Throughout the world men have built churches, synogogues, mosques, temples, and shrines of all sorts, designed for various religious functions. Religious people would do better to respect each other's right to differing beliefs and practices rather than to scoff at or quarrel over them. Instead, let all peoples exchange their religious experiences in amicable dialogue. By extending the hand of friendship to others, without trace of ungodly discrimination between men of differing religious beliefs, God's world may become more united unto His glory and man's peace.

For instance, the Jewish faith requires more consideration from the followers of Christ since it is the forerunner of Christianity. Indeed, much should be explored toward bringing about more dialogue and mutual cooperation in good works between Christians and Jews. For too long and in too many places there has existed a Jewish and a Christian "ghetto" mentality of suspicion and separation on the parts of both groups, even though both are believers in the Old Testament, the word of Jahweh. Openness toward the cultural heritages of Judaism and of Christianity provides a good beginning for appreciation of their common religious heritage. "Shalom" is a word filled with the blessings of peace.

The Church's mission endeavors have acquired a new dimension. The drive for the conversion of non-believers, while just as desirable, is more like an invitation to explore the faith. It stems from beholding Christianity's inner true values and outer good works. While sincerely respecting the good and holy elements found in the great non-Christian religions, the Christian's dialogue with those of other faiths is to be more than verbal; it must be a dialogue of the heart and of action as well. Consequently, Christians should study the languages, history, culture, religious tenets, and practices of non-Christian religions, particularly those of the middle and far East. While preserving the integrity of the Christian apostolic faith, greater efforts must be devoted to understanding and respecting those religions which are not in the Judeo-Christian tradition. The various religions, assuredly, enjoy the full right to prosper and to serve the Lord God peacefully while respecting the same rights of others.

313. Promoting Dialogue and Peace among People of All Religions

In our times, when every day men are being drawn closer together and the ties between various peoples are being multiplied, the Church is giving deeper study to her relationship with non-Christian religions. In her task of fostering unity and love among men, and even among nations, she gives primary consideration in this document to what human beings have in common and to what promotes fellowship among them.

For all peoples comprise a single community, and have a single origin, since God made the whole race of men dwell over the entire face of the earth (cf. Acts 17:26). One also is their final goal: God. His providence, His manifestations of goodness, and His saving designs extend to all men (cf. Wis. 8:1; Acts 14:17; Rom. 2:6-7; 1 Tim. 2:4) against the day when the elect will be united in that Holy City ablaze with the splendor of God, where the nations will walk in His light (cf. Apoc. 21:23 f.).

Men look to the various religions for answers to those profound mysteries of the human condition which, today even as in olden times, deeply stir the human heart: What is a man? What is the meaning and the purpose of our life? What is goodness and what is sin? What gives rise to our sorrows and to what intent? Where lies the path to true happiness? What is the truth about death, judgment, and retribution beyond the grave? What, finally, is that ultimate and unutterable mystery which engulfs our being, and whence we take our rise, and whither our journey leads us? (Non-Christians, No.1)

314. People Searching for Manifestations of God's Goodness

From ancient times down to the present, there has existed among diverse peoples a certain perception of that hidden power which hovers over the course of things and over the events of human life; at times, indeed, recognition can be found of a Supreme Divinity and of a Supreme Father too. Such a perception and such a recognition instill the lives of these peoples with a profound religious sense. Religions bound up with cultural advancement have struggled to reply to these same questions with more refined concepts and in more highly developed language. (Non-Christians, No.2)

315. The Catholic Church Respects All True and Holy Religious Beliefs

The Catholic Church rejects nothing which is true and holy in these religions. She looks with sincere respect upon those ways of conduct and of life, those rules and teachings which, though differing in many particulars from what she holds and sets forth, nevertheless often reflect a ray of that Truth which enlightens all men. Indeed, she proclaims and must ever proclaim Christ, "the way, the truth, and the life" (John 14:6), in whom men find the fullness of religious life, and in whom God has reconciled all things to Himself (cf. 2 Cor. 5:18-19).

The Church therefore has this exhortation for her sons: prudently and lovingly, through dialogue and collaboration with the followers of other religions, and in witness of Christian faith and life, acknowledge, preserve, and promote the spiritual and moral goods found among these men, as well as the values in their society and culture. (Non-Christians, No.2)

316. Jewish People and the Christian Evaluation

As holy Scripture testifies, Jerusalem did not recognize the time of her visitation (cf. Lk. 19:44), nor did the Jews in large number accept the gospel; indeed, not a few opposed the spreading of it (cf. Rom. 11:28). Nevertheless, according to the Apostle, the Jews still remain most dear to God because of their fathers, for He does not repent of the gifts He makes nor of the calls He issues (cf. Rom. 11:28-29). In company with the prophets and the same Apostle, the Church awaits that day, known to God alone, on which all peoples will address the Lord in a single voice and "serve him with one accord" (Soph. 3:9; cf. Is. 66:23; Ps. 65:4; Rom. 11:11-32).

Since the spiritual patrimony common to Christians and Jews

10

is thus so great, this sacred Synod wishes to foster and recommend that mutual understanding and respect which is the fruit above all of biblical and theological studies, and of brotherly dialogues.

True, authorities of the Jews and those who followed their lead pressed for the death of Christ (cf. Jn. 19:6); still, what happened in His passion cannot be blamed upon all the Jews then living, without distinction, nor upon the Jews of today. Although the Church is the new people of God, the Jews should not be presented as repudiated or cursed by God, as if such views followed from the holy Scriptures. All should take pains, then, lest in catechetical instruction and in the preaching of God's Word they teach anything out of harmony with the truth of the gospel and the spirit of Christ.

The Church repudiates all persecutions against any man. Moreover, mindful of her common patrimony with the Jews, and motivated by the gospel's spiritual love and by no political considerations, she deplores the hatred, persecutions, and displays of anti-Semitism directed against the Jews at any time and from any source.

Besides, as the Church has always held and continues to hold, Christ in His boundless love freely underwent His passion and death because of the sins of all men, so that all might attain salvation. It is, therefore, the duty of the Church's preaching to proclaim the cross of Christ as the sign of God's all-embracing love and as the fountain from which every grace flows. *(Non-Christians, No.4)*

317. Avoiding Discrimination Due to Race, Color, Condition, or Religion

We cannot in truthfulness call upon that God who is the Father of all if we refuse to act in a brotherly way toward certain men, created though they be to God's image. A man's relationship with God the Father and his relationship with his brother men are so linked together that Scripture says: "He who does not love does not know God" (1 Jn. 4:8).

The ground is therefore removed from every theory or practice which leads to a distinction between men or peoples in the matter of human dignity and the rights which flow from it.

As a consequence, the Church rejects, as foreign to the mind of Christ, any discrimination against men or harassment of them because of their race, color, condition of life, or religion.

Accordingly, following in the footsteps of the holy Apostles Peter and Paul, this sacred Synod ardently implores the Christian faithful to "maintain good fellowship among the nations" (1 Pet. 2:12), and, if possible, as far as in them lies, to keep peace with all men (cf. Rom. 12:18), so that they may truly be sons of the Father who is in heaven (cf. Mt. 5:45). *(Non-Christians, No.5)*

Great confidence must be placed on the activity of the Holy Spirit in the world today. While fully believing that the Catholic faith contains the fullness of God's revelation, and while hoping to share Christianity with others, the convinced Catholic should, at the same time, respect the religious convictions of others. The divine Voice behind the Council continues to call all men to the Church, but It summons gently and invites graciously. The spirit of religious freedom and open dialogue with all sincere peoples of the earth has again been proclaimed. With true zeal, our witnessing to the faith and our acts of charity may best win others to join our ranks and enjoy, in the freedom the Holy Spirit imparts, the full blessings of the Christian way of life.

Chapter XII

BUILDING A BETTER WORLD

Together in God's Love

The primary mission of the Church is to proclaim Christ and His teachings for mankind's salvation, thereby to establish His kingdom in the lives of men. Nevertheless, the Church is vitally interested in helping all men to build a better world in the temporal order, both because it befits the dignity of man and likewise benefits his spiritual attainment. A stable human life helps to prepare people for acceptance of religious values. The temporal work and spiritual mission of the Church are closely intertwined, for it is most difficult for men who are burdened by misery and hunger, injustice and oppression to be interested in spiritual values or to accept the gospel message.

On the other hand, it is precisely by inculcation of the spiritual and moral values taught by Christianity that men will be led to build a better world in the temporal order by respecting the dignity and rights of their fellow men and by practicing justice and charity toward them. The conciliar passages present the blueprint for building a better human society solidly based on the practical applications of the divine order to the end that social justice and peace may prevail within the city of man as the effects of mutual cooperation, respect and charity.

Divine love is active in the world. It becomes effective in those who will accept it and live by its norms, such as by helping others. But man is free to accept or reject God's action in his life. If the Christian foundation of true love of God and of others was solidly established throughout the world, then universal justice, stability, and peace would reign. To be productive, love must be guided by truth along the course of justice to the goal of stable and peaceful human living. Otherwise the supposed love becomes weighted with meaningless and transient sentimentality. Love's test is the action it induces rather than the words it uses. Love for God and one another should manifest itself in the thousand-and-one practical ways which present themselves in daily life. Whether Christian charity is shown on a person-to-person basis, within the close circle of family and friends, or to our fellow man on the broader scale of the social order, this love must help to unify people on all levels and in all areas of life. For it is in the harmony brought about by love that our age may hope to find the justice and peace it seeks, rather than in mere empty treaties, armaments, or the promises of temporary leaders.

To put into practice the Catholic teachings on justice and charity within the social order requires an open mind and an open heart, both to follow the principles of Christian social justice and to accept the inevitable sacrifices which these grand ideals demand. The conciliar passages pull together the central teachings of the social encyclicals over the past seventy-five years; they also draw upon history, anthropology, sociology, and the doctrinal and moral principles of Christianity as applied to the current and future needs of the world.

All Christians have crucial decisions to make throughout the maturing years of their following of Christ regarding the practical applications of Christian principles in the social order. In forming one's conscience before taking action in a given situation regarding social justice, it is well to consider what the general over-all consequences of one's position on a given issue may have on the total social program of the Church. United in the same desire for human betterment, Christians can differ in the means best suited to bring about appropriate solutions to practical current problems. Hence, the abiding principles of the Church and the guidance of her shepherds provide the best guarantee for coordinated effort in areas of Christian social action. For this needed apostolate to produce worthwhile effects it should begin with prayerful knowledge of facts, continue with courageous sacrifice, and end with prudent and persistent action.

The Christian community is not expected to improve everyone's life in every aspect. Nevertheless, the mature Christian can become involved in whatever way is open − by prayer, by interest, by knowledge and by action − through cooperation with others for helping to improve the lot and the lives of the needy. Christianity can shed much light on the guiding principles for making the world more humanly decent to live in and to make it more worthy as the vestibule to heaven. United in love for God, men must work together to improve the material and spiritual standards of human living throughout the world (Section 1). The stronger the bonds of unity become among mankind, the more this crusade of hope will spread around the world under the banner of Christ which reads, "love one another — in honesty, justice, helpfulness, charity and peace". It is in this spirit that Vatican II offers for serious consideration the fundamental Christian principles capable of transforming mankind and thereby raising our world to serve as a more fitting stepping stone to everlasting life. It is by improving family-life, the socioeconomic, the national and international aspects of human living (Sections 2, 3, 4, 5) that men build a better world together in God.

The Son of Man is the Savior of mankind. His presence and His teachings should inspire Christians to work with others toward establishing an improved human society based on equality of opportunity for everyone, on practical applications of social justice, and on selfless charity toward one another. The followers of Christ are to be witnesses to the operations of His grace and love which contain the dynamic power for helping to uplift our own lives and the lives of others in whatever opportunities are available. The city of man is God's city too, for His people dwell therein. Both divine and human love should impel us to cooperate for an improved and more peaceful world with justice for all, decent living for all, and consideration for one another as children of the same heavenly Father. Charity and, as a consequence, the unity of mankind in the 20th century inspire hope for the world's improvement and its peace.

1. THE LOVE OF GOD CAN UNITE MAN AND IMPROVE LIFE IN THE WORLD

A. Christ at Work in the Hearts of Men

God's love for us is so expansive and unending that its constant unfolding will be our deepest delight in eternity. In our present life, His love is the source of our action; it transmits itself through those who make divine love both operative in their own lives and effective in the practical aspects of social living. God's love even goes so far as to give us a participation in His own attributes. By the divine gift of intelligence man can know, discover, invent and, in a sense, create. By the gift of volition man is free to choose and determine the course of his life and his actions. Thus, through Christ's costly redemption and the Holy Spirit's constant activity for the welfare and sanctification of mankind, God's love is an ever-present event in the world.

The Christian believes that Christ is at work in the hearts of those who accept Him. Also, through Christian eyes, involvement in the social needs of contemporary times is essentially the witnessing to God's desire that people establish justice and charity in the world. God's love for man sent the Son of Man to restore human nobility. This Savior gave us the Beatitudes as the guiding norm for Christian social activity. Christ expects His Church-community to implement the gospel message by engaging in the spiritual and corporal works of mercy and by pursuing meaningful activities in the field of Christian social action.

318. God's Love for Man's Life and Brotherhood

For God's Word, through whom all things were made, was Himself made flesh and dwelt on the earth of men. Thus He entered the world's history as a perfect man, taking that history up into Himself and summarizing it. He Himself revealed to us that "God is love" (1 Jn. 4:8). At the same time He taught us that the new command of love was the basic law of human perfection and hence of the world's transformation.

To those, therefore, who believe in divine love, He gives assurance that the way of love lies open to all men and that the effort to establish a universal brotherhood is not a hopeless one. He cautions them at the same time that this love is not something to be reserved for important matters, but must be pursued chiefly in the ordinary circumstances of life. *(World, No.38)*

319. Christ Works in the Hearts of Men through His Spirit

Undergoing death itself for all of us sinners, He taught us by example that we too must shoulder that cross which the world and the flesh inflict upon those who search after peace and justice. Appointed Lord by His resurrection and given plenary power in heaven and on earth, Christ is now at work in the hearts of men through the energy of His Spirit. He arouses not only a desire for the age to come, but, by that very fact, He animates, purifies, and strengthens those noble longings too by which the human family strives to make its life more human and to render the whole earth submissive to this goal. *(World, No.38)*

320. The Laity Infusing the Spirit of Christ in the World

The apostolate of the social milieu, that is, the effort to infuse a Christian spirit into the mentality, customs, laws, and structures of the community in which a person lives, is so much the duty and responsibility of the laity that it can never be properly performed by others. In this area the laity can exercise the apostolate of like toward like. It is here that laymen add to the testimony of life the testimony of their speech; it is here in the arena of their labor, profession, studies, residence, leisure, and companionship that laymen have a special opportunity to help their brothers. *(Laity, No.13)*

321. The Laity Witnessing to God's Works and Desires for the World

Each individual layman must stand before the world as a witness to the resurrection and life of the Lord Jesus and as a sign that God lives. As a body and individually, the laity must do their part to nourish the world with spiritual fruits (cf. Gal. 5:22), and to spread abroad in it that spirit by which are animated those poor, meek, and peacemaking men whom the Lord in the gospel calls blessed (cf. Mt. 5:3-9). In a word, "what the soul is to the body, let Christians be to the world." *(Church, No.38)*

B. The Solidarity of Mankind Can Increase Through Unity in Christ

The human race is essentially and universally one. Although composed of a variety of several backgrounds, cultures, colors and customs, all men partake of the solidarity of mankind with equal rights and dignity under the fatherhood of God.

The harmonization of human society can be achieved through the coordinated efforts of all men. In these times of world-wide tensions and fast-changing structures, civil law by itself is inadequate to bring about the desired solidarity of all men. Such a vast undertaking cannot be merely legislated into existence; it must proceed from an inner movement animating men's minds and hearts in their concerted aspirations for unity and peaceful living. The Son of Man offers us a staggering ideal for unity among all mankind, since He identifies Himself with all men of all nations, even the most needful and abandoned. He also admonishes His followers to care about others as the distinctive indication that they are truly His people.

The meaning of Christian witness has its culmination in our living in such phase with God's love that others discern His influence upon us. Christian witness should reflect the principles of the gospels in all practical aspects of the social order. Our conscious efforts should be directed toward the improvement of human relations in all areas — of family life and social, economic, interracial, political, national, and international development. The Church has a definite interest and place in the various aspects of the social order everywhere, yet her special mission transcends all temporal societies and is bound to no particular nation, culture or civilization. Consequently, the Christian Church-community may well be the most ideally suited supra-national society for proposing the most beneficial principles for the unification of mankind.

322. Genuine Progress Should Improve Human Relationships

One of the salient features of the modern world is the growing interdependence of men one on the other, a development very largely promoted by modern technical advances. Nevertheless, brotherly dialogue among men does not reach its perfection on the level of technical progress, but on the deeper level of interpersonal relationships. These demand a mutual respect for the full spiritual dignity of the person. Christian revelation contributes greatly to the promotion of this communion between persons, and at the same time leads us to a deeper understanding of the laws of social life which the Creator has written into man's spiritual and moral nature. *(World, No.23)*

323. True Love Unites Men in Their Heavenly Father

God, who has fatherly concern for everyone, has willed that all men should constitute one family and treat one another in a spirit of brotherhood. For having been created in the image of God, who "from one man has created the whole human race and made them live all over the face of the earth" (Acts 17:26), all men are called to one and the same goal, namely, God Himself.

For this reason, love for God and neighbor is the first and greatest commandment. Sacred Scripture, however, teaches us that the love of God cannot be separated from love of neighbor: "If there is any other commandment, it is summed up in this saying, Thou shalt love thy neighbor as thyself. . . . Love therefore is the fulfillment of the Law" (Rom. 13:9-10; cf. 1 Jn. 4:20). To men growing daily more dependent on one another, and to a world becoming more unified every day, this truth proves to be of paramount importance.

Indeed, the Lord Jesus, when He prayed to the Father, "that all may be one ... as we are one" (Jn. 17:21-22) opened up vistas closed to human reason. For He implied a certain likeness between the union of the divine Persons, and in the union of God's sons in truth and charity. This likeness reveals that man, who is the only creature on earth which God willed for itself, cannot fully find himself except through a sincere gift of himself. *(World, No.24)*

324. The Growing Inter-Dependence among Groups in the World

Every day human interdependence grows more tightly drawn and spreads by degrees over the whole world. As a result the common good, that is, the sum of those conditions of social life which allow social groups and their individual members relatively thorough and ready access to their own fulfillment, today takes on an increasingly universal complexion and consequently involves rights and duties with respect to the whole human race. Every social group must take account of the needs and legitimate aspirations of other groups, and even of the general welfare of the entire human family. *(World, No.26)*

325. Christianity Strengthens the Bonds of Unity among Mankind

The union of the human family is greatly fortified and fulfilled by the unity, founded on Christ, of the family of God's sons.

Christ, to be sure, gave His Church no proper mission in the political, economic, or social order. The purpose which He set before her is a religious one. But out of this religious mission itself come a function, a light, and an energy which can serve to structure and consolidate the human community according to the divine law. As a matter of fact, when circumstances of time and place create the need, she can and indeed should initiate activities on behalf of all men. This is particularly true of activities designed for the needy, such as the works of mercy and similar undertakings.

The Church further recognizes that worthy elements are found in today's social movements, especially an evolution toward unity, a process of wholesome socialization and of association in civic and economic realms. For the promotion of unity belongs to the innermost nature of the Church, since she is, "by her relationship with Christ, both a sacramental sign and an instrument of intimate union with God, and of the unity of all mankind." *(World, No.42)*

326. The Church Offers Mankind the Cementing Principles for Unity

Thus she shows the world that an authentic union, social and external, results from a union of minds and hearts, namely, from that faith and charity by which her own unity is unbreakably rooted in the Holy Spirit. For the force which the Church can inject into the modern society of man consists in that faith and charity put into vital practice, not in any external dominion exercised by merely human means.

Moreover, in virtue of her mission and nature, she is bound to no particular form of human culture, nor to any political, economic, or social system. Hence the Church by her very universality can be a very close bond between diverse human communities and nations, provided these trust her and truly acknowledge her right to true freedom in fulfilling her mission. For this reason, the Church admonishes her own sons, but also humanity as a whole, to overcome all strife between nations and races in this family spirit of God's children, and in the same way, to give internal strength to human associations which are just. *(World, No. 42)*

2. CHRISTIAN PRINCIPLES ON MARRIAGE, THE FAMILY, AND YOUTH'S FORMATION

A. Norms Pertaining to Christian Marriage and the Family

Before considering the conciliar passages on marriage, it will serve as a background to review some ideas on parents' responsibilities in the home. True human love has within it a participation in the divine. The cementing principle which binds the family is comparable to the unity between Christ and His Church. Recalling that the family is the natural and basic unit of society, parents should cherish and protect their God-given rights over their children as a trust from the Lord. In addition to providing for the physical, intellectual and cultural well-being of the family, the primary obligation of parents is to maintain their mutual love and to attend to the Christian formation of their children. First by their own example of a truly Christian life, and then by instructing, protecting and guiding their young ones, parents are to form the Christ like way of life in their family. This is the greatest heritage parents could leave to their children, since a well-rounded Catholic life is the best preparation for life's struggles and for future happiness.

The father is the protector and provider of his family. These responsibilities embrace not only the temporal needs and interests of the entire family, but the spiritual progress of each as well. Paternal love impels fathers to plan and work in order to provide for the future of their sons and daughters. Moreover, well-meaning fathers will try to provide for their children the best home surroundings and the best education. But in their calculations of what is best and of what their children need most, fathers of families are reminded that their own personal example, intimate companionship, and careful guidance are the best possible provisions for their sons and daughters. Children need what their father can be to them, more than what he can give to them.

The mother is the heart of a home, as the father is its head. In addition to conducting an orderly household, mothers should cultivate those qualities which foster the wholesome and peaceful development of growing boys and girls within a Christian atmosphere. It is the deep-seated beliefs of mothers that strengthen their children in faith; it is the steady confidence of mothers that calms the fears of the young through hope; it is the constant affection of mothers that brings peace into the lives of young people who only develop properly under the warming rays of love. Mothers need the determination, courage and wisdom that flows from prayerfulness to be all that God asks of them in the daily, weekly, and yearly Christian formation of their young ones. Motherly wisdom will require its keenest sense of patient understanding when dealing with the unpredictable moods, whims and activities of their teen-age children.

Christ blesses the mutual love of husband and wife at the altar in the sacrament of matrimony, from which derives the graces throughout Christian married-life for making correct decisions affecting the temporal and eternal welfare of the entire family. Responsible parenthood is, obviously, the buttress of Christian marriage and family life. Numerous decisions must be made by Christian parents. These involve decisions regarding financial affairs, educational advancement, cultural attainment, religious practices and devotions, birth instigation or limitation, and many other intimate, personal, family and social concerns. There are some occasions when diligent parents must rely more strongly upon the grace of God and the guidance of the Church. With such assistance, Catholic husbands and wives can form their consciences correctly in the light of God's laws and carry out their decisions as best they can. arents should consider matters pertaining to the welfare of the entire family with the aid of natural and divine norms as currently interpreted by authentic authority in the Church-community. Industrious parents should strive to discharge their arduous tasks with courage, faith, and peace in the love and service of our Lord, and to inculcate these same virtues in their children, so cherished by Christ and the Church.

The generation and formation by parents of other witnesses to Christ is among the noblest achievements possible to man. In addition to forming in their children the fullest human qualities, truly Christian parents furnish the security of mutual love and the stability of well-developed religious faith. These are vital for true intellectual and moral development of the children entrusted by God to the loving care of parents.

327. Married Love Is a Reflection of Divine Love

Authentic married love is caught up into divine love and is governed and enriched by Christ's redeeming power and the saving activity of the Church. Thus this love can lead the spouses to God with powerful effect and can aid and strengthen them in the sublime office of being a father or a mother.

For this reason, Christian spouses have a special sacrament by which they are fortified and receive a kind of consecration in the duties and dignity of their state. By virtue of this sacrament, as spouses fulfill their conjugal and family obligations, they are penetrated with the spirit of Christ. This spirit suffuses their whole lives with faith, hope, and charity. Thus they increasingly advance their own perfection, as well as their mutual sanctification, and hence contribute jointly to the glory of God. *(World, No.48)*

328. Total Mutual Giving in Marriage

Such love, merging the human with the divine, leads the spouses to a free and mutual gift of themselves, a gift proving itself by gentle affection and by deed. Such love pervades the whole of their lives. Indeed, by its generous activity it grows better and grows greater. Therefore it far excels mere erotic inclination, which, selfishly pursued, soon enough fades wretchedly away.

This love is uniquely expressed and perfected through the marital act. The actions within marriage by which the couple are united intimately and chastely are noble and worthy ones. Expressed in a manner which is truly human, these actions signify and promote that mutual self-giving by which spouses enrich each other with a joyful and a thankful will.

Sealed by mutual faithfulness and hallowed above all by Christ's sacrament, this love remains steadfastly true in body and in mind, in bright days or dark. It will never by profaned by adultery or divorce. Firmly established by the Lord, the unity of marriage will radiate from the equal personal dignity of wife and husband, a dignity acknowledged by mutual and total love. *(World, No.49)*

329. The Decisive Factors for Obtaining Responsible Parenthood

Parents should regard as their proper mission the task of transmitting human life and educating those to whom it has been transmitted. They should realize that they are thereby cooperators with the love of God the Creator, and are, so to speak, the interpreters of that love. Thus they will fulfill their task with human and Christian responsibility. With docile reverence toward God, they will come to the right decision by common counsel and effort.

They will thoughtfully take into account both their own welfare and that of their children, those already born and those which may be foreseen. For this accounting they will reckon with both the material and the spiritual conditions of the times as well as of their state in life. Finally, they will consult the interests of the family group, of temporal society, and of the Church herself.

The parents themselves should ultimately make this judgment, in the sight of God. But in their manner of acting, spouses should be aware that they cannot proceed arbitrarily. They must always be governed according to a conscience dutifully conformed to the divine law itself, and should be submissive toward the Church's teaching office, which authentically interprets that law in the light of the gospel. That divine law reveals and protects the integral meaning of conjugal love, and impels it toward a truly human fulfillment. *(World, No.50)*

330. Regulating the Size of Families

This Council realizes that certain modern conditions often keep couples from arranging their married lives harmoniously, and that they find themselves in circumstances where at least temporarily the size of their families should not be increased. As a result, the faithful exercise of love and the full intimacy of their lives are hard to maintain. But where the intimacy of married life is broken off, it is not rare for its faithfulness to be imperiled and its quality of fruitfulness ruined. For then the upbringing of the children and the courage to accept new ones are both endangered.

To these problems there are those who presume to offer dishonorable solutions. Indeed, they do not recoil from the taking of life. But the Church issues the reminder that a true contradiction cannot exist between the divine laws pertaining to the transmission of life and those pertaining to the fostering of authentic conjugal love.

For God, the Lord of life, has conferred on men the surpassing ministry of safeguarding life—a ministry which must be fulfilled in a manner which is worthy of man. Therefore from the moment of its conception life must be guarded with the greatest care, while abortion and infanticide are unspeakable crimes. The sexual characteristics of man and the human faculty of reproduction wonderfully exceed the dispositions of lower forms of life. Hence the acts themselves which are proper to conjugal love and which are exercised in accord with genuine human dignity must be honored with great reverence. *(World, No.51)*

331. Harmonizing Conjugal Love with Respect for Human Life

Therefore when there is question of harmonizing conjugal love with the responsible transmission of life, the moral aspect of any procedure does not depend solely on sincere intentions or on an evaluation of motives. It must be determined by objective standards. These, based on the nature of the human person and his acts, preserve the full sense of mutual self-giving and human procreation in the context of true love. Such a goal cannot be achieved unless the virtue of conjugal chastity is sincerely practiced. Relying on these principles, sons of the Church may not undertake methods of regulating procreation which are found blameworthy by the teaching authority of the Church in its unfolding of the divine law.

Everyone should be persuaded that human life and the task of transmitting it are not realities bound up with this world alone. Hence they cannot be measured or perceived only in terms of it, but always have a bearing on the eternal destiny of men. *(World, No.51)*

332. The Responsibility to Make Honest Moral Judgments Regarding Conception

Many people assert that it is absolutely necessary for population growth to be radically reduced everywhere or at least in certain nations. They say this must be done by every possible means and by every kind of government intervention. Hence this Council exhorts all to beware against solutions contradicting the moral law, solutions which have been promoted publicly or privately, and sometimes actually imposed.

For in view of the inalienable human right to marry and beget children, the question of how many children should be born belongs to the honest judgment of parents. The question can in no way be committed to the decision of government. Now since the judgment of the parents supposes a rightly formed conscience, it is highly important that every one be given the opportunity to practice upright and truly human responsibility. This responsibility respects the divine law and takes account of circumstances and the times. It requires that educational and social conditions in various places be changed for the better, and especially that religious instruction or at least full moral training be provided.

Human beings should also be judiciously informed of scientific advances in the exploration of methods by which spouses can be helped in arranging the number of their children. The reliability of these methods should be adequately proven and their harmony with the moral order should be clear. *(World, No.87)*

333. Family Life Is the School of Humanity

The family is a kind of school of deeper humanity. But if it is to achieve the full flowering of its life and mission, it needs the kindly communion of minds and the joint deliberation of spouses, as well as the painstaking cooperation of parents in the education of their children. The active presence of the father is highly beneficial to their formation. The children, especially the younger among them, need the care of their mother at home. This domestic role of hers must be safely preserved, though the legitimate social progress of women should not be underrated on that account.

Children should be so educated that as adults they can, with a mature sense of responsibility, follow their vocation, including a religious one, and choose their state of life. If they marry, they can thereby establish their family in favorable moral, social, and economic conditions. Parents or guardians should by prudent advice provide guidance to their young with respect to founding a family, and the young ought to listen gladly. At the same time no pressure, direct or indirect, should be put on the young to make them enter marriage or choose a specific partner.

Thus the family is the foundation of society. In it the various generations come together and help one another to grow wiser and to harmonize personal rights with the other requirements of social life. All those, therefore, who exercise influence over communities and social groups should work efficiently for the welfare of marriage and the family. *(World, No.52)*

B. Christian Education of Children and Youth

Before assimilating the Council passages on the formal education of the young, it will be profitable to consider some over-all aspects of their Christian formation in contemporary circumstances. Today's children and youth are living within the newer structures emerging both in society and in the life of the Church as well. The Holy Spirit works within the contemporary human situation, and the growing generation must understand their times in order to become mature Christians of this new age. Children and adolescents are learning fast these days, are taking increased initiative, and consequently may be expected to take on responsibilities in the future far different from those their forefathers were required to shoulder. Although the young people of today did not create the conditions in which they must now live, they are, nevertheless, required to carve out satisfactory human lives in accordance with the truths of Christianity. To help them achieve this goal is largely the burden of Christian education.

These are times of deep-seated change in circumstances and popular attitudes. Young people must, therefore, be prepared and trained to adapt to the times or be left behind in this fast-moving world. As young children of former generations studied their lessons using a pencil and pad, the young of future generations will be learning through computerized means and televised transmissions. Today's children must be well-prepared for tomorrow's demands on them.

Whatever may be the differing attitudes toward life or the means of expressing them, every effort must be made to assist young people and their elders in bridging the communication-gap between the generations. Adults can become overly afraid of younger people, considering them as a real threat to established modes of life. Youth, on the other hand, can look upon their elders as obstacles to "progress" and resistant to newer ideas. Intercommunication between persons of diverse views requires real, not pretended, listening on both sides if truth is to emerge. In open dialogue, derogatory adjectives cause static just as condemnatory generalities cause disharmony. Name-calling and distrust between the generations causes friction and separation. Not all young people are "rebellious and irreligious" nor are all adults "domineering and unreasonable." Part of the renewal expected in the Church-community will derive from respect for traditional standards as well as for appraisal of newer approaches. Most youths want some order but without domination, some discipline when it is reasonably based on truth rather than mere appeal to authority, and some adult guidance when convinced that their elders know where they are going and can prove the correctness of their position. Each generation must learn to respect and profit from what the other has to offer. The Council asks all to maintain an open mind, a listening ear, a discerning eye, and understanding heart toward others.

Regarding specific ideals about youth's formation and education, adults should re-evaluate the Church's educational system, the existing youth programs and organizations, liturgical celebrations for the young, and the manner of presenting Christian doctrine and morality in the light of modern life and the trends pointed out by Vatican II. The future Christian community must not derive from outside forces; it must develop dynamically from the Church of today for the youth of this and coming generations.

Through whatever institutions in the future the Christian education of the young may be imparted, Christ has enjoined upon His followers the serious obligation of teaching others His saving truths until the end of time. Whether this teaching is accomplished at home or in schools or in centers, the Christian education and formation of children and youth is of prime importance. True education must aim primarily at preparing a person to live in the realization that he is a creature of God, with the duty of living by God's norms now so that he may one day enjoy his eternal destiny. In short, the primary function of true education must ultimately be the formation of Christian character. Hence, to form the perfect man of Christ-like character is the proper and immediate aim of Christian education. Included in this ideal is the perfecting of youth's natural abilities and powers, chiefly the intellect and the will, which become more properly developed under the elevating influence of God's grace. Young people would then be better prepared to cope with the particular difficulties of living as true Christians under the conditions of modern times and in the face of any circumstances of their personal or local environment.

It follows as a consequence of this aim that the scope of Catholic education must embrace the whole of human living, since all of life should be directed toward the Creator. The physical, intellectual, cultural and religious development of youth, as well as their individual, domestic and social relationships, are included within the scope of Christian education. Such education embraces all spheres and aspects of human living, in order to elevate, regulate and perfect the natural by means of the supernatural. It is the integrated man, soul united to body in a marvelous way, who must be educated for time and for eternity. Man comes from God, must live God's way, and is destined for God. All phases of human life — physical, intellectual, emotional, aesthetic, moral and religious — have a bearing on the purpose of life and, consequently, on the education of children for life. So also has every form of social living within the family, the Church, and the school; within the local community, the nation, and the solidarity of all nations. The religious and moral formation of youth is not merely one phase of their education. Their service of God and of their fellow man should be the outstanding motives for a richer and happier life. Such a well-rounded education would then produce spiritually vigorous Catholic young men and women who are intelligent, cultured, healthy, vocationally prepared, social-minded, and patriotic.

The true product of Catholic education must maintain a supernatural character which is deeply imbued with the spirit and the grace of Christ. Such a person of developed but controlled natural powers would be deeply interested in the activities of this life, which he would make more perfect by elevating his actions to the supernatural order. In this way his actions would make more noble all that is finest in human life. The products of Christian education must be young men and women of sound judgment, of high principles, and of strong Christ-like character.

334. Some Guidelines for the Education of Children and Adolescents

Since every man of whatever race, condition, and age is endowed with the dignity of a person, he has an inalienable right to an education corresponding to his proper destiny and suited to his native talents, his sex, his cultural background, and his ancestral heritage. At the same time, this education should pave the way to brotherly association with other peoples, so that genuine unity and peace on earth may be promoted. For a true education aims at the formation of the human person with respect to his ultimate goal, and simultaneously with respect to the good of those societies of which, as a man, he is a member, and in whose responsibilities, as an adult, he will share.

As a consequence, with the help of advances in psychology and in the art and science of teaching, children and young people should be assisted in the harmonious development of their physical, moral, and intellectual endowments. Surmounting hardships with a gallant and steady heart, they should be helped to acquire gradually a more mature sense of responsibility toward ennobling their own lives through constant effort, and toward pursuing authentic freedom. As they advance in years, they should be given positive and prudent sexual education. Moreover, they should be trained to take their part in social life, so that by proper instruction in necessary and useful skills they can become actively involved in various community organizations, be ready for dialogue with others, and be willing to act energetically on behalf of the common good. (*Education, No.1*)

335. Basic Aims of Christian Education and Character Formation

Since every Christian has become a new creature by rebirth from water and the Holy Spirit, so that he may be called what he truly is, a child of God, he is entitled to a Christian education. Such an education does not merely strive to foster in the human person the maturity already described. Rather, its principal aims are these: that as the baptized person is gradually introduced into a knowledge of the mystery of salvation, he may daily grow more conscious of the gift of faith which he has received; that he may learn to adore God the Father in spirit and in truth (cf. Jn. 4:23), especially through liturgical worship; that he may be trained to conduct his personal life in righteousness and in the sanctity of truth, according to his new standard of manhood (Eph. 4:22-24).

Thus, indeed, he may grow into manhood according to the mature measure of Christ (cf. Eph. 4:13), and devote himself to the upbuilding of the Mystical Body. Moreover, aware of his calling, he should grow accustomed to giving witness to the hope that is in him

(1 Pet. 3:15), and to promoting that Christian transformation of the world by which natural values, viewed in the full perspective of humanity as redeemed by Christ, may contribute to the good of society as a whole. Therefore this holy Synod reminds pastors of souls of their acutely serious duty to make every effort to see that all the faithful enjoy a Christian education of this sort, especially young people, who are the hope of the Church. *(Education, No.2)*

336. Parent's Responsibility for Their Childrens' Christian Education

Since parents have conferred life on their children, they have a most solemn obligation to educate their offspring. Hence, parents must be acknowledged as the first and foremost educators of their children. Their role as educators is so decisive that scarcely anything can compensate for their failure in it. For it devolves on parents to create a family atmosphere so animated with love and reverence for God and men that a well-rounded personal and social development will be fostered among the children. Hence, the family is the first school of those social virtues which every society needs.

It is particularly in the Christian family, enriched by the grace and the office of the sacrament of matrimony, that from their earliest years children should be taught, according to the faith received in baptism, to have a knowledge of God, to worship Him, and to love their neighbor. Here, too, they gain their first experience of wholesome human companionship and of the Church. Finally, it is through the family that they are gradually introduced into civic partnership with their fellow men, and into the People of God. Let parents, then, clearly recognize how vital a truly Christian family is for the life and development of God's own people. *(Education, No.3)*

337. The Religious and Moral Training of Children and Youth

The Church is keenly aware of her very grave obligation to give zealous attention to the moral and religious education of all her children. To those large numbers of them who are being trained in schools which are not Catholic, she needs to be present with her special affection and helpfulness. This she does through the living witness of those who teach and direct such students, through the apostolic activity of their schoolmates, but most of all through the services of the priests and laymen who transmit to them the doctrine of salvation in a way suited to their age and circumstances, and who afford them spiritual assistance through programs which are appropriate under the prevailing conditions of time and setting.

The Church reminds parents of the serious duty which is theirs of taking every opportunity—or of making the opportunity—for their children to be able to enjoy these helps and to pace their development as Christians with their growth as citizens of the world. For this reason, the Church gives high praise to those civil authorities and civil societies that show regard for the pluralistic character of modern society, and take into account the right of religious liberty, by helping families in such a way that in all schools the education of their children can be carried out according to the moral and religious convictions of each family. *(Education, No. 7)*

338. Teaching Others, Especially Youth, Both Obedience and Self Reliance

Many pressures are brought to bear upon men of our day, to the point where the danger arises lest they lose the possibility of acting on their own judgment. On the other hand, not a few can be found who seem inclined to use the name of freedom as the pretext for refusing to submit to authority and for making light of the duty of obedience.

Therefore, this Vatican Synod urges everyone, especially those who are charged with the task of educating others, to do their utmost to form men who will respect the moral order and be obedient to lawful authority. Let them form men too who will be lovers of true freedom—men, in other words, who will come to decisions on their own judgment and in the light of truth, govern their activities with a sense of responsibility, and strive after what is true and right, willing always to join with others in cooperative effort.

Religious freedom, therefore, ought to have this further purpose and aim, namely, that men may come to act with greater responsibility in fulfilling their duties in community life. *(Freedom, No. 8)*

339. The Function of Catholic Schools

Among all the agencies of education the school has a special importance. By virtue of its very purpose, while it cultivates the intellect with unremitting attention, the school ripens the capacity for right judgment, provides an introduction into the cultural heritage won by past generations, promotes a sense of values, and readies for professional life. By creating friendly contacts between students of diverse temperament and background, the school fosters among them a willingness to understand one another. Moreover, the school sets up a kind of center whose operation and progress deserve to engage the joint participation of families, teachers, various kinds of cultural, civic, and religious groups, civil society, and the entire human community. *(Education, No.5)*

340. Teachers' Function in Catholic Schools

But let teachers realize that to the greatest possible extent they determine whether the Catholic school can bring its goals and undertakings to fruition. They should, therefore, be trained with particular care so that they may be enriched with both secular and religious knowledge, appropriately certified, and may be equipped with an educational skill which reflects modern-day findings. Bound by charity to one another and to their students, and penetrated by an apostolic spirit, let them give witness to Christ, the unique Teacher, by their lives as well as by their teachings. *(Education, No.8)*

341. The State's Function in Education

For the rest, it is incumbent upon the state to provide all citizens with the opportunity to acquire an appropriate degree of cultural enrichment, and with the proper preparation for exercising their civic duties and rights. Therefore, the state itself ought to protect the right of children to receive an adequate schooling. It should be vigilant about the ability of teachers and the excellence of their training. It should look after the health of students and, in general, promote the whole school enterprise. But it must keep in mind the principle of subsidiarity, so that no kind of school monopoly arises. For such a monopoly would militate against the native rights of the human person, the development and spread of culture itself, the peaceful association of citizens, and the pluralism which exists today in very many societies. *(Education, No.6)*

3. CHRISTIAN STANDARDS FOR
THE SOCIO-ECONOMIC ORDER

A. Protection of Human Dignity and
Justice Amid Economic Progress

Everyone is involved, at least to some degree, in the socio-economic order as social beings living in some form of community and having material needs which require fulfillment. Families, as well as the unmarried, must sustain themselves in the work-a-day world through the necessity of earning a living and improving the cultural level of all concerned.

The purpose and end of created goods, of economic and political systems, and indeed of all true human associations is the welfare of the human beings for whom they exist. Christian teaching loudly proclaims that the dignity and improvement of the human person must be maintained along with the advancement of the socio-economic order. Man is the source, the center, and the purpose of all production, agricultural and industrial. He must not be made a mere instrument of economic productivity. Furthermore, the rising expectations of humanity for progress and a more equitable distribution of the productiveness of the world are legitimate aspirations. Human labor should advance man's total development. Consequently, the economic order should help man to fulfill not only his material needs but also his spiritual requirements.

Winding all through the documents of the Council is the consistent plea that the dignity of every human being be respected. Possibly in no other area are men ground down and their human respect pulverized so badly as in the area of social and economic injustices. Although statistics merely approximate the reality of the situation, it may help to reflect briefly on some projected figures about the future of man with the implication that we must strive to improve the economic conditions throughout the world now.

Of the present 120 nations of the world, by the year 2,000 there will be about 6,000,000,000 people on the earth. Of this figure it is estimated that around two billion people will be living luxuriously or comfortably. At the same time there will be another two billion living moderately well through hard work. However, unless more is accomplished to improve the living conditions of the poor, a minimum of one-third of the human beings on the earth will be suffering from varying degrees of poverty, destitution, ignorance, starvation, disease, misery and frustration. This horrendous condition seems concentrated in Asia, Africa and Latin America, the lands requiring our greatest concern and missionary endeavors. The human dignity of the downtrodden must be uplifted in the socio-economic order. This is the will of Christ as expressly proclaimed by His Church, particularly in an age of vast agricultural and industrial potential for the improvement of the human condition of the world's people.

Christ came primarily to bring about the salvation of mankind. Yet that salvation also entails helping people live in the world with decency, freedom, justice and peace. Although the Church was not founded to solve all problems or feed all people, she most assuredly yearns to help all people with regard to their practical problems and human requirements. The followers of Christ are required by Him to be vitally concerned with establishing a universally just and stable social order for every human being.

342. More Universal Social Justice Is Required in Socio-Economic Areas

In the socio-economic realm, too, the dignity and total vocation of the human person must be honored and advanced along with the welfare of society as a whole. For man is the source, the center, and the purpose of all socio-economic life.

As in other areas of social life, modern economy is marked by man's increasing domination over nature, by closer and more intense relationships between citizens, groups, and countries and by their mutual dependence, and by more frequent intervention on the part of government. At the same time progress in the methods of production and in the exchange of goods and services has made the economy an apt instrument for meeting the intensified needs of the human family more successfully.

Reasons for anxiety, however, are not lacking. Many people, especially in economically advanced areas, seem to be hypnotized, as it were, by economics, so that almost their entire personal and social life is permeated with a certain economic outlook. These people can be found both in nations which favor a collective economy as well as in others. (World, No.63)

343. The Economic Order Should Also Advance Man's Cultural and Spiritual Needs

Today, more than ever before, progress in the production of agricultural and industrial goods and in the rendering of services is rightly aimed at making provision for the growth of a people and at meeting the rising expectations of the human race. Therefore, technical progress must be fostered, along with a spirit of initiative, an eagerness to create and expand enterprises, the adaptation of methods of production, and the strenuous efforts of all who engage in production—in a word, all the elements making for such development.

The fundamental purpose of this productivity must not be the mere multiplication of products. It must not be profit or domination. Rather, it must be the service of man, and indeed of the whole man, viewed in terms of his material needs and the demands of his intellectual, moral, spiritual, and religious life. And when we say man, we mean every man whatsoever and every group of men, of whatever race and from whatever part of the world. Consequently, economic activity is to be carried out according to its own methods and laws but within the limits of morality, so that God's plan for mankind can be realized. *(World, No.64)*

344. Requirements of Individuals Must Be Regarded

Growth must not be allowed merely to follow a kind of automatic course resulting from the economic activity of individuals. Nor must it be entrusted solely to the authority of government. Hence, theories which obstruct the necessary reforms in the name of a false liberty must be branded as erroneous. The same is true of those theories which subordinate the basic rights of individual persons and groups to the collective organization of production.

Citizens, for their part, should remember that they have the right and the duty, which must be recognized by civil authority, to contribute according to their ability to the true progress of their own community. Especially in underdeveloped areas, where all resources must be put to urgent use, those men gravely endanger the public good who allow their resources to remain unproductive or who deprive their community of the material and spiritual aid it needs. The personal right of migration, however, is not to be impugned. *(World, No.65)*

345. Human Labor Should Enhance Total Human Development

Human labor which is expended in the production and exchange of goods or in the performance of economic services is superior to the other elements of economic life. For the latter have only the nature of tools.

Whether it is engaged in independently or paid for by someone else, this labor comes immediately from the person. In a sense, the person stamps the things of nature with his seal and subdues them to his will. It is ordinarily by his labor that a man supports himself and his family, is joined to his fellow men and serves them, and is enabled to exercise genuine charity and be a partner in the work of bringing God's creation to perfection. Indeed, we hold that by offering his labor to God a man becomes associated with the redemptive work itself of Jesus Christ, who conferred an eminent dignity on labor when at Nazareth He worked with His own hands. *(World, No.67)*

B. Concerning A More Equitable Socio-Economic Order

The grace of God operates within man's interior being; the goods of earth influence man's exterior living. Both the spiritual and the material aspects of man's life must be gratified to attain the Christian ideal. To achieve balanced human development, man must render to life's material needs what is required and to life's spiritual needs what is essential. The founding of the kingdom of God on earth includes the establishment of a just social and economic order of which equal opportunity is an essential ingredient.

Since our Savior poured Himself out for mankind's salvation, His followers imitate the perfection of their Lord's sacrifice by giving more and more of themselves to the betterment of humanity in His name. In striving to perfect the social and economic order, man further develops his resemblance to God. We here summarize some central aspects of a just socio-economic order as presented throughout the documents of Vatican II.

1. All men are created with equal dignity in the image of God and have the right to attain salvation in decent circumstances. God destined the earth and everything it contains for the use of all mankind so that all created things would be shared fairly, in justice inspired by charity.

2. Nevertheless, vast numbers of people are deprived of the abso-

lute necessities of life while some live in luxury and squander their wealth. Such imbalance is unjust and engenders unrest and endangers world peace. At times these immense economic inequalities are linked with individual and social discrimination against others.

3. In order to rectify these imbalances, increased production and more equitable distribution of goods are required. This becomes particularly urgent now, as the world's population is growing at an accelerated rate. Economic progress is an urgent necessity, provided the increased production becomes more widely distributed, especially with the poorer people sharing in the increase.

4. The ultimate and basic purpose of economic production goes beyond the satisfaction of material needs reaching to the service of all mankind and considering not only man's material needs but also his intellectual, cultural, moral and spiritual requirements. If economic development does not develop the whole man, then it becomes suspect as to the true worth of increased production.

5. In order to have true economic development, it is essential that as many people as possible participate in the direction and sharing of that development. On the international plane, all nations should be considered; on the level of groups or among individuals, the harmonious linking with public authorities should be properly coordinated, and government — as well as groups or individuals — should not monopolize the sources of productivity.

6. The right to private ownership is innate but it must always be considerate of the common good and the equal rights of others. Developed nations must assist under-developed nations to uplift themselves since the goods of the earth are for all mankind's betterment materially, culturally, and spiritually.

7. Workers should be involved in the process of decision-making and should share equitably in the profits of the common enterprise, while at the same time recognizing the rights and due profits of management and corporate ownership.

8. Finally, human labor is man's right and duty and it is superior to all other elements of economic productivity. Employment must be provided and labor must be diligently rendered for which an equitable remuneration must be given as suitable for raising one's family in dignity, with educational opportunity and the means for attaining the cultural and spiritual advancement of the entire family. Christians believe in the dignity of human labors for, through the homage of work offered to God, man is associated with the redemptive mission of Jesus Christ.

Obviously, unjust discrimination against others, inequitable compensation for honest labor, objectionable working conditions, monopoly for the means of production, an unfair share in profits, and all such inequities cry to heaven for rectification. The human suffering that results from injustices in the socio-economic order are incalculable in extension and excruciating in dimension. In a truly Christian society, the underprivileged will be given every opportunity for improvement. The poor, disadvantaged, oppressed, and the weak must be objects of deep concern to the followers of Christ. Having Himself experienced suffering and frustration from injustice, the Savior of mankind desires that the cross of social and economic injustice be eliminated from the face of the earth.

346. Conditions Which Foster Total Development of Workers

From all these considerations there arise every man's duty to labor faithfully and also his right to work. It is the duty of society, moreover, according to the circumstances prevailing in it, and in keeping with its proper role, to help its citizens find opportunities for adequate employment. Finally, payment for labor must be such as to furnish a man with the means to cultivate his own material, social, cultural, and spiritual life worthily, and that of his dependents. What this payment should be will vary according to each man's assignment and productivity, the conditions of his place of employment, and the common good.

The opportunity should also be afforded to workers to develop their own abilities and personalities through the work they perform. Though they should apply their time and energy to their employment with a due sense of responsibility, all workers should also enjoy sufficient rest and leisure to cultivate their family, cultural, social, and religious life. They should also have the opportunity to develop on their own the resources and potentialities to which, perhaps, their professional work gives but little scope. (World, No. 67)

347. God's Norms for the Proper Use of Created Goods by Man

God intended the earth and all that it contains for the use of every human being and people. Thus, as all men follow justice and unite in charity, created goods should abound for them on a reasonable basis. Whatever the forms of ownership may be, as adapted to the legitimate institutions of people according to diverse and changeable circumstances, attention must always be paid to the universal purpose for which created goods are meant. In using them, therefore, a man should regard his lawful possessions not merely as his own but also as common property in the sense that they should accrue to the benefit of not only himself but of others. *(World, No. 69)*

348. Economic Inequalities and Discrimination Degrade the Social Order

If the demands of justice and equity are to be satisfied, vigorous efforts must be made, without violence to the rights of persons or to the natural characteristics of each country, to remove as quickly as possible the immense economic inequalities which now exist. In many cases, these are worsening and are connected with individual and group discrimination. *(World, No. 66)*

349. The Right to Share in the Necessities of Life

For the rest, the right to have a share of earthly goods sufficient for oneself and one's family belongs to everyone. The Fathers and Doctors of the Church held this view, teaching that men are obliged to come to the relief of the poor, and to do so not merely out of their superfluous goods. If a person is in extreme necessity, he has the right to take from the riches of others what he himself needs. Since there are so many people in this world afflicted with hunger, this sacred Council urges all, both individuals and governments, to remember the saying of the Fathers: "Feed the man dying of hunger, because if you have not fed him you have killed him." According to their ability, let all individuals and governments undertake a genuine sharing of their goods. Let them use these goods especially to provide individuals and nations with the means for helping and developing themselves. *(World, No. 69)*

350. Equal Opportunity for All with Provision for the Future

The distribution of goods should be directed toward providing employment and sufficient income for the people of today and of the future. Whether individuals, groups, or public authorities make the decisions concerning this distribution and the planning of the economy, they are bound to keep these objectives in mind. They must realize their serious obligation of seeing to it that provision is made for the necessities of a decent life on the part of individuals and of the whole community. They must also look out for the future and establish a proper balance between the needs of present-day consumption, both individual and collective, and the necessity of distributing goods on behalf of the coming generation. They should also bear constantly in mind the urgent needs of underdeveloped countries and regions. In financial transactions they should beware of hurting the welfare of their own country or of other countries. Care should also be taken lest the economically weak countries unjustly suffer loss from a change in the value of money. *(World, No. 70)*

351. Christians Should Be Motivated by Charity to Establish Socio-Economic Justice

Christians who take an active part in modern socio-economic development and defend justice and charity should be convinced that they can make a great contribution to the prosperity of mankind and the peace of the world. Whether they do so as individuals or in association, let their example be a shining one. After acquiring whatever skills and experience are absolutely necessary, they should in faithfulness to Christ and His gospel observe the right order of values in their earthly activities. Thus their whole lives, both individual and social, will be permeated with the spirit of the beatitudes, notably with the spirit of poverty.

Whoever in obedience to Christ seeks first the kingdom of God will as a consequence receive a stronger and purer love for helping all his brothers and for perfecting the work of justice under the inspiration of charity. *(World, No. 72)*

4. CHRISTIAN IDEALS WITHIN
THE NATIONAL COMMUNITY

A. Unity and Stability Within
the National Community

By first discussing the notion of community, the Council gives the concept of the State more depth, showing that authority is a reality which derives from within the national political community, not external to it or imposed upon it. The purpose of political authority is first and foremost the promotion of the common good, in whose name every act of authority should be performed and every separate power organism set up. Hence, government must aim to provide the best conditions for complete development of its citizens. Fully aware of his own dignity, rights, and opinions while respecting the same in others, each person in the national community should be given the opportunity to fulfill his life on all levels — economic, social, cultural, educational, religious, and political. Genuine democracy, though not restricted to any particular form, seems in line with man's social calling. Certainly a totalitarian government which may offer mere trappings of freedom while in practice depriving its people of their liberties is contrary to the natural rights of self-determination. Government is established for the service of its citizens, and the human person has transcendent rights which cannot be absorbed by the State.

On the other hand, civil obedience to a just government must be given as a truly human activity based on the use of one's intellect and moral judgment. Such obliged obedience does not excuse a person from assuming his rightful obligations with human dignity, in justice, and through charity which represents the fullness of the law and even transcends it. Hence, the function of government is to provide the conditions for the full development of the human personalities of those governed. Citizens should feel that they are united with their legitimate civil authorities, and they should cooperate with them in promoting the common good of the national community. In an ideal national structure all the citizens would feel that they have an integral share in the government to which they freely give their loyalty, respect and cooperation and from which they can rightfully expect to receive equal protection of rights and equitable opportunities for total human development. Under such conditions, patriotism has ever been an adjunct of Christianity and an obligation of its adherents.

In a national community that provides stability through unity of concerted effort men advance toward their fullest intellectual, cultural, economic, religious, and political attainment in accordance with the Christian ideal. The followers of Christ realize that they are members of two great societies, namely their country and their Church, and they strive to fulfill their obligations within each.

352. Unity within the National Political Community Governed by Legitimate Authority

Many different people go to make up the political community, and these can lawfully incline toward diverse ways of doing things. Now, if the political community is not to be torn to pieces as each man follows his own viewpoint, authority is needed. This authority must dispose the energies of the whole citizenry toward the common good, not mechanically or despotically, but primarily as a moral force which depends on freedom and the conscientious discharge of the burdens of any office which has been undertaken.

It is therefore obvious that the political community and public authority are based on human nature and hence belong to an order of things divinely foreordained. At the same time the choice of government and the method of selecting leaders is left to the free will of citizens.

It also follows that political authority, whether in the community as such or in institutions representing the state, must always be exercised within the limits of morality and on behalf of the dynamically conceived common good, according to a juridical order enjoying legal status. When such is the case, citizens are conscience-bound to obey. This fact clearly reveals the responsibility, dignity, and importance of those who govern. (World, No. 74)

353. The Roles of Government, Citizens, and Groups in the National Community

If conscientious cooperation between citizens is to achieve its happy effect in the normal course of public affairs, a positive system of law is required. In it should be established a division of governmental roles and institutions and, at the same time, an effective and independent system for the protection of rights. Let the rights of all persons, families, and associations, along with the exercise of those rights, be recognized, honored, and fostered. The same holds for those duties which bind all citizens. Among the latter should be remembered that of furnishing the commonwealth with the material and spiritual services required for the common good.

Authorities must beware of hindering family, social, or cultural groups, as well as intermediate bodies, and institutions. They must not deprive them of their own lawful and effective activity, but should rather strive to promote them willingly and in an orderly fashion. For their part, citizens both as individuals and in association should be on guard against granting government too much authority and inappropriately seeking from it excessive conveniences and advantages, with a consequent weakening of the sense of responsibility on the part of individuals, families, and social groups. (World, No. 75)

354. Rights and Duties of Individuals and of the Community

Because of the increased complexity of modern circumstances, government is more often required to intervene in social
and economic affairs, by way of bringing about conditions more
likely to help citizens and groups freely attain to complete human
fulfillment with greater effect. The proper relationship between
socialization on the one hand and personal independence and development on the other can be variously interpreted according to the
locales in question and the degree of progress achieved by a given
people.

When the exercise of rights is temporarily curtailed on behalf
of the common good, it should be restored as quickly as possible
after the emergency passes. In any case it harms humanity when
government takes on totalitarian or dictatorial forms injurious to
the rights of persons or social groups.

Citizens should develop a generous and loyal devotion to their
country, but without any narrowing of mind. In other words, they
must always look simultaneously to the welfare of the whole human
family, which is tied together by the manifold bonds linking races,
peoples, and nations.

Let all Christians appreciate their special and personal vocation in the political community. This vocation requires that they
give conspicuous example of devotion to the sense of duty and of
service to the advancement of the common good. Thus they can
also show in practice how authority is to be harmonized with freedom, personal initiative with consideration for the bonds uniting
the whole social body, and necessary unity with beneficial diversity.
(World, No.75)

B. Relations Between the Church and National Communities

The Church's sanctifying mission transcends all specific forms of
government, as the Christian community is comprised of citizens of all
nations, cultures and traditions. The Church and the various national
communities in which she exists are interiorly independent, but exteriorly dependent upon one another. In addition, it may well be that,
because of her transcendental function, the Church can bring great
benefits to those nations which welcome her unifying influence. Mutual
cooperation between the State and the Church can benefit both the

temporal and eternal well-being of the people they both serve. Each operates in their own sphere of competence, purpose and mission from God, from whom all legitimate authority ultimately derives its binding power.

The Christian Church has no mere earthly ambitions. Consequently, no national political community need fear her, nor should they obstruct her work among the citizens of any country. Moreover, this is an era in which the Church is striving to have deeper dialogue with all forms of government, ideologies, and movements which attempt to better the condition of people's lives. While the Church cannot become completely "secular" in the sinister sense, the Council does urge all Christians to become involved in whatever aspects of the secular world are available to them. Without explicitly intending to convert others, the Christian will certainly make every effort to uplift the human situation and help to bring out the true, good, and beautiful elements in the various communities. Just as others enjoy the right to freedom of opinion and expression in a free society, so also do Christians have the same right to witness to Christ and His Church in the various communities of the world.

355. Relations Between the Church and the Political Community

It is highly important, especially in pluralistic societies, that a proper view exist of the relation between the political community and the Church. Thus the faithful will be able to make a clear distinction between what a Christian conscience leads them to do in their own name as citizens, whether as individuals or in association, and what they do in the name of the Church and in union with her shepherds.

The role and competence of the Church being what it is, she must in no way be confused with the political community, nor bound to any political system. For she is at once a sign and a safeguard of the transcendence of the human person.

In their proper spheres, the political community and the Church are mutually independent and self-governing. Yet, by a different title, each serves the personal and social vocation of the same human beings. This service can be more effectively rendered for the good of all, if each works better for wholesome mutual cooperation, depending on the circumstances of time and place. For man is not restricted to the temporal sphere. While living in history he fully maintains his eternal vocation. (World, No.76)

356. The Church Supports Whatever Is Truly Helpful for the Human Community

There are, indeed, close links between earthly affairs and those aspects of man's condition which transcend this world. The Church herself employs the things of time to the degree that her own proper mission demands. Still she does not lodge her hope in privileges conferred by civil authority. Indeed, she stands ready to renounce the exercise of certain legitimately acquired rights if it becomes clear that their use raises doubt about the sincerity of her witness or that new conditions of life demand some other arrangement.

But it is always and everywhere legitimate for her to preach the faith with true freedom, to teach her social doctrine, and to discharge her duty among men without hindrance. She also has the right to pass moral judgments, even on matters touching the political order, whenever basic personal rights or the salvation of souls make such judgments necessary. In so doing, she may use only those helps which accord with the gospel and with the general welfare as it changes according to time and circumstance.

Holding faithfully to the gospel and exercising her mission in the world, the Church consolidates peace among men, to God's glory. For it is her task to uncover, cherish, and ennoble all that is true, good, and beautiful in the human community. *(World, No.76)*

5. CHRISTIAN COLLABORATION WITHIN INTERNATIONAL COMMUNITIES

A. Eliminating the Causes of War for International Peace

The following extensive passages present the Council's pattern for peace. Christ has charged His followers to strive for the establishment of peace based on justice and right order in individual lives, among groups, within countries, and between all nations. Peace is illusive and must constantly be sought and maintained. The temporary absence of conflict does not guarantee a lasting peace. True peace must be founded on a more steady basis than the mere balance of military power among nations. It is by erradicating the causes of social injustice that the likelihood of warfare diminishes. Disarmament also lessens the danger of armed conflict. Ultimately, peace is derived from within the minds and hearts of men from mutual respect, honesty and unselfishness. To relax the tensions among men through a just social order is to lessen the danger of violence.

Every individual can contribute by prayer and action toward peace, since even the smallest effort has some influence on the more universal scale of world peace. The first step consists in taking active interest to improve conditions on the level of one's local community. When this action becomes multiplied by that of others it improves conditions everywhere by lessening tensions, arguments and conflict that much more. On the broader scale, more effort must be made to establish some international authority with power to intercede and arbitrate disputes before they blow up into military action. The search for international peace is an absolute imperative, for the awesome alternative is the possible total devastation of mankind.

The service of one's country in some way should be expected of all citizens according to their capacity. However, in addition to serving with the armed forces there are other ways of serving one's country. There is an expanding concern for those who sincerely object in conscience to taking part in armed conflict. Reflecting the right of religious freedom, objection in conscience to personal involvement in military conflict looks toward respect for certain individual choices. When these choices bear witness to an authentic sense of human values in a higher order, such as freedom to follow one's convictions when faced with physical violence, the general quality of conscientious objectors would seem sufficient to elicit tolerant legislation in their favor from the entire community in whose name laws are passed. Furthermore, chaplains who have served with the armed forces, can testify that there really are some courageous and patriotic young men who sincerely have an innate revulsion for physical violence and cannot bring themselves to take part in warfare or its preparation. Our society has room for divergent convictions, and the consciences of all should be respected by law in areas of vital concern.

The Council passages provide many guidelines for practical action toward helping to bring about conditions for peace in the world. It would be fatalistic, hence unchristian, to maintain that there must always be contentions and wars among men. Christians must cooperate with all sincere men for the acquisition of peace among the children of God, striving to bring about that ultimate condition in the world when Christ will be able to present to the Father the peoples of all nations at peace.

357. Peace, the Longing of Mankind, Must Be Achieved

In our generation when men continue to be afflicted by acute hardships and anxieties arising from ongoing wars or the threat of them, the whole human family has reached an hour of supreme crisis in its advance toward maturity. Moving gradually together and everywhere more conscious already of its oneness, this family cannot accomplish its task of constructing for all men everywhere a world more genuinely human unless each person devotes himself with renewed determination to the reality of peace. Thus it happens that the gospel message, which is in harmony with the loftier strivings and aspirations of the human race, takes on a new luster in our day as it declares that the artisans of peace are blessed, "for they shall be called children of God" (Mt. 5:9).

Consequently, as it points out the authentic and most noble meaning of peace and condemns the frightfulness of war, this Council fervently desires to summon Christians to cooperate with all men in making secure among themselves a peace based on justice and love, and in setting up agencies of peace. This Christians should do with the help of Christ, the Author of peace. *(World, No.77)*

358. Basic Conditions for a Lasting Peace

Peace is not merely the absence of war. Nor can it be reduced solely to the maintenance of a balance of power between enemies. Nor is it brought about by dictatorship. Instead, it is rightly and appropriately called "an enterprise of justice" (Is. 32:7). Peace results from that harmony built into human society by its divine Founder, and actualized by men as they thirst after ever greater justice.

The common good of men is in its basic sense determined by the eternal law. Still the concrete demands of this common good are constantly changing as time goes on. Hence peace is never attained once and for all, but must be built up ceaselessly. Moreover, since the human will is unsteady, and wounded by sin, the achievement of peace requires that everyone constantly master his passions and that lawful authority keep vigilant.

But such is not enough. This peace cannot be obtained on earth unless personal values are safeguarded and men freely and trustingly share with one another the riches of their inner spirits and their talents. A firm determination to respect other men and peoples and their dignity, as well as the studied practice of brotherhood, are absolutely necessary for the establishment of peace. Hence peace is likewise the fruit of love, which goes beyond what justice can provide. *(World, No.78)*

359. Motives for Establishing Peace with Justice

That earthly peace which arises from love of neighbor symbolizes and results from the peace of Christ who comes forth from God the Father. For by His cross the incarnate Son, the Prince of Peace, reconciled all men with God. By thus restoring the unity of all men in one people and one body, He slew hatred in His own flesh. After being lifted on high by His resurrection, He poured the Spirit of love into the hearts of men.

For this reason, all Christians are urgently summoned "to practice the truth in love" (Eph. 4:15) and to join with all true peacemakers in pleading for peace and bringing it about.

Motivated by this same spirit, we cannot fail to praise those who renounce the use of violence in the vindication of their rights and who resort to methods of defense which are otherwise available to weaker parties too, provided that this can be done without injury to the rights and duties of others or of the community itself.

Insofar as men are sinful, the threat of war hangs over them, and hang over them it will until the return of Christ. But to the extent that men vanquish sin by a union of love, they will vanquish violence as well, and make these words come true: "They shall beat their swords into plowshares and their spears into pruning hooks; one nation shall not raise the sword against another, nor shall they train for war again" (Is. 2:4). *(World, No.78)*

360. The Morality and Immorality of Military Action

Certainly, war has not been rooted out of human affairs. As long as the danger of war remains and there is no competent and sufficiently powerful authority at the international level, governments cannot be denied the right to legitimate defense once every means of peaceful settlement has been exhausted. Therefore, government authorities and others who share public responsibility have the duty to protect the welfare of the people entrusted to their care and to conduct such grave matters soberly.

But it is one thing to undertake military action for the just defense of the people, and something else again to seek the subjugation of other nations. Nor does the possession of war potential make every military or political use of it lawful. Neither does the mere fact that war has unhappily begun mean that all is fair between the warring parties.

Those who are pledged to the service of their country as members of its armed forces should regard themselves as agents of security and freedom on behalf of their people. As long as they fulfill this role properly, they are making a genuine contribution to the establishment of peace. *(World, No.79)*

361. Total Warfare Is Fully Condemned

The horror and perversity of war are immensely magnified by the multiplication of scientific weapons. For acts of war involving these weapons can inflict massive and indiscriminate destruction far exceeding the bounds of legitimate defense. Indeed, if the kind of instruments which can now be found in the armories of the great nations were to be employed to their fullest, an almost total and altogether reciprocal slaughter of each side by the other would follow, not to mention the widespread devastation which would take place in the world and the deadly aftereffects which would be spawned by the use of such weapons.

All these considerations compel us to undertake an evaluation of war with an entirely new attitude. The men of our time must realize that they will have to give a somber reckoning for their deeds of war. For the course of the future will depend largely on the decisions they make today.

With these truths in mind, this most holy Synod makes its own the condemnations of total war already pronounced by recent Popes, and issues the following declaration:

Any act of war aimed indiscriminately at the destruction of entire cities or of extensive areas along with their population is a crime against God and man himself. It merits unequivocal and unhesitating condemnation.

The unique hazard of modern warfare consists in this: it provides those who possess modern scientific weapons with a kind of occasion for perpetrating just such abominations. Moreover, through a certain inexorable chain of events, it can urge men on to the most atrocious decisions. That such in fact may never happen in the future, the bishops of the whole world, in unity assembled, beg all men, especially government officials and military leaders, to give unremitting thought to the awesome responsibility which is theirs before God and the entire human race. *(World, No.80)*

306 EXPLORING VATICAN II

362. The Military Arms Race Is a Treacherous Trap for Humanity

While extravagant sums are being spent for the furnishing of every new weapon, an adequate remedy cannot be provided for the multiple miseries afflicting the whole modern world. Disagreements between nations are not really and radically healed. On the contrary other parts of the world are infected with them. New approaches initiated by reformed attitudes must be adopted to remove this trap and to restore genuine peace by emancipating the world from its crushing anxiety.

Therefore, it must be said again: the arms race is an utterly treacherous trap for humanity, and one which injures the poor to an intolerable degree. It is much to be feared that if this race persists, it will eventually spawn all the lethal ruin whose path it is now making ready.

Warned by the calamities which the human race has made possible, let us make use of the interlude granted us from above and in which we rejoice. In greater awareness of our own responsibility let us find means for resolving our disputes in a manner more worthy of man. Divine Providence urgently demands of us that we free ourselves from the age-old slavery of war. But if we refuse to make this effort, we do not know where the evil road we have ventured upon will lead us. *(World, No.81)*

363. International Action for Avoiding Wars Is Essential

It is our clear duty, then, to strain every muscle as we work for the time when all war can be completely outlawed by international consent. This goal undoubtedly requires the establishment of some universal public authority acknowledged as such by all, and endowed with effective power to safeguard, on the behalf of all, security, regard for justice, and respect for rights.

But before this hoped-for authority can be set up, the highest existing international centers must devote themselves vigorously to the pursuit of better means for obtaining common security. Peace must be born of mutual trust between nations rather than imposed on them through fear of one another's weapons. Hence everyone must labor to put an end at last to the arms race, and to make a true beginning of disarmament, not indeed a unilateral disarmament, but one proceeding at an equal pace according to agreement, and backed up by authentic and workable safeguards. *(World, No.82)*

364. Individual as Well as Governmental Efforts for Disarmament and Peace

The problems of peace and of disarmament have already been the subject of extensive, strenuous, and relentless examination. Together with international meetings dealing with these problems, such studies should be regarded as the first steps toward solving these serious questions. They should be promoted with even greater urgency in the hope that they will yield practical results in the future.

Nevertheless, men should take heed not to entrust themselves only to the efforts of others, while remaining careless about their own attitudes. For government officials, who must simultaneously guarantee the good of their own people and promote the universal good, depend on public opinion and feeling to the greatest possible extent. It does them no good to work at building peace so long as feelings of hostility, contempt, and distrust, as well as racial hatred and unbending ideologies, continue to divide men and place them in opposing camps.

Hence arises a surpassing need for renewed education of attitudes and for new inspiration in the area of public opinion. Those who are dedicated to the work of education, particularly of the young, or who mold public opinion, should regard as their most weighty task the effort to instruct all in fresh sentiments of peace. Indeed, every one of us should have a change of heart as we regard the entire world and those tasks which we can perform in unison for the betterment of our race.

But we should not let false hope deceive us. For enmities and hatred must be put away and firm, honest agreements concerning world peace reached in the future. Otherwise, for all its marvelous knowledge, humanity, which is already in the middle of a grave crisis, will perhaps be brought to that mournful hour in which it will experience no peace other than the dreadful peace of death.

But while we say this, the Church of Christ takes her stand in the midst of the anxiety of this age, and does not cease to hope with the utmost confidence. She intends to propose to our age over and over again, in season and out of season, this apostolic message: "Behold, now is the acceptable time" for a change of heart; "behold, now is the day of salvation!" *(World, No.82)*

B. Establishing a Better World in God

Just as Christ longed to save the whole world from sin, death, and debasement, so also the world-wide Council speaks the mind of Christ in terms of the global or "universal" Catholic mission of His Church. Although Christians comprise only a percentage of the peoples of the earth, it has been a constant effort of the Church to work for the unification of all men in Christ Jesus. Working together with all men, movements, and agencies, the Church longs to help establish a truly international community with justice, cooperation, good-will, and a peacefully progressive social order for all mankind.

From the Christian viewpoint of life, the spiritual and material aspects of the human situation are inter-related as objects of apostolic endeavor. God reveals Himself to man as love and it is precisely in this love that the Lord reveals each man unto himself, opening up a deeper insight into his inner being. New advances in man's life-experience bring him deeper knowledge of divine love in his regard. Furthermore, the same God who is man's creator is also his redeemer. It is the same God who is Lord of man's salvation history who likewise works through human history. Hence the Church is, in Christ, like a sacramental sign of a very closely-knit union with God which looks toward the unity of the whole human race in Him. Consequently, where true human progress exists in the social development of man it may be considered as happening with the assistance of the Spirit of God at work in the world. When we strive to build a better world together in God's love, we are fostering the work of the Holy Spirit toward the establishment of the kingdom of Christ.

In briefest terms, this building of an improved world on Christian principles might be listed in the following areas, each of which would require further expansion and implementation in order to be effective.

1. Spiritual realities must be acknowledged in men's lives, and the trend toward the complete secularization of life offset by man's realization that it is God who is the source of all true power in a world created for humanity's own betterment. In this spirit man's temporal improvement advances his spiritual welfare.

2. Because men are formed in the divine image, every form of human degradation must be wiped out. Devastating poverty, degrading illiteracy, and debilitating health must be eliminated. Job training and opportunity along with wider economic productivity must be fostered on all local, national, and international levels, particularly among disadvantaged people.

3. In addition to increased educational opportunity, cultural advancements must become widespread bringing the advantages of history, literature, drama, music and all the creative arts to the peoples of the world. To this end, libraries, museums, and cultural centers should be established, especially where not available in the poorer towns and villages of the world.

4. The complex problems of racial and class contentions must be resolved, and prejudice and discrimination replaced by fair labor, housing, educational, social and cultural opportunities for all.

5. The causes of crime and delinquency should be exposed and removed, and the communities freed of vice, such as promiscuity, narcotics, alcoholism, gangsterism and other deteriorations of public standards and morals, particularly detrimental to the young.

6. Respect for law and order must be inculcated and enforced. A wholesome sense of patriotism should be fostered which would also relate to other countries and consider international relationships among all peoples.

7. Some international agency must be formed and empowered to outlaw war and enforce peace among nations through arbitration of differences and curtailment of armed conflict.

8. To establish ideal cooperation among all nations of the world, the more developed nations must assist the less developed countries, which in turn should even help those nations which are worse off than they are to emerge from primitive standards of living. If each nation helped to raise the standards of those behind them, the spirit of mutual assistance would relax suspicions of taking advantage one of the other and would expand the sense of unity among all nations. If justice and charity are to become the norms, then it is not only the more wealthy nations which must give, but rather every nation has something to share with those less developed. Scientific, technological, agricultural, industrial, economic, social, and cultural sharing by every nation would help to build a better world in which each nation would give an equitable percentage of what it has in order to uplift those less well-off in the family of nations.

9. Catholics should cooperate with all individuals and with organized agencies at the local, national, and international levels to promote world-wide social, economic, educational, political, and cultural assistance to others in need.

10. The mission efforts of the Church require even wider extension, particularly in the less developed areas of the world, as in Asia, Africa, and in sections of Central and South America. To foster this

mission expansion, Church laws and practices should be made more adaptable throughout the various parts of the world for the spread of the gospel of Christ everywhere.

Everyone is invited to cooperate in good works with others and with international agencies which aim toward improving the condition of men throughout the world. The bureaus of the United Nations on world poverty, health and education, as well as the Papal commission pertaining to world justice, development and peace, serve as models for other agencies to foster organized assistance. Young adults are especially requested to lend their talents, time, and energy to help make this a more decent world in the name of the God of all mankind.

Despite the ideological, political, cultural, economic, and religious differences among the various nations of the world, men are drawing closer together in their common aspirations for equality, justice, solidarity, and peace. All over the earth there is expectation of a greater human existence in this world. Men are longing to live as respectable persons with secure possession of life's necessities, a greater chance to acquire knowledge and culture, and a wider freedom for self and group determination with improvement of life for all in an atmosphere of peaceful development.

This is a crucial era for Christianity. The secular elements in the world are energetically moving ahead. The Christian community must not lag behind, for it is the Church of Christ's ever-dynamic gospel message for man's welfare and salvation. The course marked out by the Second Vatican Council must not be altered by obstruction of its aims, or lethargy toward its trends, or mockery to its intent. From within the ranks of the Church harm can be done by calling the Council a feeble attempt to catch up with the times or to look upon it as just another move of the "establishment". It is likewise detrimental to the efforts of the great Council to suspect its directives as tinged with secularism, humanism, utopianism, relativism, or to tag it with other unfounded "isms". This Council has committed the Church-community to join with all people of goodwill in the common effort to build a better world.

The "signs of the times" are seen for the most part as "signs of God's workings" to improve the condition of mankind throughout the world − in food, health, housing, employment, education and so on − with a spirit of brotherly friendship in God in the various practical aspects of human living. All of this should certainly prepare men to accept Christ's revelation for ultimate salvation. In the surge for community improvement, the importance of the individual's spiritual life is in no way lessened; rather it must become even more intensive through prayer, self-denial, liturgical participation, and self-giving toward others for the sake of God. Christ died that men might rise from the grip of sin, death, and degradation as unbecoming to images of His heavenly Father. By cooperating together in God to build a better human world men can more readily attain their eternal salvation which is available for all by the Redeemer of all.

365. The Laity's Global Mission for the Church

Now, in view of the progress of social institutions and the fast-moving peace of modern society, the global nature of the Church's mission requires that apostolic enterprises of Catholics should increasingly develop organized forms at the international level. Catholic international organizations will more effectively achieve their purpose if the groups comprising them, as well as their members, are involved more closely and individually in these international organizations.

As long as the proper relationship is kept to Church authorities, the laity have the right to found and run such associations and to join those already existing. Yet the scattering of energies must be avoided. This waste occurs when new associations and projects are promoted without a sufficient reason, or if antiquated associations or methods are retained beyond their period of usefulness. Nor is it always fitting to make an indiscriminate transfer to other nations of forms of the apostolate that have been used in one nation. (Laity, No.19)

366. Practical Solutions for the Problems of Nations

Today the bonds of mutual dependence become increasingly close between all citizens and all the peoples of the world. The universal common good needs to be intelligently pursued and more effectively achieved. Hence it is now necessary for the family of nations to create for themselves an order which corresponds to modern obligations, particularly with reference to those numerous regions still laboring under intolerable need.

For the attainment of these goals, agencies of the international community should do their part to provide for the various necessities of men. In the field of social life this means food, health, education, and employment. In certain situations which can obtain anywhere, it means the general need to promote the growth of developing nations, to attend to the hardships of refugees scattered throughout the world, or to assist migrants and their families.

The international agencies, both universal and regional, which already exist assuredly deserve well of the human race. These stand forth as the first attempts to lay international foundations under the whole human community for the solving of the critical problems of our age, the promotion of global progress, and the prevention of any kind of war. The Church rejoices at the spirit of true fraternity flourishing between Christians and non-Christians in all these areas. This spirit strives to see that ever more intense efforts are made for the relief of the world's enormous miseries. *(World, No.84)*

367. Governments, Population Growth and Improving Standards of Living

International cooperation becomes supremely necessary with respect to those peoples who, in addition to many other problems, are today often enough burdened in a special way with the difficulties stemming from a rapid population growth. There is an urgent need for all nations, especially the richer ones, to cooperate fully and intensely in an exploration as to how there can be prepared and distributed to the human community whatever is required for the livelihood and proper training of men. Some peoples, indeed, would greatly better their conditions of life if they could be duly trained to abandon ancient methods of farming in favor of modern techniques. With necessary prudence they should adapt these techniques to their own situations. In addition they need to establish a better social order and regulate the distribution of land with greater fairness.

Within the limits of their own competence, government officials have rights and duties with regard to the population problems of their won nation, for instance, in the matter of social legislation as it affects families, of migration to cities, of information relative to the condition and needs of the nation. Since the minds of men are so powerfully disturbed about this problem, the Council also desires that, especially in universities, Catholic experts in all these aspects should skillfully pursue their studies and projects and give them an ever wider scope. *(World, No.87)*

368. Christian Collaboration to Establish a Better World

Christians should collaborate willingly and wholeheartedly in establishing an international order involving genuine respect for all freedoms and amicable brotherhood between all men. This objective is all the more pressing since the greater part of the world is still suffering from so much poverty that it is as if Christ Himself were crying out in these poor to beg the charity of the disciples.

Some nations with a majority of citizens who are counted as Christians have an abundance of this world's goods, while others are deprived of the necessities of life and are tormented with hunger, disease, and every kind of misery. This situation must not be allowed to continue, to the scandal of humanity. For the spirit of poverty and of charity are the glory and authentication of the Church of Christ. *(World, No.88)*

369. The Christians' Call to Serve the Poor and Needy

Christians, especially young people, are to be praised and supported, therefore, when they volunteer their services to help other men and nations. Indeed, it is the duty of the whole People of God, following the word and example of the bishops, to do their utmost to alleviate the sufferings of the modern age. As was the ancient custom in the Church, they should meet this obligation out of the substance of their goods, and not only out of what is superfluous.

Without being inflexible and completely uniform, the collection and distribution of aid should be conducted in an orderly fashion in dioceses, nations, and throughout the entire world. Wherever it seems appropriate, this activity of Catholics should be carried on in unison with other Christian brothers. For the spirit of charity does not forbid but rather requires that charitable activity be exercised in a provident and orderly manner. Therefore, it is essential for those who intend to dedicate themselves to the service of the developing nations to be properly trained in suitable institutions. *(World, No.88)*

370. Christian Involvement, Especially of Youth, in Contemporary Needs

In pursuit of her divine mission, the Church preaches the gospel to all men and dispenses the treasures of grace. Thus, by imparting knowledge of the divine and natural law, she everywhere contributes to strengthening peace and to placing brotherly relations between individuals and peoples on solid ground. Therefore, to encourage and stimulate cooperation among men, the Church must be thoroughly present in the midst of the community of nations. She must achieve such a presence both through her public institutions and through the full and sincere collaboration of all Christians, a collaboration motivated solely by the desire to be of service to all.

This goal will come about more effectively if the faithful themselves, conscious of their responsibility as men and as Christians, strive to stir up in their own area of influence a willingness to cooperate readily with the international community. In both religious and civic education, special care must be given to the proper formation of youth in this respect. *(World, No.89)*

371. Catholic Cooperation with All Men to Build a Better World

Finally, this Council desires that by way of fulfilling their role properly in the international community, Catholics should seek to cooperate actively and in a positive manner both with their separated brothers, who together with them profess the gospel of love, and with all men thirsting for true peace.

In view of the immense hardships which still afflict the majority of men today, the Council regards it as most opportune that some agency of the universal Church be set up for the world-wide promotion of justice for the poor and of Christ's kind of love for them. The role of such an organization will be to stimulate the Catholic community to foster progress in needy regions, and social justice on the international scene. *(World, No. 90)*

God is always at work in the world for man's benefit. Christianity is God's fullest "economy," serving as a framework for the unfolding of His love and His design for man's welfare. God has willed that men become His partner in the development of the world. The mystery of building a better world is akin to the mystery of Christ's incarnation. He uplifted mankind by becoming Himself a man, and in that very process He redeemed the world. In a similar way the Church enters into intimate association with humanity. By becoming one with mankind the Church becomes more human and thereby more capable of making divine-like the peoples of the earth.

Hopefully, the followers of Christ will not become tarnished but rather will gain more luster by rubbing shoulders with all genuine secular interests of life. The Church is not lessening her true grandeur by moving through the streets and alleys of the earth. She is acquiring deeper insights, more practical contacts, and, as befits her calling, is sacrificing herself all the more for mankind's welfare and salvation. The Church constantly refuses to shrivel up and be consigned to a rocking chair to watch the world pass by without so much as a nod to her saving influence. The Church has true life and wishes to share it most abundantly with all who will accept it. She is the gracious mother of fair love, of true light, and of ultimate salvation, with kindly and understanding ways, modern and temperate means, divine and human resources, and temporal as well as eternal interests. For the benefit of all mankind, the Church of the Vatican II era is making more effective in the world the presence of Christ, – the loving Savior of mankind.

Summary of Part Four – WITNESS

This fourth and final part of the book sought to send Christians forth as witnesses of Christ and the Christian way of life in the communities of the world. The Holy Spirit of truth, whom the Father sent in Christ's name, is actively at work in the world preparing man for salvation. The Spirit of Christ continues this work through our Christian vitality and involvement in helping our fellow-man (Chapter XI). Since God is love, all men should combine in love for him, and for each other, in a mighty crescendo of effort toward the building of a better world in the practical aspects of life (Chapter XII). This fourth part has presented the essential principles for Christian living in the contemporary social order of the Vatican II era for the welfare of mankind and the greater glory of God, as the following passage beautifully reflects.

372. May Witness Show Completer Involvement of Christians in the World's Communities

Mindful of the Lord's saying: "By this will all men know that you are my disciples, if you have love for one another" (Jn. 13:35), Christians cannot yearn for anything more ardently than to serve the men of the modern world ever more generously and effectively. Therefore, holding faithfully to the gospel and benefiting from its resources, and united with every man who loves and practices justice, Christians have shouldered a gigantic task demanding fulfillment in this world. Concerning this task they must give a reckoning to Him who will judge every man on the last day.

Not everyone who cries, "Lord, Lord," will enter into the kingdom of heaven, but those who do the Father's will and take a strong grip on the work at hand. Now, the Father wills that in all men we recognize Christ our brother and love Him effectively in word and in deed. By thus giving witness to the truth, we will share with others the mystery of the heavenly Father's love. As a consequence, men throughout the world will be aroused to a lively hope — the gift of the Holy Spirit — that they will finally be caught up in peace and utter happiness in that fatherland radiant with the splendor of the Lord.

"Now, to him who is able to accomplish all things in a measure far beyond what we ask or conceive, in keeping with the power that is at work in us — to him be glory in the Church and in Christ Jesus down through all the ages of time without end. Amen" (Eph. 3:20-21). *(World, No.93)*

CONCLUDING SUMMARY

Achieving Vatican II's Four Main Goals

To assist in accomplishing the Council's aims, this book, EX-PLORING VATICAN II, is intended as an aid for Christian living in this current age. The Council's main goals are organized within the four parts of the book, bearing the designations as Renewal, Commitment, Unity and Witness. Reflecting on Christian life today, the followers of Christ are urged to deepen their spiritual renewal (Part One), strengthen their commitment to Christ's cause (Part Two), and enliven their unity in the worship of God (Part Three), from which they can thereafter be full witnesses of Christianity in the contemporary world (Part Four).

Renewal, the rejuvenation of Christian vitality in modern times, is, like the breath of life itself, constantly essential for a healthy spiritual existence in the Church-community (Part One). A human person is a remarkable being possessing a marvelous potential for good, with each of us created to love and be loved in the image of our gracious and loving Lord. To live as God's own people responding to His call (Chapter I), while maintaining the proper balance between the sacred and the secular interests of life (Chapter II), prevents the shattering of human lives through sin and its degradation (Chapter III) and fosters the attainment of salvation, which is the very purpose and supreme fulfillment of man's life (Chapter IV).

It is in the service of Christ and His cause by His people that a life of Christian dedication fulfills its commitment (Part Two). Since our Lord Himself is present and effective with all individuals who respond to His loving call within His Church-community, (Chapter V), Christ's people in action become externally effective in advancing His kingdom on earth through their apostolate in the world (Chapter VI). Just as

Christ warned the early disciples, so also His guiding Church cautions His followers today to discern carefully between the movements of the Holy Spirit whom Christ sends, and the influences of evil which are in the world (Chapter VII). While Christians press on to accomplish their constant challenge to holiness of life (Chapter VIII), the Church-community ever strives to fulfill the mission entrusted to it by Christ.

The relevance of ecumenism's unifying results and of the liturgy's sanctifying effects is most appropriate today for strengthening the bonds of faith, hope, and charity among the People of God as our Savior desires (Part Three). Ecumenism, or unity among the followers of Christ, is a command from the Lord who insisted, even unto His death, that His people be unified as He and the Father are united (Chapter IX). The consummation of Christian unity is achieved when Christ's paschal mystery becomes fully effective through man's complete and consistent participation in His sacred and fruitful liturgical rites and celebrations (Chapter X), beyond which lies only the eternal liturgy of heaven.

The mature followers of Christ will witness in the world their love for the Lord Jesus, and, through Him, their love for all peoples of the earth. In this spirit, Christians should assist their least brethren in the practical aspects of life on this globe and toward the eternal life beyond with God (Part Four). Today's Pentecost of the Holy Spirit is actively at work inspiring the People of God to respond to their Lord's promptings (Chapter XI), in whose name and by whose strength they can cooperate with all men of good will to build a better world together in the love of God Almighty (Chapter XII). The involvement of Christians, and indeed, of all good people, in uplifting the spirit and condition of mankind throughout the world, comprises proof of their love of God and of their religious witness to His love in the world.

Vatican Council II will, undoubtedly, not be the last word in the development of the dynamic gospel message or of the ever-current Church of Christ. This Council is, however, the contemporary application of the gospels for Christians in modern times. The present era offers great opportunity to be truly alive in Christ and to glimpse the vision of tomorrow by exploring the Vatican II Church of today. Our Creator's world is opening up vast new horizons of hope for our own age and for future generations. The betterment and salvation of mankind, through Christ Jesus, our Savior, is all the more to the praise, service and greater glory of God.

SUPPLEMENT

THE JESUIT WAY FOR ASSISTING CONTEMPORARY CHRISTIANS

Relating the Spiritual Exercises of St. Ignatius Loyola
to the Spirit of Vatican II

The supplement is not essential to the full use of this book for private reading, group discussion, or personal meditation. It will be useful, however, for those who conduct or make religious retreats of various kinds, based on the Spiritual Exercises of St. Ignatius.

Briefly, the Spiritual Exercises are a Christ-centered system of meditations with a man-oriented objective; they assist people to become more alive in Christ. The genius of the Exercises is that they are based on sacred Scripture and they apply the dynamics of salvation history while appropriating the effects of Christ's paschal mystery for the spiritual lives of the exercitants. This Ignatian system of meditations, organized in four major stages, called "weeks", also contains pastoral guidelines for helping Christians to cooperate with the Holy Spirit's promptings in their following of Christ. The Exercises are the Jesuit way for assisting people to live the Christian life as applied to the Vatican II era.

This supplement offers some relevant points regarding the adaptation, the application, and the dynamism of the Ignatian Exercises for current needs in the light of Vatican Council II. It is hoped that the relevancy of the Spiritual Exercises will, through *Exploring Vatican II,* become more evident and more fruitful for promoting Christian living in contemporary circumstances.

1. The Adaptation of the Spiritual Exercises After Vatican II

Although the Spiritual Exercises were originated by Saint Ignatius in the 16th century, they belong to the universal Church and remain, with some accommodations, particularly well-suited to the needs of the 20th century. Pope Paul VI, from the See of Peter, saw the Spiritual Exercises as extremely relevant for fostering Christian living in the Vatican II era. His Holiness gave some pointed norms for the adaptation of the Exercises to the needs of the times.

"Retreat directors must never cease to deepen their understanding of the doctrinal and spiritual riches of the Ignatian text, and to express those riches in terms of the theology of Vatican Council II . . . . The director should present the insights of the Exercises. . . . in the theological context with which modern laymen will be familiar." [1]

"Some are said to doubt the relevancy and effectiveness of the Exercises in the present time; even in your Society there are said to be some who do not think highly of them. How badly they are mistaken! The Exercises, rooted as they are in the pure spirit of the gospel, must be considered even today as most useful and effective. Would that they were ever more widely used! The service which the Society has rendered to the Church through the Exercises can scarcely be sufficiently praised. It is clear, however, that the Exercises, like other things in the Church, must be accommodated to the present times. I wish that excellent and well-edited books of the Exercises might be widely diffused . . . . " [2]

"It would be very deplorable if the Spiritual Exercises, precisely because of the wonderful and outstanding structure which Saint Ignatius gave them, should degenerate into a formalistic and, I dare say, lazy repetition of the outline. The depth of the doctrine, the wealth and applicability of the spiritual values that they contain must be carefully brought to light. A new elaboration of the Spiritual Exercises should therefore be undertaken, and we look forward to seeing this done by our zealous priests." [3]

Although the Spiritual Exercises of St. Ignatius Loyola belong to the whole Church, the Jesuits are especially entrusted with the responsibility of preparing new texts, of revising the directory to them, and of making recommendations for bringing them up to date. The General of the Society of Jesus provides some valuable guidelines for the adaptation of the Ignatian method in the light of Vatican II.

"It is evident that it would be an anachronism to continue to give the Exercises today according to plans that ignore the Council . . . . It is, therefore, not much to ask of one who lives after the great Council that he make a prolonged, intense, and untiring study of the Spiritual Exercises in the light of the actual teaching of the Church."[4]

"In the institutes (for the training of directors of the Exercises) there should be research into the genuine meaning of the Ignatian text; indeed, there should be a real reworking of the Spiritual Exercises themselves to unfold their spiritual riches to modern man, and to express them in the concepts of the theology of the Second Vatican Council . . . . May you keep in mind the sacredness of the Exercises and also the desire of St. Ignatius that the Exercises be adapted to present day situations and problems." [5]

"The study of the Exercises of Saint Ignatius is more urgent now than in the past. It is our task to review the various methods which have been introduced in the course of time, to examine the defects which have occurred, and to infuse the authentic power which in many places the Exercises seem to have lost. It is also necessary to coordinate the Spiritual Exercises with pastoral activity and to integrate into them those tendencies of the present time which accord with their nature. All this requires that we know what is principal and permanent in the Ignatian method and that we discover the way in which the Exercises should be applied to the present generation. This effort to adapt the Exercises to present conditions is necessary not only because of the objective evolution of the times, but also because of the high regard which the Church has repeatedly shown for the Exercises of Saint Ignatius." [6]

"These Exercises cannot respond to the needs of modern man unless they are integrated with the spiritual doctrine of the Council and accommodated to modern pastoral concerns. On the other hand they cannot produce their proper results unless, in giving them, the Ignatian form and structure is preserved." [7]

Following the directives of Pope Paul VI and the General of the Jesuits, members of the Society of Jesus throughout the world are urged to study how the Spiritual Exercises may be better adapted to the theology and the trends of Vatican II.

"All retreat masters, besides having a thorough understanding of the Exercises, should be well-versed in the documents of Vatican II, and every means should be used to attain this result." [8]

"On the updating of the Spiritual Exercises of St. Ignatius, we (at the International Congress on the Exercises and Vatican II) make the following observations:

A — There is no question of changing the Exercises into a manual of conciliar theology. They are and remain after Vatican II the same as they were before, a guide to the spiritual life.

B — Yet we have to distinguish between the spiritual insight and the theological mentality of Saint Ignatius. The insight is the charism (grace) given to Saint Ignatius for the Church. This is to be kept in its purity by the Society. But the theology in which this charism is expressed — the theology which it makes use of, or which was applied to it in the past — can and should be renewed according to the living consciousness which the Church has gained about the mysteries of our Faith.

C — The Exercises, then, can no longer be presented in a theological context that is foreign to that of Vatican II. For we would be unfaithful to the Church herself whom we wish to serve, and there would arise in the minds of the exercitants confusion and an unjustifiable anxiety, with serious harm to the fruit of the Exercises. On the contrary, through the Society's loyalty to the Council's 'aggiornamento', the Exercises should benefit from the renewal which ought to embrace the whole Church." [9]

Adaptation, then, to the current needs of those making the Spiritual Exercises today has become an essential of the Ignatian method in our time. The selection of the Exercises to be used and the type of retreat to be conducted depend on the contemporary requirements of the particular retreatants at hand. People make retreats for a variety of personal reasons such as for conversion, renewal, enlightenment, election and other purposes. To designate the various uses of the Spiritual Exercises, adjectives help to clarify some of their adaptations. There are elemental exercises, abbreviated exercises, the full exercises, in addition to closed retreats, dialogue retreats, theme retreats, enlightenment retreats, etc. [10] The selection of material for meditation and consideration on a retreat depends on the needs of the retreatants and can include a wide variety of subject-matter.

"It is agreed that, according to the mind of Saint Ignatius, the subject-matter for the instructions (and the arrangement of exercises in a retreat) can legitimately be extended to include other subjects such as the liturgy, Scripture, apologetics, the doctrines of the Council, the sacraments, Mass, etc., according to the needs expressed by the retreatants." [11]

Any religious exercises, Ignatian or otherwise, in order to be fruitful should be based on sacred Scripture and have a relationship to the living Christ in the liturgy of the Eucharist and the sacraments. The Exercises of St. Ignatius are composed from Scripture and from his experience of the spiritual life. [12] The road traveled in the four weeks of the Spiritual Exercises is intimately identified with salvation history, with its climax in the paschal mystery, which, in the theology of Vatican II, is fully expressed and lived in the sacred liturgy. [13]

"The whole dynamics of the Exercises in the four weeks is the dynamics of the paschal mystery . . . . The 'Principle and Foundation' already places before us the beginning of salvation history with God's plan for saving men. Man tries to thwart this plan through sin; but the Father's love is so great that He sends Christ to save us by His cross, and so our 'exodus' from sin to life in the Lord is brought about (first week). At the end of the second week St. Ignatius presents our Lord's entry in Jerusalem on Palm Sunday (Spiritual Exercises text n. 161). In Scripture this is considered as the prelude to the paschal event. The first contemplation of the third week is on the Lord's last supper (ns. 190, 191, 289), so basic to the paschal mystery.

The third and fourth weeks are of a particular importance as regards the paschal mystery. In them we move from an interior knowledge of our Lord (n. 104) to an identification with the suffering (n. 203) and glorified Christ (n. 221). The apostles themselves passed through these stages to a full knowledge of the mystery of Christ, and in the same way man enters the paschal event, according to the meaning of St. Paul's teaching about this mystery." [14]

The documents issued from Vatican Council II are filled with quotations, references, and the spirit and application of sacred Scripture. These documents also contain much of the currently developed theology. They provide excellent source material for conducting or making retreats in contemporary times. Consequently, the conciliar passages which pertain to Christian living in modern times have been arranged for use in various kinds of retreats. The following section shows how the parts and chapters of this book reflect the weeks and meditations of the Spiritual Exercises of St. Ignatius.

2. The Application of the Spiritual Exercises with the Aid of This Book EXPLORING VATICAN II

Reflections on Christian Living Today (Modeled on the Ignatian Exercises)

The organization of this book fits the framework of the four weeks and the area of the more commonly employed meditations of the Spiritual Exercises of St. Ignatius. A brief explanation will show how this book may be used in conjunction with the Exercises for conducting or making a retreat with contemporary tones.

It is taken for granted that the retreat director would follow the basics of the Exercises, and would use sacred Scripture widely while judiciously employing the material from Vatican II. At the end of the introduction to each chapter there is a central theme which may easily be converted to the grace of the corresponding meditation. Likewise, each chapter contains a concluding reflection which, with slight expansion, can be widened into a suitable prayer or colloquy with which to conclude a meditation. To obtain the fullest impact of the Spiritual Exercises, St. Ignatius advised that the exercitant should not proceed further until he has gleaned the desired fruit week by week in the progressive stages provided for his ripening spiritual life. Consequently, the summary of each part in this book can serve as a review of the corresponding "week" as well as presenting matter for repeating some of the meditations when this is deemed appropriate.

Each chapter contains so much material for meditation that selectivity will, obviously, be required. There is ample matter for several retreats. Countless meditations could be made from the Vatican II passages with their numerous scriptural references.

PART ONE – RENEWAL, The Rejuvenation of Christian Vitality in Modern Times

(THE FIRST WEEK: Spiritual Exercises text, No. 1 - 90) [15]

Part one of the book, *Exploring Vatican II,* may be adapted to the first week of the Exercises. The method of presenting the Exercises of this week wholly from a philosophical approach of first causes seems unsuited to many, especially young adults, in modern times. A scriptural approach in conjunction with the current needs of man as expounded in the documents of Vatican II will make the presentation of the first-week meditations more contemporary. [16]

"The teachings of Vatican II have enriched and thrown much light on the Ignatian Exercises. They have also brought us to study the dynamic unity of the Exercises. Consequently, the genuine Spiritual Exercises, deeply imbued as they are with the doctrine of the Council, can be a very strong pastoral instrument to promote the spiritual renewal desired by Vatican II. For through the Exercises the way is open to attaining the sanctity which, according to the Council, every one must strive to attain in accordance with his state in life . . . ." [17]

The material for meditation during the first week is contained in four chapters. The Principle and Foundation is a brief statement of God's loving plan for man in the history of salvation by our living as God's people today (Chapter I). Man's active response to God's love will consist in great measure in the wise use of created things and human institutions or in integrating the secular and the sacred through spiritual wisdom (Chapter II). Renewal in both the individual's life and that of the community is presented (Chapter III), wherein there is ample material for consideration on the effects of and remedies for personal and communal sin. Whatever aspects of escatology will most benefit the exercitant should be offered for meditation on the last things, life's fulfillment and finality (Chapter IV).

The Ignatian Exercises are an excellent method for communicating God's love as contained in the Vatican II messages which call for personal and community rejuvenation of Christian vitality in modern times.

Chapter I

LIVING AS GOD'S PEOPLE TODAY
For Meaningful Lives

(The Principle and Foundation 1; A Statement of Salvation History and
Human Experience; Spiritual Exercises text, No. 23)

The Principle and Foundation in the Spiritual Exercises is a compact statement summarizing the history of salvation and containing a compendium of human experience in the spiritual life. The presentation of the Principle and Foundation to retreatants should not be merely philosophical; it must be scriptural, theological, and contemporary. The first act of the history of salvation is the revelation and communication of divine love to mankind. Man's generosity must freely respond to the goodness of God who reveals Himself in creation, in the individual's life, and in His Church-community.

The Principle and Foundation exercise, as it flows from the Ignatian experience, is based on the way of salvation which contains the call, the covenant, and the paschal passover of the People of God who fulfill their purpose in life according to God's plan. [18]

"The history of salvation offers a most apt prospective under which the Exercises could and ought to be given. Directors of the Exercises should familiarize themselves with this approach, for it has in it a profitable method for making contact with the modern mind. In particular, salvation history opens to us the entire divine plan in our regard and invites us to enter into it through the ecclesial and sacramental life." [19]

In the current age of secular humanism which attempts to find meaning for human life devoid of divine purpose, the retreatants may require some consideration of preambles to the faith even before considering the Principle and Foundation in the Exercises. Since a retreat of spiritual experiences is conducted for people in their current and concrete circumstances, this chapter or meditation begins with a consideration of God's interest in the problems of modern man (Section 1). Salvation history is then briefly presented (Section 2) within the perspective of the People of God responding to the will, love, and plan of their Lord (Section 3).

Chapter II

INTEGRATING THE SECULAR AND THE SACRED –
Through Wisdom in Our Times

(The Principle and Foundation 2; The Proper Use of Creatures, etc.; Spiritual Exercises text, No. 23)

The problem of integrating the secular and the sacred is as old as the history of salvation. The solution lies in using wisely all created things according to God's plan, for this results in life's improvement and sanctification, which leads toward the attainment of eternal life. This chapter, considering the contemporary condition of man in the world, presents the proper use of creatures within the Christian existential perspective.

"The nature of the Foundation and its contents should have an existential consideration (what is going on? what is man doing in this world?) which can resound to the aspirations of our times. Notice that the concern here is man as free; this is close to modern thought about man." [20]

Indeed, man responds to God precisely in the human conditions of life in the secular world as it is. Hopefully, the Christian uplifts human society by reason of his wise choices in the light of the divine and natural laws and their legitimate application in specific areas of life.

It will require the wisdom which comes from prayer and detachment in order to integrate throughout life the secular creatures of God and the sacred intentions God has for their proper use. A peaceful life can only be established by following the right order intended by God for man's life (Section 1). Establishing the proper harmony between the secular and the sacred, as the Vatican II passages point out, not only assures a happy eternal life but also benefits human living on earth (Section 2). To use creatures wisely is to serve God well in both the sacred and the secular realms, integrating both in Him.

Chapter III

PREVENTING SHATTERED LIVES –
Of Personal and Communal Sin

(Sin in General and in One's Life; Spiritual Exercises text, Nos. 45-65)

This chapter treats of sin in the dimensions both of one's personal life and of the community, as do the meditations on sin in the Spiritual Exercises. With the flare and vivid language of the 16th century, St. Ignatius presented the considerations of sin's effects on the individual with its ramifications on the health of the human community in general.

"The biblical themes proposed by Saint Ignatius are suited to the understanding of the mystery of sin as it is operative in today's world and as it afflicts humanity. This sin overcomes us and constitutes the 'mystery of iniquity' which is also represented by a superhuman reality, with which Christ himself engaged in battle." [21]

In 20th century language, Vatican II considers the effects of personal sin which men commit in their lives and the effects of communal injustices and imbalances which exist in the world. There are both personal and global effects of culpable sin involved in the transgression of God's designs for man's highest activity occasioned by failing to follow a right conscience individually or collectively (Section 1). The affront or indignity which sin causes to God's laws, to man's true worth, and to the community is next considered (Section 2). In the Christian spirit of hope to improve man's life and to prevent shattered lives, the Church offers aids for the renewal of mankind in God (Section 3).

Chapter IV

LIFE'S FULFILLMENT AND FINALITY –
Through Eternal Values

(Escatology; the Last Things – Death, Resurrection, Heaven, Hell; Spiritual Exercises text, Nos. 65-72)

It is important that man understands the true purpose of life; it is essential that he attain life's goal, his salvation. This chapter treats of the life hereafter, man's attainment of eternal salvation and transformation, which is his ultimate purpose of life on earth.

The Ignatian meditations on life's finality leave much room for incorporating the latest theological developments regarding the ultimate fulfillment of human existence, and of the world, in the newer life that awaits those whose love for God and man endures (Section 1). While he strives for eternal life, man's assignment from God is to establish with Christ His kingdom on earth, which includes improvement of the human condition (Section 2).

This is the briefest chapter in the book, but it contains a most important lesson for life on earth, because it motivates and orientates man toward attaining his true eternal life with Christ and his loved ones.

PART TWO – COMMITMENT, The Service of Christ's Cause by His People Today

(THE SECOND WEEK; Spiritual Exercises text, Nos. 91-189)

Part two of this book corresponds to the second week of the Spiritual Exercises. The person who is making a retreat in the Ignatian pattern is called upon to contemplate the life and teachings of Christ in order that he or she may become more united with our Lord and more committed to His cause in today's world. The Spiritual Exercises help people to follow Christ more closely in the spirit and precepts of the gospel. The mysteries of the life of Christ which are chosen for contemplation should pertain to the practical needs of the retreatants in the circumstances of their Christian vocation in daily life.

The meditation on the kingdom (Chapter V) prepares the exercitant for personal commitment to Christ and His cause in the apostolate of contemporary times.

"The value of the interior offering made in the meditation on Christ's kingdom should not be extolled by distinguishing it from its apostolic implication. For according to Saint Ignatius the efficacy of the apostolate necessarily depends on the authentic spiritual offering of oneself to Christ; this offering is the most thoroughly Ignatian source of the whole apostolate." [22]

The meditations on the Incarnation and the life of Christ as applied to lay people and others ultimately pertain to their Christian apostolate (Chapter VI). The meditations on the Two Standards (Chapter VII), the Three Classes of Men and the Three Degrees of loving service have an inter-relationship.

"The three meditations − on the Two Standards, the Three Classes of Men and Three Degrees of Love − are very important today because they express universal experience. This becomes clear in the light of the universal call to sanctity. These meditations are not individualistic, but rather their context and purpose are apostolic. Taken together they form a whole unit. Their purpose is to actualize the 'sentire' (the sense of feeling truth deeply) of Saint Ignatius. This state is necessary for every Jesuit and laymen, both for making the election and for engaging in a genuine apostolate."[23]

Part two of this book, like the second week or stage of the Exercises helps to form, under the benign working of the Holy Spirit, the mature modern Christian dedicated to the service of Christ and His cause. No matter what else the experience of making the Ignatian Exercises may produce, greater personal holiness should always result (Chapter VIII). As a consequence of holiness a more fruitful apostolate may spread throughout the world.

Chapter V

CHRIST'S PRESENCE AMONG HIS PEOPLE −
His Kingdom and His Church

(The Kingdom of Christ; Spiritual Exercises text, Nos. 91-99. Also, Guidelines for an Authentic Catholic Outlook, Nos. 352-370)

Some may look upon Christ as the embodiment of religious principles; others, more correctly, experience Him personally both in His divine nearness and in His holy Church with her liturgy, blessings, and helpfulness. To those who respond generously to Christ's call He is the more present; for, to experience Christ's presence is to fall in love with His cause, His people, His Church.

"The contemporary nature of the mysteries of Christ are not merely past events, but are truly present today in the glorified Christ, and in Him they are efficacious for us. Consequently, the contemplation of the mysteries of Christ's life opens the way to a personal contact with Christ Himself, living and working in the Church and dwelling in the hearts of His disciples. Modern studies of Scripture show that the evangelists were aware of that active presence of the glorified Christ, living in the Church, and that they had the current needs of the churches in mind." [24]

Once an individual or a group of Christians becomes fully committed to our Lord, they become heralds of Christ's message to the world. This is the mission or calling of His followers to the apostolate.

"Since the mystery of Christ is the mystery of Him who was sent by the Father and who sends the Church as He Himself was sent, in the meditation of the kingdom there should be no opposition between one's personal offering to Christ and one's consecration to the apostolate. This supposes, of course, that the apostolate be not identified only with merely external activities of whatever kind, even generous ones." [25]

Christ truly dwells among His people, and this is a constantly unfolding mystery (Section 1). Catholics believe that their Christian community has been entrusted with the fullness of Christ's revelation and with all the means for salvation's attainment, in which all mankind is invited to share (Section 2). Service is the keynote of commitment, as it is of the responsibility of religious leaders in the Church (Section 3). As with the clergy and religious, so also with the laity, their integral role in the Church derives from their active commitment to Christ in His priestly, prophetic and kingly roles (Section 4). Christ's presence among His people comprises His kingdom on earth.

Chapter VI

CHRIST'S PEOPLE IN ACTION –
The Laity's Apostolate

(The Effects of Christ's Incarnation in Action;
Spiritual Exercises text, Nos. 101-126)

The meditation on the Incarnation of Christ prepares for and is augmented by subsequent meditations on the life of Christ as applicable to the retreatants' lives. These Ignatian meditations consider Christ as calling His people in order to further His saving mission throughout the towns and cities of the whole world, among every race of men in all that they think or say or do. Once a Christian has been incorporated in Christ, the action of the Holy Spirit continues to further the apostolate.

"The experience of the Holy Spirit through an infused inner attraction is an experience within the Church, the 'sacrament of Christ'. The Church nourishes and authenticates this experience in the contemplation leading to the election and confirming it, and in the election itself, whether it be made intuitively or by reasoning. The norm is, according to this, to have the same sentiments within the Church as those which are in Christ Jesus." [26]

When people become dedicated to furthering our Lord's mission in their lives, then the incarnate Lord increases His redemptive work in the world more fully through them (Section 1). The incarnational Church extends the effects of Christ's redemption by the salvific activity of the Holy Spirit in the Church's members (Section 2). In order to be effective in their apostolate the faithful require solid formation to fulfill their essential mission (Section 3).

Chapter VII

DISCERNING THE SPIRIT OF CHRIST —
In The Signs of The Times

(The Two Standards; Spiritual Exercises text, Nos. 136-148. Also, Discerning Between Good and Evil Influences, Nos. 313-336)

People can easily be led astray by their own self love or by the worldly attractions which entice them from their main goal. Evil spirits, as acknowledged in holy Scripture and as evidenced by Christ's struggle for man's welfare, still attempt to deceive mankind with lies and distortions of reality. Life is not lived in a vacuum of unreality, nor does the Holy Spirit work in the clouds. Both human life and the Holy Spirit operate in the daily circumstances of ordinary living. In order to assure that Christ's ways prevail throughout life, people need discernment to ascertain wherein the good or the evil influences may predominate. Obviously, the followers of Christ will make every effort to follow His ways, otherwise disorder, sin, and unhappiness will predominate.

"Since the responsibility of every member of the People of God is being more and more consciously felt, and is growing day by day in keeping with the mind of the Council, the faithful followers of Christ should be zealously initiated through the Exercises into true personal discernment, following the spirit of the Church, in the very act of discerning and choosing." [27]

The knowledge of evil can come from revelation, observation, prayer, or spiritual wisdom; it should not derive from personal experience. The knowledge of evil helps people to avoid it, as the knowledge and desire of good leads to the acquisition of virtue.

"The knowledge of the will of God is achieved gradually, by means of the discernment of spirits. It is God who reveals himself to man in the Holy Spirit, through illuminations and constant inspirations in man's soul. With this in mind, we must consider the election in the supernatural order, that is, inasmuch as it is the work of the Holy Spirit. It presupposes a climate of intense prayer and full openness to the movements of the Holy Spirit." [28]

Hence, this chapter presents for meditation an analysis of some of the signs and conditions of the times (Section 1). It points out the harrowing emptiness of atheism and irreligion (Section 2), and provides some basic solutions to the needs of the times (Section 3).

Chapter VIII

THE CONSTANT CHRISTIAN COMMITMENT –
The Call to Holiness

(The Universal Call to Sanctity; The Three Types of Christians, The Three Levels of Love, and the Election; Spiritual Exercises text, Nos. 149-189)

Christians have a constant vocation to follow Christ in holiness throughout their lives. This is what election means; the free personal and full response to Christ's call and His cause.

"The Ignatian Exercises get their organic, dynamic unity from the Election. But we must consider the Election in its full biblical sense (Is. 43:1-17; Deut. 5). This means that we choose or 'elect'

God because God has chosen us beforehand. I do not bring about my own vocation or union with Christ; God has granted even to me a share in that call which is extended to all mankind, and even to the whole cosmos, in Christ. It is not a question of a merely ethical or psychological act of my own free choice, but of a divine initiative toward my liberty, received in a thankful, filial spirit. It is in this sense that we choose Christ poor, Christ lowly, Christ crucified." [29]

What others have accomplished in the service of Christ we also can strive to do with His help, provided we rely on His grace, His friendship, and His promise of future glorification.

"The election as an event should be considered in the light of the history of salvation. On man's side, then, it means a generous response, an 'exodus' to perfection from a less perfect state, or a conversion ('metanoia' in its fuller, biblical sense). Concretely, it means the paschal mystery of Christ: a continuous process, a movement of the spirit in which a real configuration to Christ Jesus poor, lowly, stripped, crucified, is applied to the individual. This 'Christ-formation' is the basis and the source of our Easter exultation in the risen Christ." [30]

This calling from Christ requires a response from His followers, which means to live the gospel message leading to genuine holiness of life (Section 1). The fuller our dedication to Christ and His cause becomes, the more complete will be our commitment (Section 2). For our assistance in following Christ more completely we recall the inspiration and example of the Blessed Mother (Section 3) whose complete dedication to the will of God won for her the highest attainment of sanctity among human beings. She can be of the greatest assistance in helping today's Christians in their quest for holiness.

PART THREE – UNITY, The Relevance of Ecumenism and the Liturgy in our Age

(THE THIRD WEEK: Spiritual Exercises text, Nos. 190-217)

Part three contains material from the Council aptly suited for use in the third week of the Exercises. The redemptive events in our Lord's life contain the central mysteries of man's salvation. His sacred passion, death, and resurrection provide the basic source for man's unity in

Christ, and for his essential sharing in the effects of our Redeemer's paschal mystery, particularly as contained in the sacred liturgy. The function of worship of God entails practical applications of the great commandment to love the Lord and, in Him to be united in love with one's neighbor. Such was our Lord's bequest, which He especially emphasized prior to His redemptive death. The practice of ecumenism and the summit of Christianity — the sacred liturgy — are especially relevant to our age in which it is so emphatically imperative for mankind to become united in God. Unison among Christians reaches its peak when there can be united worship of the Lord in the liturgical life of the Church-community.

In addition to reviewing the historical passion and death of our Lord, the retreatants could profitably meditate on the present-day suffering within the Mystical Body of Christ, and, indeed, the whole world. Hence, one vastly important aspect of "suffering with Christ" is contained in the anguish to alleviate the disunity among Christians, and in the world at large, through the practice of ecumenism. Moreover, the fullness of Christian vitality and the victory of Christ lie in man's living within the spirit and graces of His paschal mystery, through participation in the sacred liturgy.

"The paschal mystery, which the Second Vatican Council considers the synthesis of the Christian life, was prefigured in many ways, so that Christ is really the fulfillment of life, and in Him we truly enter the fullness of time (cf. 1 Cor. 10, 1-11).

By the paschal mystery we understand the mystery of Christ which embraces His whole life in His 'kenosis' and in His glory, and at the same time, the mystery of Christ who is the Head of the Mystical Body in the present reality until its fulfillment in heaven. Therefore the paschal mystery is the mystery of Christ the Head, Mediator, Revealer and Redeemer. In this mystery we turn our attention, explicitly, to the internal bond between Christ's death and His resurrection, a bond which through the Father's will, was the means of our initiation into the life of the Father and into our reconciliation with Him. This mystery presents the victory of Christ and of the Christian." [31]

Arranged in climactic order, the chapters containing the conciliar passages for the third week profoundly reflect not only Christ's passion-time plea for unity, especially among His followers (Chapter

IX), but particularly the need for man's active sharing in Christ's paschal mystery through participation in the sacred liturgy of the Mass and the sacraments (Chapter X).

Chapter IX

CHRIST'S DEATH–PLEA FOR UNITY –
Among His People Everywhere

(The Last Supper and Passion of Christ; Spiritual Exercises text, Nos. 190-207)

Suffering will never be completely wiped out on this earth. It can, however, have profound sanctifying effects in peoples lives. Nevertheless, the Christian effort should ever strive to remove sin and alleviate suffering in the world, regardless of how far-reaching such a goal may seem. In a real sense, the passion of Christ continues in the world through the suffering of His people. Christ, as it were, suffers in His suffering brethren, even the very least man or woman, youth or child. Another way in which the passion of Christ continues in the world of today is in the sin, injustice, and disunity which exist.

An important sign to the world that Christ's followers have dynamic vitality must come from their power of unity in Him through love. Consequently, this chapter can easily be extended to apply to meditations on the redemptive passion and death of our Lord. One of the most potent themes of Vatican II, with far reaching significance, is the fostering of Christian unity (Section 1). In order that this vital ecumenical movement may grow in fertile ground and produce lasting fruit, there are basic requirements for its advancement and practice (Section 2). Within this great movement the various Eastern and Western rites should also join in open dialogue (Section 3) toward that unity of faith so desired by Christ, our Savior.

Chapter X

CHRIST'S PASCHAL MYSTERY TODAY –
Alive in the Liturgy

(The Paschal Mystery of Christ; Spiritual Exercises text, Nos. 208-217)

The meditations on the paschal mystery of Christ bring the exercitant deeply into the course of salvation history as a living event in contemporary times.

"Salvation history, which is itself the mystery of Christ (cf. Vat. II, Liturgy, Nos. 16, 35), coincides with the paschal mystery in so far as this history is considered not merely as a phenomenon, but ontologically.

By the phrase to live the paschal mystery we mean that man receives Christ by faith, is engulfed in Him sacramentally through baptism (cf. Rom. 6, 3) and grows in union with Him by the whole sacramental life, especially by the Eucharist, and finally conforms himself in his own moral-religious life to Christ dead and risen, to the extent that the sanctifying action of the Spirit of Christ is not obstructed by the inordinate will of man.

The relation between the Exercises and the paschal mystery is a particular instance of this truth. The Exercises help us to participate in the paschal mystery in our spiritual life, or to live it in ourselves. Perhaps the Ignatian Exercises are singled out by the Church from among the other 'exercises' because it was the express wish of St. Ignatius that man pass spiritually through the same way that the Father wanted the Son to 'pass through'." [32]

The fruits of our redemption come to us most effectively through our participation in the liturgical rites of the Church. Particularly in the Eucharistic sacrifice, the sacraments, and through living the spirit of sacred Scripture, Christ becomes most actively present among His people. In contemporary retreats, the nexus between liturgical rites and the Exercises must be stressed.

"In the Exercises there is a relationship between the contemplations of Christ's mysteries and the liturgy, the center of which is the Eucharist. In liturgical action, the mysteries of Christ's life become for us, in some sense, present and actual: 'Today Christ is born.' Therefore, it is very important that the liturgy be celebrated every day during the Exercises, and that a homily be given then. In the liturgy sacred Scripture is read and presented in an ecclesial gathering and paschal setting. Modern studies in Scripture show that this is the atmosphere in which the gospels were written." [33]

"The Exercises call for a daily assistance at Mass and Vespers (n. 20); they look for and promote a profound sacramental life (n. 44; 354); they promote especially a personal 'living presence' of the paschal mystery. It is in this living presence especially that a deep and active participation in the Liturgy consists. The Exercises finally can lead to a community life, as intended by Christ in the gospel and in His kingdom. Furthermore, there are in the Exercises many accords with liturgical prayer and thought:

a.　St. Ignatius gives the first place to divine worship (n. 3).
b.　Likewise he wants a full response from the exercitant (nn. 91, 98).
c.　The Exercises instill a spirit of self-abnegation which corresponds to the baptismal spirituality of death and resurrection (n. 97).
d.　The Exercises teach how God is found in creatures, which is the very foundation of sacrament and liturgy (n. 230, ff).
e.　The Exercises show a certain parallelism with the liturgical year (nn. 261, ff).
f.　In the Exercises when the triple colloquy is introduced, Christ is presented as Mediator to the Father, just as in liturgical prayer (nn. 109, 147).
g.　The struggle of Christians with unclean spirits, which is mentioned everywhere in the liturgy, appears also in the Exercises (nn. 136, ff).
h.　The Word of God is valued most highly both in the liturgy and in the Exercises.
i.　Both the liturgy and the Exercises earnestly encourage the Christian to become the Servant of his brothers (n. 95)." [34]

The liturgy is the work of Christ celebrated in the Church to foster the worship of God through the sanctification of people's lives. The Exercises, in their sanctifying process, prepare retreatants to participate more fruitfully in this liturgical work of Christ.

"The Constitution on the Liturgy (n. 11) reminds us that personal dispositions are necessary for participating in the liturgical mysteries with profit. It also teaches (n. 9) that the very ministry of the Word, as it actually is in the Exercises, prepares for a more efficacious participation of the faithful in the sacred liturgy. For this reason, the Spiritual Exercises can render a great service to today's Church, to help her obtain a deeper spiritual awareness of the liturgical life of grace." [35]

Meditations in the third week of the exercises can be most suitably made from *The Constitution on the Sacred Liturgy,* for Christ's paschal mystery becomes most effective for us through participation in liturgical actions (Section 1). The retreatant will profit greatly from meditation on Christ's presence in liturgical actions, particularly in the Eucharistic celebration and in the sacraments (Section 2). There is an element of warm majesty in the sacred liturgy which should be enhanced (Section 3) by prayer, music, art-forms, and ornamentation, as duly authorized for divine worship.

PART FOUR – WITNESS, The Involvement of Christians in Uplifting Communities of the World

(THE FOURTH WEEK: Spiritual Exercises text, Nos. 218-237)

The Ignatian Exercises of the fourth week can well be enhanced for contemporary retreats by including the conciliar material in Part Four of this book. When the Christian truly lives the spirit of the paschal mystery of the risen Christ, he becomes a witness of the gospel in his life to the benefit of the communities in which he lives. The Spiritual Exercises seek to assist the Christian, under the influence of the Holy Spirit, to become a true ' person" in Christ, prepared to take his or her place in the various communities of the world as circumstances allow.

"Concerning the sense of community stressed by Vatican II, it is true that we are confronted by a problem of religious psychology which does not seem to be immediately solved through the Exercises. For it is clear that the Exercises properly made are Exercises for men as individuals. But in the Church today there is a profound desire for community life. The aspiration is for a conversion which transcends the individual dimension, a conversion of a whole group,

342 EXPLORING VATICAN II

a conversion effected in and through community. This religious experience is alien to many Jesuits, since we may have been formed in a different religious tradition. But unless we are careful, there is danger that we will not understand the language that our contemporary world speaks." [36]

"It will help to remember that the Christian should not be an 'individualist', one cut off from others, but rather a 'person', one who can communicate with others. But one becomes a person only in communication with others. And 'personality' is not weakened or suppressed in community, but on the contrary it grows. In the Exercises, therefore, it is necessary to foster the Christian person, one who can communicate with God and with Christ; with Christ as a person and as a community of persons, (as in His Mystical Body, the Church-community.") [37]

The action toward achieving salvation is an outcome of Christ's paschal mystery. Strictly speaking, our Lord's passion, death, resurrection, and ascension, − from which derives the descent of the Holy Spirit − are events intimately connected for man's salvation. But man must reason and consider matters carefully, discursively, step by step. Hence, while not overlooking the risen life of Christ in the third week of the Exercises, St. Ignatius, in that week, stresses the sacred passion and death of our Lord, reserving for the fourth week the stronger emphasis on Christ glorified. The important bond between the third and fourth weeks of the Exercises is the paschal aspect of the meditations on the life of our risen Saviour.

"The internal link between the third and fourth weeks under the dynamic 'paschal' aspect is seen in the fact that in the third week there is an allusion to the divinity which is 'hidden' (n. 196), and in the fourth week we hear of the divinity which is 'manifested', the same 'which during the passion seemed to be hidden', (n. 223).

To live the paschal mystery in the third and fourth weeks means to enter into the 'passion' not only in feeling but in effect as well, and to live the death of Christ in our mortal existence together with the life of the glorified Christ, who by His ascension sends us the Spirit who cries in us 'Abba', Father. For the gift of the Holy Spirit depends on the glorification of Christ (cf. Jn 7, 39)." [38]

Christ has risen, ascended into heaven, and, as He promised, has sent the Holy Spirit in a fuller outpouring to advance His cause among mankind until the end of time. Hence, today as earlier, the world is experiencing a genuine, godly activity or Pentecost of the Holy Spirit at work (Chapter XI). Once the Christian-community becomes open to the graces of this Holy Spirit it becomes involved in building a better world together with others to the greater glory of God (Chapter XII). This enthusiasm for life crystalizes the contemplation for divine love with which the Ignatian Exercises conclude in a grand crescendo of praise to God for the wonders of His world and the workings of His love.

Chapter XI

TODAY'S PENTECOST OF THE SPIRIT –
At Work in God's People

(The Risen Christ's Mission Now; Spiritual Exercises text, Nos. 218-229)

Once the historical reality of Christ's resurrection and ascension and their significance are realized by the Christian it leads directly into awareness of the present effectiveness of our Lord's risen life in our lives today. The saving action of our Lord continues through the working of the Holy Spirit whom Christ continually sends to complete His mission among His people.

"The movement of the Holy Spirit, which is the heart of the Exercises' impact, is greatly clarified by the theological teaching of Vatican II, which places a principal source of the action of the Spirit in the people of God. All the Fathers (at the International Congress on the Spiritual Exercises) agreed on the primacy of the work of the Holy Spirit in the Exercises. They saw the necessity of urging on the retreatants an alert consciousness of this action." [39]

Directors of the Spiritual Exercises are aware, of course, that the retreatants should be open to the free movements of the Holy Spirit's promptings in the human soul. Indeed, the very rooting out of sin makes the soul more free to respond to the benign actions of the Holy Spirit in one's personal life and in a community of Christians.

"The constant personal communication between director and retreatant is completely coordinated with and subordinate to the movement of the Holy Spirit, who molds the retreatant to the image of Christ, the Lord and Eternal King. This movement must be diligently prepared for, discerned, explained, and allowed free play. A careful preparation of the retreatant for personal communication with God is conducive to this end.

The Director reverently assists this internal movement of the Holy Spirit by urging earnest prayer, leaving it to God to correct disordered affections, by offering Exercises that are appropriate in matter and method for the agitations caused by diverse spirits, by never going ahead without having obtained the result that was sought, by allowing the Creator to act directly on the creature with His invitations and choices.

Thus the Director, in his dialogue with the retreatant who is approaching or even attaining to God, will be an effective minister of the wonderful deeds which the Spirit works in the history of every member of the people of God, both individually and universally." [40]

"All (at the International Congress on the Spiritual Exercises) agreed on the primacy of the working of the Holy Spirit, and on the need for a renewed awareness of His working, both in personal prayer and in discernment of spirits.

It was further felt that we should earnestly promote facilities with longer personal prayer and frequent meetings with the retreat-director, or at least Exercises for homogeneous groups in numbers proportionate to the number of directors.

It was also pointed out that the director's role as representative of the Church in helping the retreatant must be more clearly understood and explained. For the director shares in the Ignatian charism of the Spiritual Exercises, which has been solemnly endorsed by the Church; he exercises this charism with the Church's commission and approval and makes his own experience of the Exercises take deep root — i.e., his personal experience of Christ in the Exercises." [41]

The mission of the Holy Spirit in the world today (Section 1), as ever, carries on the saving work of Christ, who, in turn, calls upon His followers to be witnesses to Him and His teachings through their apostolic works (Section 2). This work can best be carried out in an atmosphere of peace and freedom as the work of the Holy Spirit appears to prosper better in this kind of environment (Section 3).

Chapter XII

BUILDING A BETTER WORLD —
Together in God's Love

(Contemplation for Obtaining Divine Love; Spiritual Exercises text, Nos. 230-237)

The presence of God, continually creating, redeeming, and sanctifying, floods the world with His love, for all who will partake of His goodness. It is man's privilege to use the works of God's love and unite in building a better human existence both for his greater happiness and for God's greater glory.

"The Ignatian contemplation on divine love is at the same time a recapitulation of all that has gone before in the Exercises and a preparation of the exercitant for his future. It brings the exercitant to contemplate the mystery of divine love, which means to know intimately and perfectly the History of Salvation and the paschal mystery; at the same time it induces him to turn his own life into an exercise of true love. Everything that Saint Ignatius has on this is in perfect accord with what we get from the Vatican II Constitution on the place of the Church in the world.

The purpose and importance of the contemplation on divine love is such that it should never be omitted even in the lower grade of retreats. And it should be given the most suitable place, which we think is at the end of the retreat, because the rhythm of the Exercises and the Exercises themselves lead up to it.

There is no doubt that this contemplation on divine love can be expressed in 'Christocentric' terms, starting from the 'restoration' of all things in Christ; this will give depth to the love of the neighbor and to the theology of earthly realities. Moreover, it can even be developed 'ecclesiocentrically', since the Church is the presence of Christ, the mystery of Christ, among us." [42]

When Christians actively live with divine love in them they become God's Church-community of worship and service, which, of course, includes participation in the practical social activities and projects for improving the lives of people in concrete ways. Since the Church is essentially the mystery of the presence of Christ in the Christian-community existing in the world, all aspects of peoples' lives – domestic, socio-economic, national and international – merit the concern of the followers of Christ from the motive of divine love as the foundation-stone of their lives.

"This exercise or contemplation for obtaining divine love has a remarkable power to make created things relative and external, and if this is well grasped it will initiate in us an excellent way of life. It can also prepare the way for dialogue.

It is in the attitude produced by Saint Ignatius in this contemplation for obtaining divine love that the perseverance of the exercitant must find its support. This perseverance will be effective if it proceeds rightly from within us, then outwardly toward our surroundings; and not as some would have it, from the outside world inwardly to us.

Although in the Exercises Saint Ignatius speaks explicitly of man only in his relation to his own external circumstances, it is clear that implicitly there is question also of his part in economic, political, and social structures, which are very much the concern of the Second Vatican Council." [43]

While the basics of the Spiritual Exercises must be maintained to enable them to produce their intended effects, these Exercises are always to be conducted according to current theological teachings and adapted to the present needs of the retreatants. As Vatican II presents the world-wide vision for today and tomorrow, so also the Ignatian Exercises are to expand the souls of those who make them, assisting the exercitants to grasp the universal dimension of individual and collective problems, just as God Himself might look upon the total life of a person and the whole surface of the globe of this world.

"It is necessary that those things which we can call 'Ignatian constants' be retained, but in their exposition, the director must accommodate himself to the needs of the soul, the capacity of the person, and the mentality of this age.

The objective Ignatian process ought to be based, as Ignatius bases it, on salvific facts, not on abstract concepts. The universal dimension should always be preserved, i.e., the problems of the exercitant should be seen as part of and in the universal perspective of world problems." [44]

The love of God for man, when acknowledged and returned to Him, is capable of uniting mankind and effecting the improvement of all human life in this world (Section 1). This union and improvement would show forth the greatness of our God and give greater meaning to the redemptive love of His divine Son, our Redeemer and Lord. Indeed, this will be a better world when people live by Christ's teachings and rely on His grace for their improvement of human standards of living in accordance with Christian ideals in the domestic, socio-economic, national, and international communities throughout the world (Sections 2, 3, 4, 5).

Vatican II's pastoral messages for contemporary Christians contain a treasury of material for our contemplation and benefit. Obviously, neither the retreatant nor the director would use the time of a closed retreat simply to study the conciliar passages. Nevertheless, it is hardly conceivable that St. Ignatius would direct a retreat which would ignore the teachings and trends of the Church for the retreatants of his time. Among the characteristics of the Ignatian Exercises are adaptability to the exercitant's needs and applicability to the current requirements of the Church-community. The Vatican II era is that in which the contemporary Christian must live and be a witness of the dynamic gospel-message. The documents and trends of Vatican Council II will find effective implementation in the Spiritual Exercises of St. Ignatius Loyola for the People of God today.

3. The Dynamism of the Spiritual Exercises for Modern Times

Like the small book of the Spiritual Exercises of St. Ignatius Loyola, this supplement merely indicates leads for exercising one's own spiritual insights, while reflecting on the chapters which contain key passages from the great Vatican Council. Hopefully, the book will stand by itself as a reflective and prayerful approach to the study of the Council messages. Yet, it is believed that the dynamism of the Spiritual Exercises gives the work its impelling power for assisting contemporary Christians to know, love, and serve their Lord more wholeheartedly in modern times.

As with many instruments of the Church in the Vatican II era, the Exercises must be up-dated in their use. However, while calling for adaptation of the Ignatian Exercises, the experts including the Holy Father and the general of the Jesuits together with regional, national and international congresses on the adaptation of the Spiritual Exercises, all make an important distinction. These authorities, after careful study both of the Exercises and the documents of Vatican II, clearly affirm the profound value of the Ignatian insight for our times. These experts also suggest a fuller exploration of the Spiritual Exercises to bring out more clearly their wealth of material in the light of current theological development and the exigencies of the times.

Consequently, deep study and reflection is required to discern, to adapt, and to apply the basics of the Spiritual Exercises to the requirements, psychology, and current doctrinal and moral development of theology for modern man in the spirit of Vatican II. Briefly, the charismatic insight of the Ignatian spiritual guidance remains most practical for assisting the People of God in modern times. However, some further research into the Ignatian Exercises may be required to clarify some of their intonations, which, while defensible, may be misconstrued by some today. Hence, the book in hand offers a contribution toward the adaptation and application of the dynamic Spiritual Exercises in the light of Vatican Council II.

Under the guiding grace of the Holy Spirit and with the assistance of their retreat master, retreatants can feel assured that the Ignatian Exercises remain dynamic for our use today. Indeed, the Spiritual Exercises have been, and still are, the most widely used and most loudly proclaimed instrument of religious exercises among several which have more recently emerged. It is not triumphalism; rather it points up the serious responsibility, particularly for Jesuits, to acknowledge the lists of saints, Popes, bishops, religious and the countless laity who have so profoundly profited by engaging in the Spiritual Exercises. An earlier Pope Paul declared that the finger of God was behind the Ignatian insight. A later Pope Paul proclaimed that he wanted the Spiritual Exercises of St. Ignatius to be used because of their great value in fostering the sanctification of people in this Vatican II era.

NOTES

1. Pope Paul VI to Richard J. Cardinal Cushing, Archbishop of Boston, on the occasion of the Convention of the National Catholic Laymen's Retreat Conference, July 25, 1966. Published by The Program to Adapt the Spiritual Exercises, 144 Grand St., Jersey City, N.J., 07302.

2. Pope Paul VI in an audience with Very Reverend Father Peter Arrupe, General of the Society of Jesus, August 12, 1965. From Reports and Recommendations of the International Congress on the Spiritual Exercises, Loyola, 1966, pgs. 4-5. Published by The Program to Adapt the Spiritual Exercises.

3. Pope Paul VI in an audience with Very Reverend Father Peter Arrupe, General of the Society of Jesus, December 29, 1965. International Congress on the Spiritual Exercises; pgs. 5-6.

4. Very Reverend Father Peter Arrupe, General of the Society of Jesus in a Letter to the Fathers Provincial of Italy, for a Conference on the Spiritual Exercises, Triuggio, Italy, June 2, 1967. International Congress on the Spiritual Exercises; pg. 3.

5. Very Reverend Father Peter Arrupe, General of the Society of Jesus, in a Letter to Participants of the Workshop on the Spiritual Exercises at Fordham University, N.Y., June 19-21, 1967. Published by The Program to Adapt the Spiritual Exercises.

6. Very Reverend Father Peter Arrupe, General of the Society of Jesus, to Participants at the International Congress on the Spiritual Exercises, Rome, August 8, 1966. International Congress on the Spiritual Exercises; pgs. 3-4.

7. Very Reverend Father Peter Arrupe, General of the Society of Jesus, to Participants at the International Congress on the Spiritual Exercises, Rome, August 8, 1966. International Congress on the Spiritual Exercises; pg. 6.

8. From "Declarations" of the International Congress on the Spiritual Exercises; pg. 12.

9. From "Summaries" of the International Congress on the Spiritual Exercises; pgs. 15-16.

10. Cf. "Theme 18" of the International Congress on the Spiritual Exercises; pgs. 64-65.

11. From "Theme 14" of the International Congress on the Spiritual Exercises; pg. 55.

12. Cf. "Declarations" of the International Congress on the Spiritual Exercises; pg. 11.

13. Cf. "Declarations" of the International Congress on the Spiritual Exercises; pg. 11.

14. From "Theme 9" of the International Congress on the Spiritual Exercises; pgs. 36-37.

15. References to the text of the Spiritual Exercises of St. Ignatius are in accordance with the numbers from the approved directory. Among several

translations of the Exercises available, that of Fr. Lewis Delmage, S.J., is recommended because of its contemporary language. "The Spiritual Exercises of St. Ignatius Loyola: An American Translation." J. F. Wagner, Inc., N.Y.; 1968. The Program to Adapt the Spiritual Exercises, 144 Grand St., Jersey City, N.J., 07302.

16. Cf. "Theme 3" of the International Congress on the Spiritual Exercises; pg. 20.

17. From "Declarations" of the International Congress on the Spiritual Exercises; pg. 11.

18. Cf. "Theme 2" of the International Congress on the Spiritual Exercises; pgs. 17-18.

19. From "Theme 3" of the International Congress on the Spiritual Exercises; pg. 20.

20. From "Theme 2" of the International Congress on the Spiritual Exercises; pg. 17.

21. From "Theme 3" of the International Congress on the Spiritual Exercises; pg. 21.

22. From "Theme 4" of the International Congress on the Spiritual Exercises; pg. 22.

23. From "Theme 7" of the International Congress on the Spiritual Exercises; pg. 30.

24. From "Themes 5 and 6" of the International Congress on the Spiritual Exercises; pg. 24.

25. From "Theme 4" of the International Congress on the Spiritual Exercises; pg. 22.

26. From "Theme 13" of the International Congress on the Spiritual Exercises; pg. 52.

27. From "Theme 13" of the International Congress on the Spiritual Exercises; pg. 53.

28. From "Theme 8" of the International Congress on the Spiritual Exercises; pgs. 31-32.

29. From "Theme 8" of the International Congress on the Spiritual Exercises; pg. 31.

30. From "Theme 8" of the International Congress on the Spiritual Exercises; pg. 32.

31. From "Theme 9" of the International Congress on the Spiritual Exercises; pg. 35.

32. From "Theme 9" of the International Congress on the Spiritual Exercises; pgs. 35-36.

33. From "Themes 5 and 6" of the International Congress on the Spiritual Exercises; pg. 25.

34. From "Theme 11" of the International Congress on the Spiritual Exercises; pgs. 43-44.

35. From "Theme 11" of the International Congress on the Spiritual Exercises; pg. 44.

36. From "Theme 11" of the International Congress on the Spiritual Exercises; pg. 42.

37. From "Theme 11" of the International Congress on the Spiritual Exercises; pg. 43.

38. From "Theme 9" of the International Congress on the Spiritual Exercises; pg. 37.

39. From "Declarations" of the International Congress on the Spiritual Exercises; pg. 10.

40. From "Theme 13" of the International Congress on the Spiritual Exercises; pgs. 50-51.

41. From "Theme 13" of the International Congress on the Spiritual Exercises; pgs. 53-54.

42. From "Theme 10" of the International Congress on the Spiritual Exercises; pg. 39.

43. From "Theme 10" of the International Congress on the Spiritual Exercises; pg. 40.

44. From "Theme 18" of the International Congress on the Spiritual Exercises; pg. 65.

STUDY GUIDE

INDEX

Presence of Christ: among His
people, 87-89
in liturgical celebrations, 217-218;
224-227
Priests: and the Church —
community, 104-108
federations of, XIX-XX
involvement in needs of people,
105
ministering to God's people, 104-
108
practical preaching of, 105
relationships with laity, 106-107;
112; 117-119
the role of today, 104-108
Problems: attitudes toward, 12-14
Progress: on earth toward heaven,
73-74
and human dignity, 289-292
Protestant: and Catholic leaders:
209-210
Providence, divine: for man's
welfare, 16-18
Prudence: of judgment and action,
XVII-XX; 147-156
Purpose: of life, 7-28
Rejuvenation: of Christian Vitality,
3-5
Relevance: of Christian activity, 128-
131
of ecumenism and liturgy, 189-191
Religion: and culture, 39-44
and freedom, 257-262
indifference toward, 156-161
to unify mankind, 193-200
Religious Life: adaptation to modern
needs, 110-111
benefits and blessings of, 109-112
renewal for current needs, 108-112
Renewal: of Chrisitan Vitality, 3-5
enthusiasm for, 3-4
of life and society, 62-66
and the Mother of Christ, 182-185
purpose of book, XVII-XVIII
Repentance: aids sanctity, 173; 181
for renewal, 62-66
Respect: dialogue proceeds from, 57-
60
Responsibility: personal with
freedom, 257-262
Resurrection: of man's body, 68-70
Retreats: for religious development,
XVIII; 140-141; 145; 321-351
Revelation: Catholic Church and, 92-
98
divine, and human life, 16-20
Rites: practices of Eastern, 218-219
various in the Church, 210-215
Sacred: integrating with secular: 29-
47
Sacrifice: for Christ's cause, 176-181

Sacraments: power within, 229-233
Saints: benefits of union with, 75-
77; 178-181
Salvation: attainable by all, 26-28
Church sacrament of, 89-91
life's goal, 67-70
of man through the Church, 92-98
and human progress, 14-16; 20-22
Satan: influence of, 147-149
Schools: forming Christian leaders,
142-143
and changes, 149-153
and man's dignity, 60-62
Scripture sacred: modern insights,
XVIII-XIX
Secular Order: integrating with
sacred, 29-47
and Christian humanism, 128-131
Secularism: as inadequate, 153-156
and religion, 29-30
Self-denial: necessity of, 218-220
Seminarians: and apostolic works,
122-123; 132-134
changes affecting, XVIII-XX; 108-
110
renewed training of, 108-110
Service: of Christ and His cause, 83-
85
of Church for man, 9-10; 92
Signs of the times: analyzing for the
Spirit, XXI; 147-167
and life's improvement, 310-311
Sin: personal and communal, 49-66
repentance for, 181
in the social order, 60-62
Sinners: conversion of, 28; 49-50;
54-57; 62-66
Single people: apostolate of, 122-
123; 137
and holiness, 173-176
Social order: assisting the needy,
137-140
changes within, 149-153
and God's blessings, 308-315
and man's dignity, 57-62
morality in, 53-54
principles of, 269-315
Society: and Church cooperating,
44-47
curing ills of, 4-5
religious freedom in, 257-262
renewal of life in, 62-66
uplifted by Christian activity, 128-
131
Socio-economic order: principles of:
289-296
Spiritual Exercises: Ignatian, XVIII;
321-351.
Spiritual life: development of, 140-
141
State: and Church relations, 299-301